Song of the Union
Emeka Ogboh

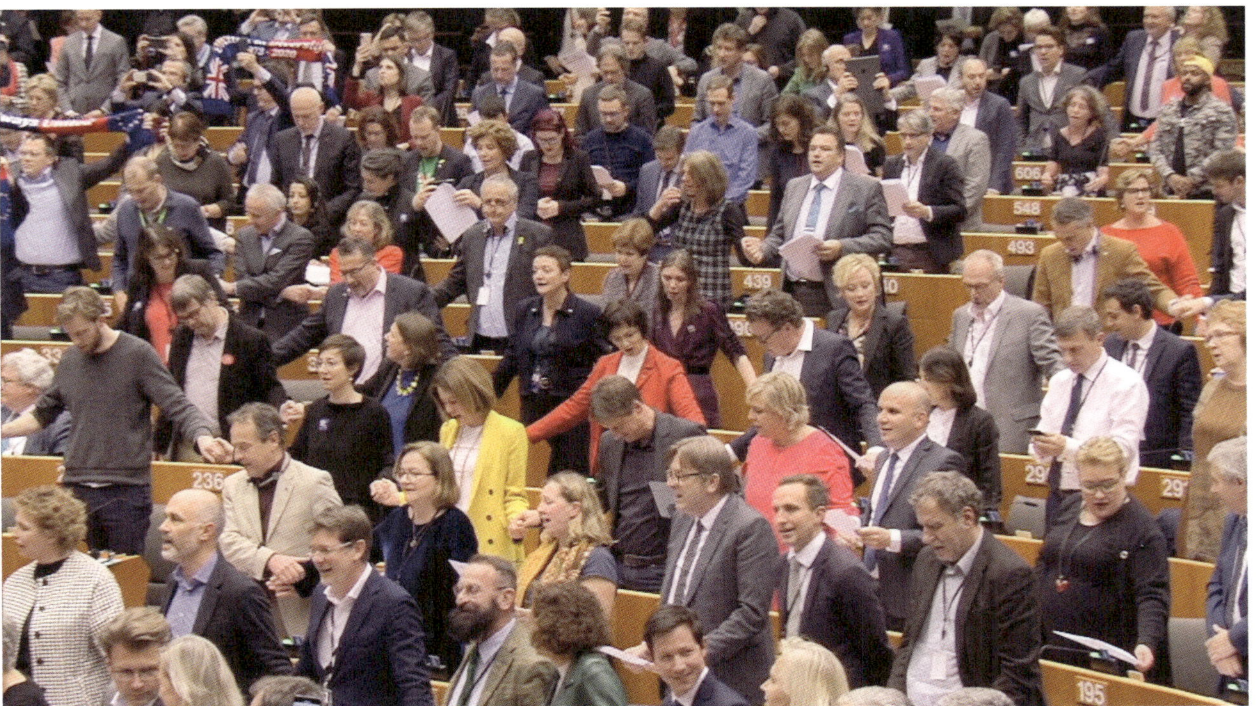

This catalogue is published by Talbot Rice
Gallery, University of Edinburgh on the
occasion of the exhibition Emeka Ogboh
'Song of the Union' curated by Tessa Giblin
as part of Edinburgh Art Festival 2021
Commissions Programme.

29 July – 29 August 2021
Burns Monument, Edinburgh

Supported by the PLACE Programme,
a partnership between Edinburgh Festivals,
Scottish Government, City of Edinburgh Council
and Creative Scotland. With additional support
from Goethe-Institut Glasgow, ifa (Institut
für Auslandsbeziehungen), Edinburgh College
of Art and Museums and Galleries Edinburgh.

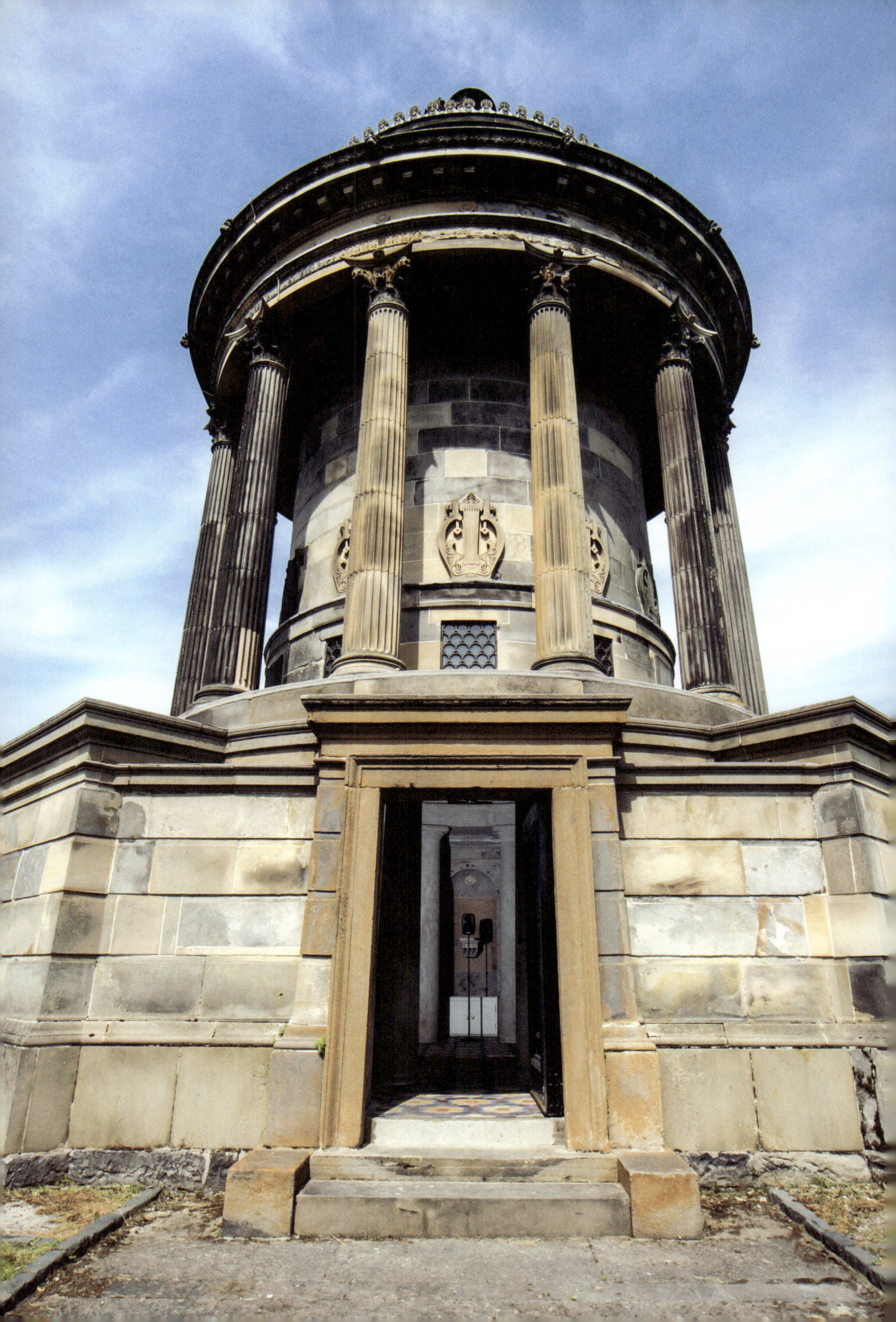

Song of the Union

Tessa Giblin, Director of Talbot Rice Gallery

It's like going into a dark room and feeling your
way through.
Emeka Ogboh, April 2021

On 29 January 2020, as the United Kingdom departed the
European Union (EU) and as a final gesture of farewell,
Members of the European Parliament (MEPs) took to their feet
in Brussels, held hands and sang Robert Burns' 'Auld Lang Syne'
– a song which has come to represent solidarity, friendship and
open doors.

When Emeka Ogboh stood in the Burns Monument in Edinburgh
and conceived of 'Song of the Union', it was just 12 days after
the event he was going to end up, in part, memorialising.
'Song of the Union' is a sound installation in which 27 singers
from the EU member states living in Scotland today, as well
as one from the recently departed UK, sing 'Auld Lang Syne' in
their mother tongue. As an artist, Ogboh has long concentrated
on sound – from the reconstruction of the soundscape of a city,
to working with songs or anthems to complicate their political
efficacy. His 'The Song of the Germans' installation is a clear
precursor to 'Song of the Union' – ten African immigrants that
reside in Berlin sing the German national anthem in their own
languages, emanating from a series of surrounding, disembodied
speakers, with individual voices emerging and converging.

Erected in 1830 to memorialise Robert Burns, Scotland's great
poet and bard, the Burns Monument overlooks Holyrood, the
current seat of the devolved Scottish Parliament and is adjacent
to the Old Royal High School – where Scotland's parliament was
to reside, had devolution been granted in the referendum of 1979.
As explored by M. J. Grant's essay in this book, 'Auld Lang Syne'
is attributed to Robert Burns; and the monument in his name
is uniquely placed between two key architectural reminders
of Scotland's political history. To understand why Ogboh found
himself to be feeling his way through a dark room in making
'Song of the Union', we have to first understand the complexity
of emotions that ran through the European Parliament in
Brussels on that day in 2020.

We beat them that day – symbolically, we won.

Molly Scott Cato (British Green Member of the European Parliament, 2014–2020)

The battle that Molly Scott Cato spoke of wasn't the battle over
the United Kingdom's Brexit vote in 2016, or the many attempts
that pro-EU politicians and activists made to halt the UK's exit
from the European Union. By 29 January 2020, the UK was just
two days away from its official exit from the European Union,
and the battle lines had been drawn over the tone of departure.

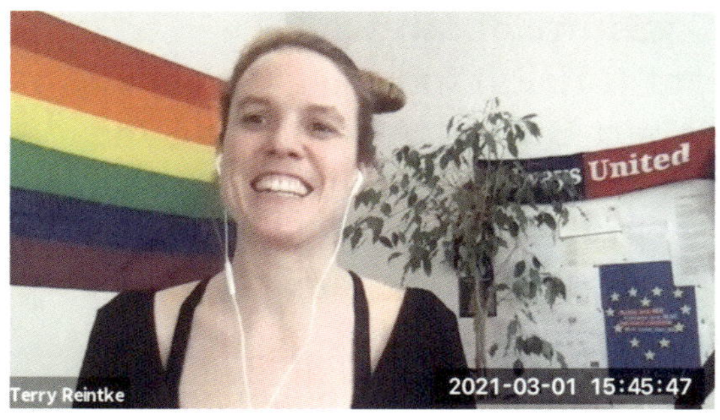
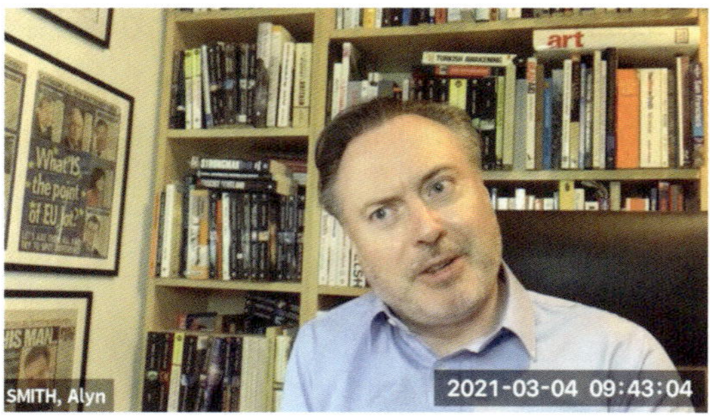
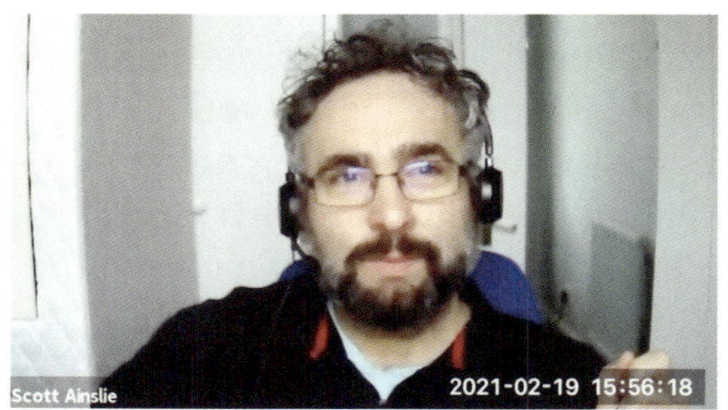
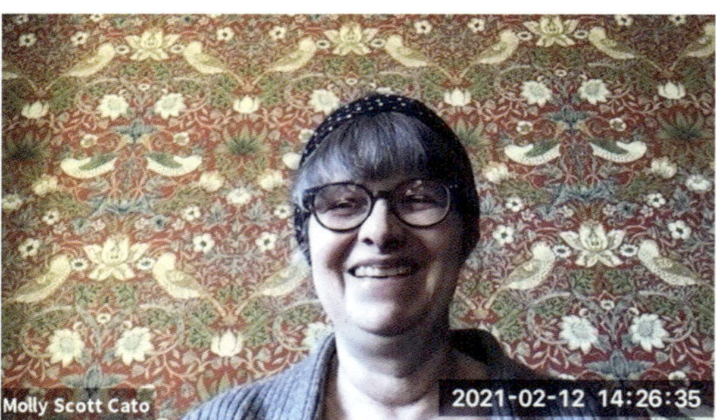
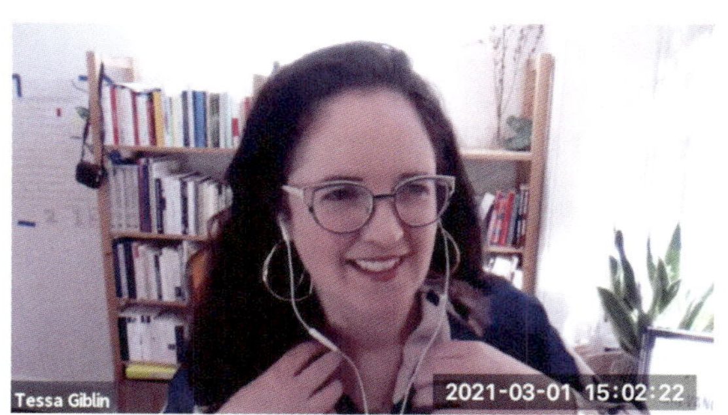
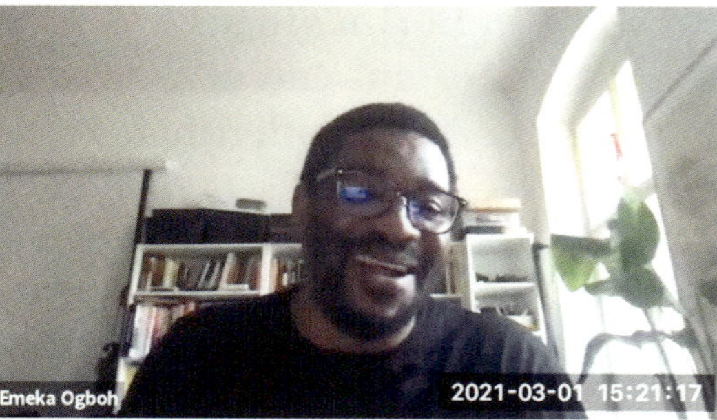

Left to right, top to bottom: Interviews with Terry Reintke, Alyn Smith, Scott Ainslie,
Molly Scott Cato, Tessa Giblin, Emeka Ogboh

On one side were the Eurosceptic Brexiteers, flamboyant and
baiting, waving miniature Union Jack flags and performatively
turning their backs on 'Ode to Joy' as it was sung to begin the
parliamentary session. Pointedly flaunting European Parliament
rules prohibiting flags in the chamber, the Brexiteers' behaviour
reflected their ongoing derision of EU bureaucracy, made
infamous during their ultimately successful campaign for

the UK to leave the EU. On the other side were the pro-EU
politicians from a number of British political parties alongside
international allies, the Greens/European Free Alliance (EFA),
and what Terry Reintke (German Green MEP) called 'a UK–EU
friendship group', including Molly Scott Cato (British Green
MEP), Alyn Smith (Scottish National Party MEP) and Scott
Ainslie (British Green MEP) among a great many others.

Alyn Smith recalled, 'As the Brexit conclusion was reaching
its crescendo we really wanted to make sure that this moment
was done in the right way, because it was going to be symbolic –
one way or another. The European project is about international
cooperation, fraternal assistance and mutual solidarity –
aspirational things.' Scott Cato reflected, 'In the European
Parliament, when we start our sessions they always played
"Ode to Joy", which symbolises bringing us together. When
the Brexit party turned their backs on the musicians, it told
me about the power of art – it frightens them, and they needed
to reject it. To me that encapsulates the power that art has in
the political sphere.' Terry Reintke, like the sitting President
of the European Commission Ursula von der Leyen, had
studied in the UK, spending a year in Edinburgh on the Erasmus
programme. 'Usually we gave speeches, which are a very political
way of interacting, but we needed to have a song that people sing
not only like an orchestra that comes in and plays, but really the
human voice, to convey a message that goes beyond just voting
or not voting for the withdrawal agreement.'

It was Reintke, a German MEP who suggested Robert
Burns' 'Auld Lang Syne', and on 29 January, after voting
on the final withdrawal agreement and accompanying speeches,
the 751-strong parliament rose and sang the Scottish song of
farewell – some tearful, some stoic, others visibly uncomfortable.
Beaming into homes, gyms and departure lounges around
the world, this was the image that captured the spirit and
tone of departure, and this was the battle that Scott Cato and
her friends had won. Later, Scott Cato described how it came
about – that, like art, it didn't just happen, it was made to
happen: 'we had the correct note on our phones, Terry's office led
on circulating the words, and Scott Ainslie, with his big booming
voice immediately gave everybody else confidence – and then
all over the chamber, other people joined in.'

The powerful emotions that underpinned the final parliamentary
session of 29 January 2020 were shared by citizens across

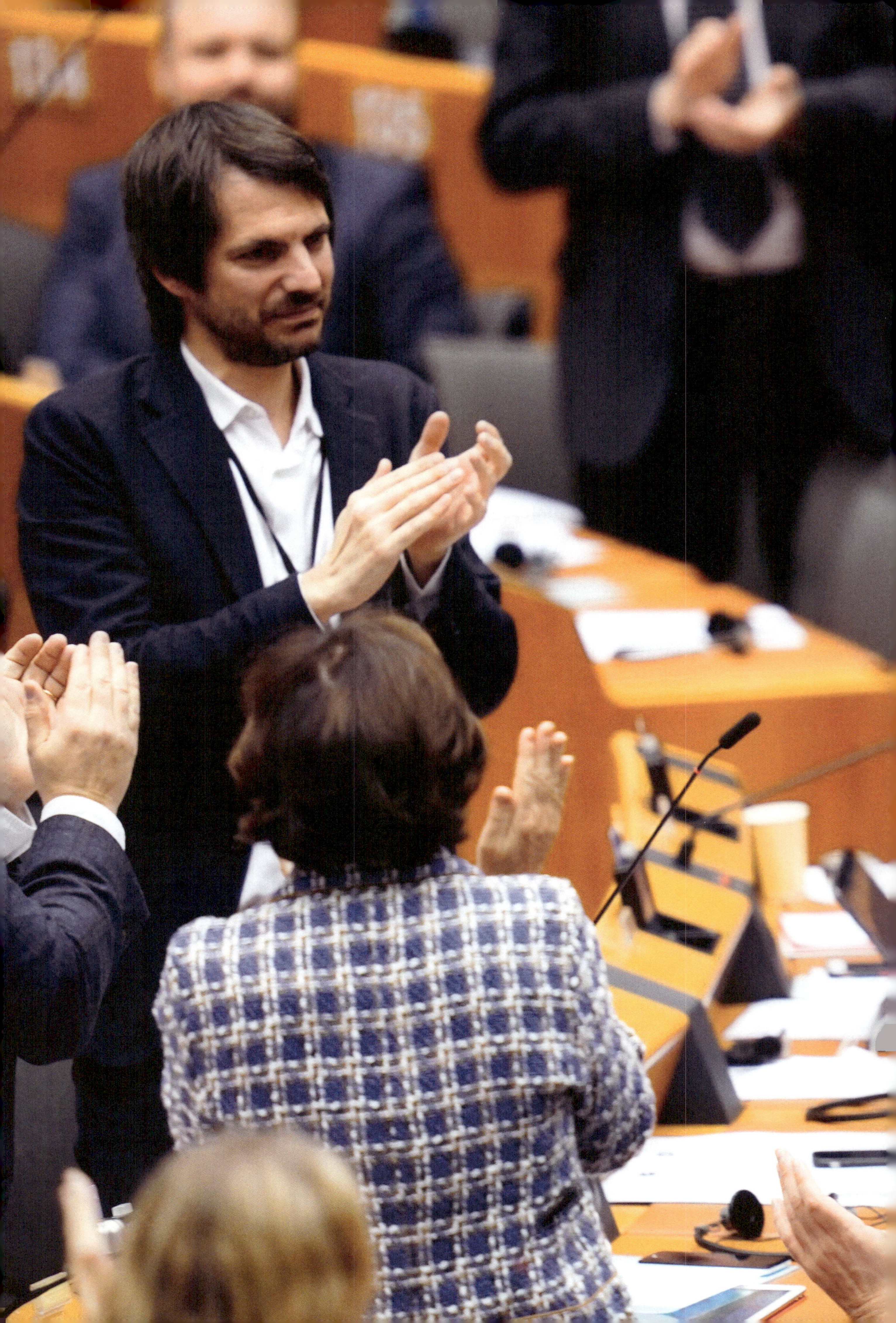

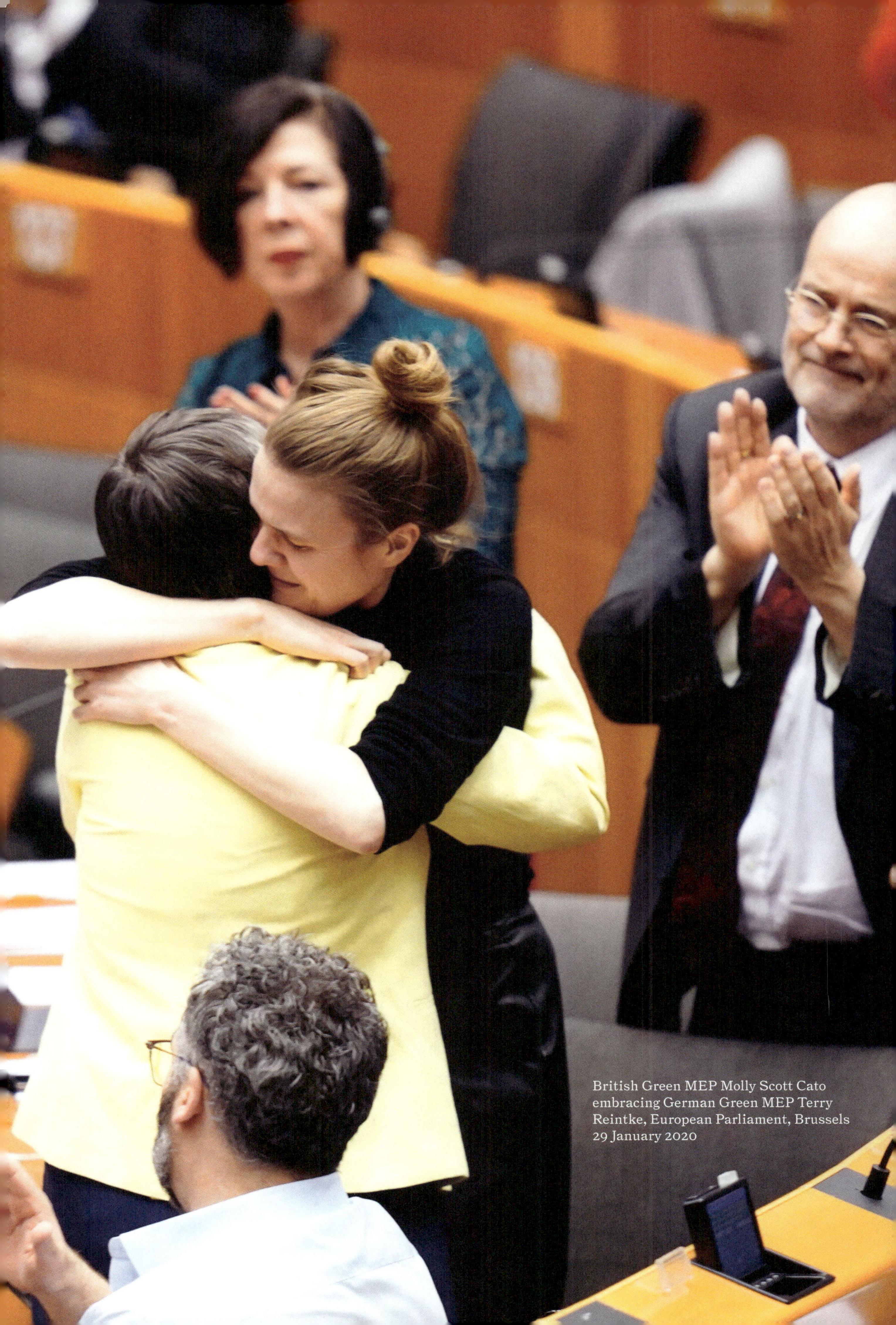

British Green MEP Molly Scott Cato
embracing German Green MEP Terry
Reintke, European Parliament, Brussels
29 January 2020

Europe and the UK. It was a time of great uncertainty: Europeans
living in the UK encountered new restrictions around their
settled status; traders struggled to comprehend potential border
restrictions for imports and exports, and British citizens living
across Europe waited for news of their own status and rights.
Northern Ireland remained unresolved and, as predicted by Willie
Doherty's photographic diptych in the *Borderlines* exhibition at
Talbot Rice Gallery in 2018, tensions flared as the much-denied
customs line was inevitably drawn through the Irish Sea.

*

> I've created this composition of different languages,
> synchronised and singing the same tempo, the same
> beats, but most likely, by the time people come to visit
> the installation, you may not even be hearing it as different
> languages. It's just going to be 'Auld Lang Syne' in your head,
> you will not even try to separate it. I'm looking at synchrony
> here. The voices will at first be separate and you might hear
> Dutch there, or German there, but at the end, you're just going
> to hear the music.
> Emeka Ogboh

This power or ability to affect lies deeply within the
consciousness of Emeka Ogboh's artwork. The artwork collects
the 28 languages of the then-EU, including Scots to represent
the UK, as this is the language in which the song was written
and continues to be sung around the world today. Ogboh has
created not only a monument to the UK's departure from the
EU, but an expression of what European unity was intended to
be in the first place. As each of the individual voices sing 'Auld
Lang Syne' in Portuguese, Latvian, Greek or French, the sense
of what this big European project has been and will continue to
be surrounds the listener. Reintke explained, 'for me, fighting
against Brexit is beyond the question of whether the UK is part
of the European Union, but about whether we, as citizens of this
world, can try to find solutions together.' That idea of unity is
what Reintke believes was overlooked by the remain campaign,
which fought to keep the UK in the EU: 'How the remain side
made the case for the European Union was very much based on
facts and figures – you know, a white heterosexual man sitting
in a talk show explaining to people why economically it's smarter
to stay part of the European Union. But this was not touching
on what a lot of people actually were asking themselves, about
a broader story that this European Union also tells, based as it

was on the ruins of the Second World War. It's a peace project. And arts and culture can really talk to people in a completely different way than I, as a politician, ever can. I can give the greatest speech in the European Parliament, but it is not going to engage people on the same level as when they hear a song, or engage in some way with cultural, artistic pieces. So, I felt, now we have to live with the consequences, we are in this mess, this withdrawal agreement is a reality, but at least let's learn from this mistake and try to attract people in a different way. And this was really behind singing "Auld Lang Syne" in the European Parliament that day. Politics in the end is also deeply emotional and deeply personal.'

Having collected lyrics for all 27 EU languages, individual singers were recorded in the sound studios of Edinburgh College of Art and Dystopia Studios, Glasgow. Working with computer programming, Ogboh engaged an algorithm to control the order and density of voices. This chance operation, interweaving language, syntax, cadence and rhythm resulted in a complex and constantly shifting soundscape, which amazes as much as it dislocates.

For many of the 27 EU citizens living in Scotland, the recording sessions were a reclamation of their voice. Only citizens of Malta, Ireland and Cyprus were allowed to vote in the 2016 Brexit referendum, so for many it was a chance to reclaim the voice that had been denied them five years ago – the results of which fundamentally changed their status in the UK forever. This isolation remains acutely acknowledged in 'Song of the Union', with the isolated, individual voices only coming together as the algorithm decides. The resultant polyphony is much like the makeup of the EU itself – divergent, while collective.

These European singers weren't the only ones to reclaim their voice through Ogboh's artwork. For Molly Scott Cato, one of the agonies of the preceding four years had been how much the Brexiteers had dominated the headlines and controlled the Brexit narrative. There was even a perspective in the European Parliament that after the final vote the British MEPs should immediately leave – muting the pro-Europeans, but also ridding themselves of the jeering Brexiteers. Singing 'Auld Lang Syne' on 29 January 2020 and cementing the tone of departure was a victory for Scott Cato and Reintke not only because it captured the headlines, but because it restored what Scott Cato felt to be the UK's authentic voice.

Is Emeka Ogboh's artwork a monument to a broken family,
or a celebration of a united vision? To those who waved their
little paper flags and habitually turned their backs on the
playing of 'Ode to Joy', perhaps it is even evidence of the
incomprehensibility of difference: different languages, compiled
on top of each other, drowning out their specificities, flattening
their individuality. For Eurosceptics, Ogboh's artwork might
even resonate with this point of view. To those who stood in the
chamber that day, held hands and sang, for whom the memory
of the moment is still raw, 'Song of the Union' is undoubtedly
a powerful, rallying call to remember what the European project
and collectivity is all about. For Emeka Ogboh, and for us at
Talbot Rice Gallery, 'Song of the Union' is an artwork about
friendship, just as 'Auld Lang Syne' is a song about friendship.
It looks forward, not back, to a time when friends might see
each other again.

The departing speeches in the European parliament included
Alyn Smith's appeal to 'leave the light on for Scotland',[1] as well
as Terry Reintke's prediction that she would 'one day see British
MEPs being re-elected to [the EU] chamber.'[2] It included Nigel
Farage (Brexit Party MEP) 'once we've left we're never coming
back'[3] and Scott Cato: 'Now is not the time to campaign to re-
join, but we must keep the dream alive. Especially for young
people who are overwhelmingly pro-European. I hold in my
heart the knowledge that one day I will be back in this chamber
celebrating our return to the heart of Europe.'[4]

For the Nigerian artist, living in Berlin and making a new work
in close collaboration with Edinburgh strangers who became
friends during a global pandemic, Ogboh's artistic vision, and the
resounding memory of those of us who had the privilege to work
with him, has been about the ability of art to tell its own defiant
story about history. As Scott Ainslie reflected, 'a song that is
extremely popular is deeply embedded in peoples' consciousness
– it has a deeper, lasting resonance, and made into a piece of art
will reverberate beyond the event itself.'

1. *Alyn Smith – 'Do No Let Scotland Down'*, 2016, www.youtube.com/watch?v=E-9iAZKLHbU

2. *One Day UK Will Return Back to EU after Brexit – Terry Reintke Eudebates
with British MEPs*, 2020, www.youtube.com/watch?v=2zgrvj_sGsw

3. *Nigel Farage's Dramatic Final Speech at the European Parliament Ahead
of the Brexit Vote | LBC*, 2020, www.youtube.com/watch?v=LIgmfpHBiDw

4. *Final Speech in the European Parliament – Molly Scott Cato MEP*, 2020,
www.youtube.com/watch?v=AJZZj6E4j38

Brexit is an undeniably complicated event for the UK and
European history, and as the essay of Kirsty Hughes in this
book illustrates – borne of a great many decisions and policies
that remain unresolved. Producing art during enforced lockdown
and ongoing separation is teaching us a lot – resoundingly, that
our human connections across the globe are deeper and more
resonant than we may have feared. There's a politic to friendship
just as there is in national identity. Standing in the middle of
those disembodied speakers, Europeans and British citizens
will recognise their language – but will this language be what
we identify with the most? This is a song after all, and songs
are powerful carriers of emotion, gesture and message. When
listening to these 28 unique performances, through the veil of
language we encounter style, gender, age, timbre and passion.
In this book, Bonaventure Soh Bejeng Ndikung writes about the
capacity that language has for possession: 'to be wholly gripped
by something, akin to the religious sense of being possessed by
a spirit, which is to say one is completely consumed.' Engulfed
by the waves of languages around you, you might not know what
it says, but you'll know what it means.

    Should auld acquaintance be forgot
    And never brought to mind?
    Should auld acquaintance be forgot
    And auld lang syne.

    For auld lang syne my jo,
    For auld lang syne.
    We'll tak a cup o' kindness yet
    For auld lang syne.

All quotes by Molly Scott Cato come from an interview between Tessa Giblin and Scott Cato
on 12 February 2021. All quotes by Scott Ainslie come from an interview between Tessa Giblin
and Ainslie on 19 February 2021. All quotes by Alyn Smith come from an interview between
Tessa Giblin and Smith on 4 March 2021. All quotes by Emeka Ogboh and Terry Reintke come
from an interview between Tessa Giblin, Reintke and Ogboh on 1 March 2021.

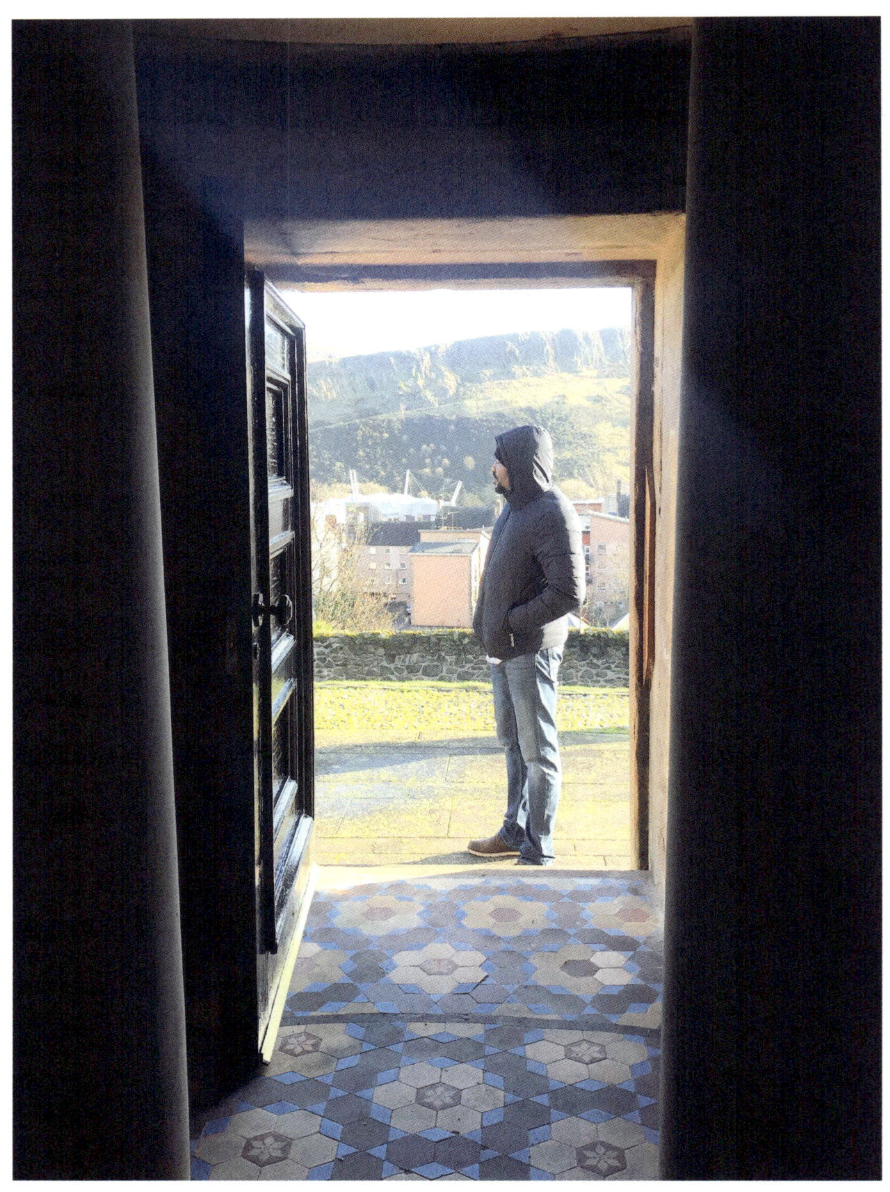

Emeka Ogboh at Burns Monument, Edinburgh, February 2020

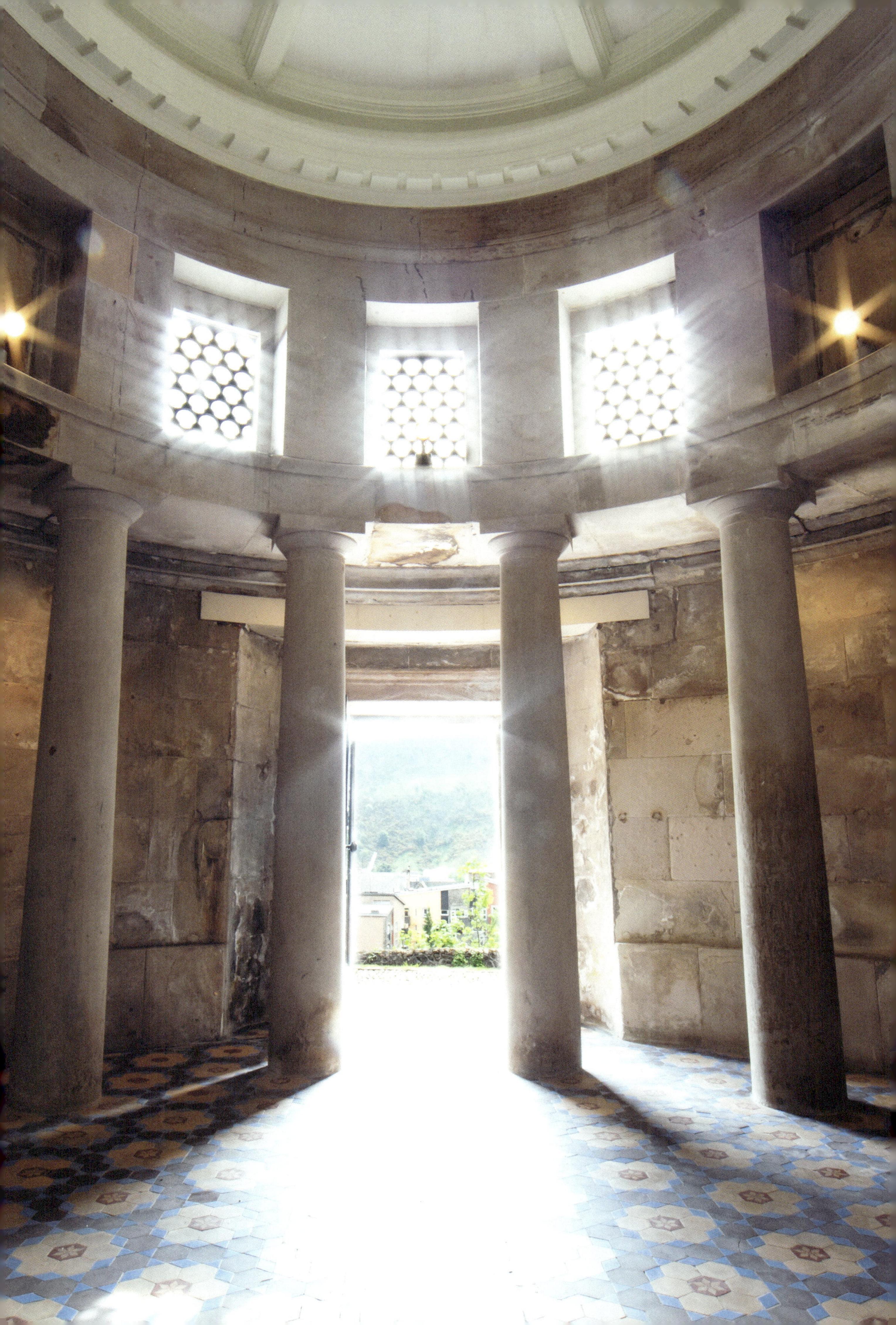

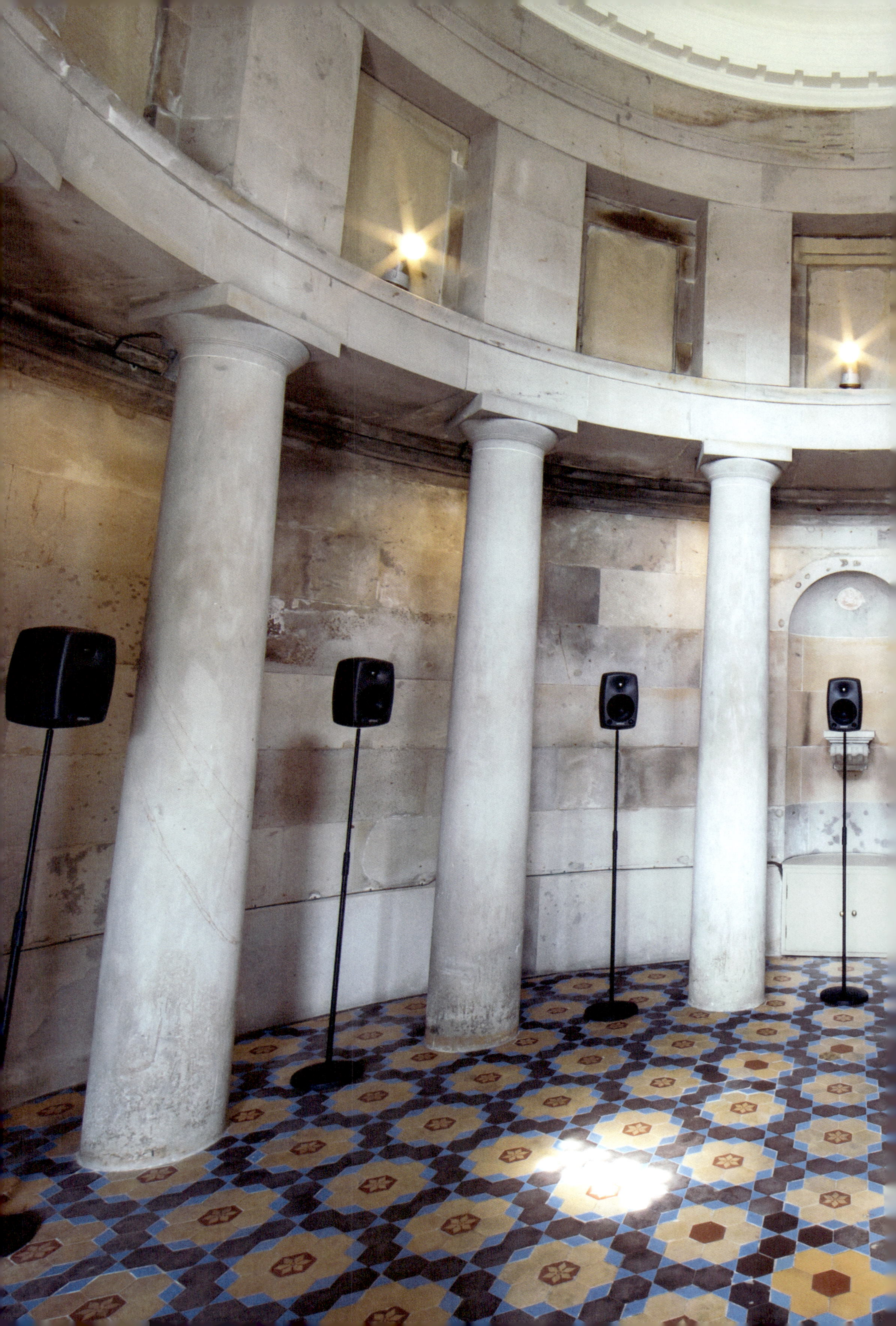

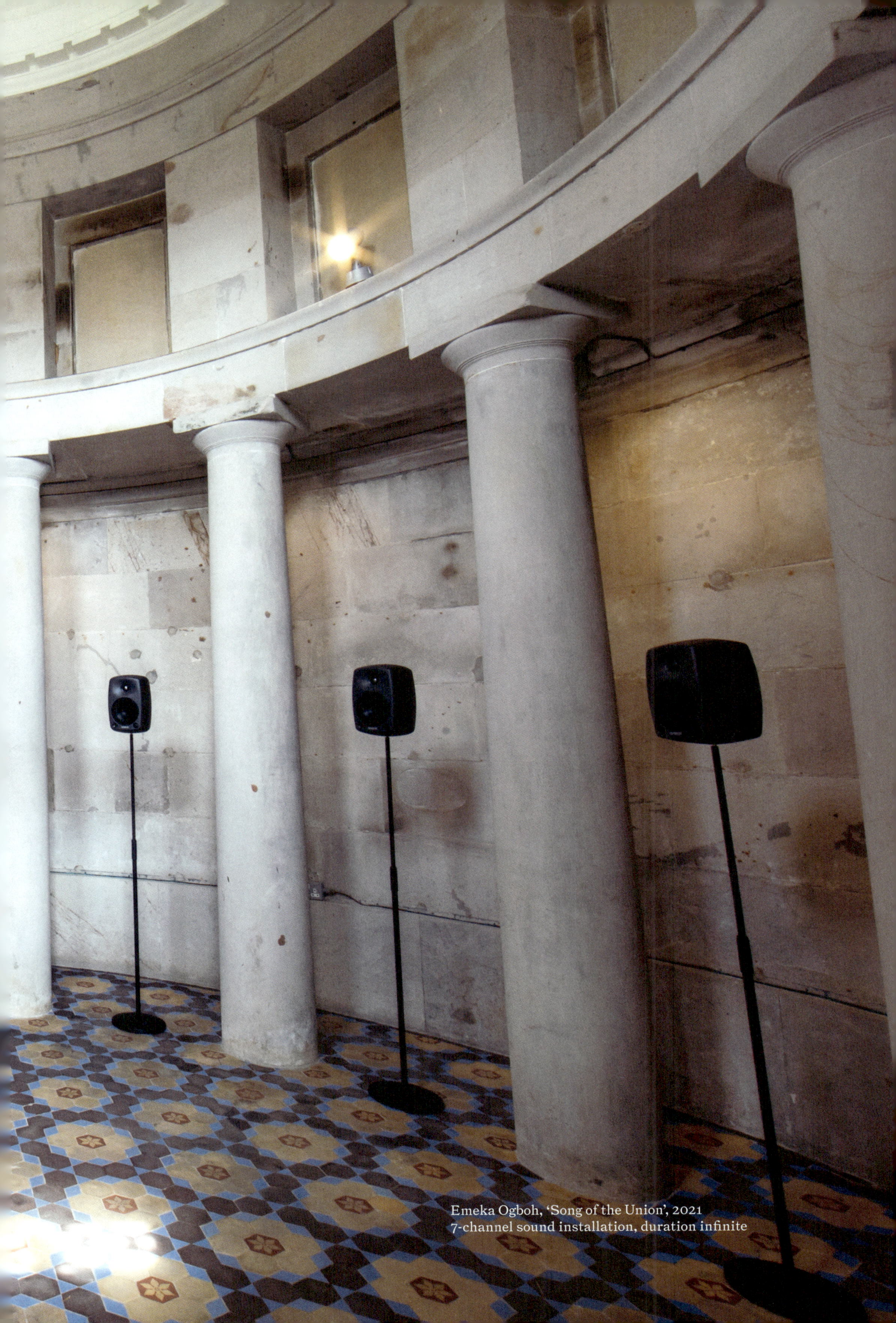

Emeka Ogboh, 'Song of the Union', 2021
7-channel sound installation, duration infinite

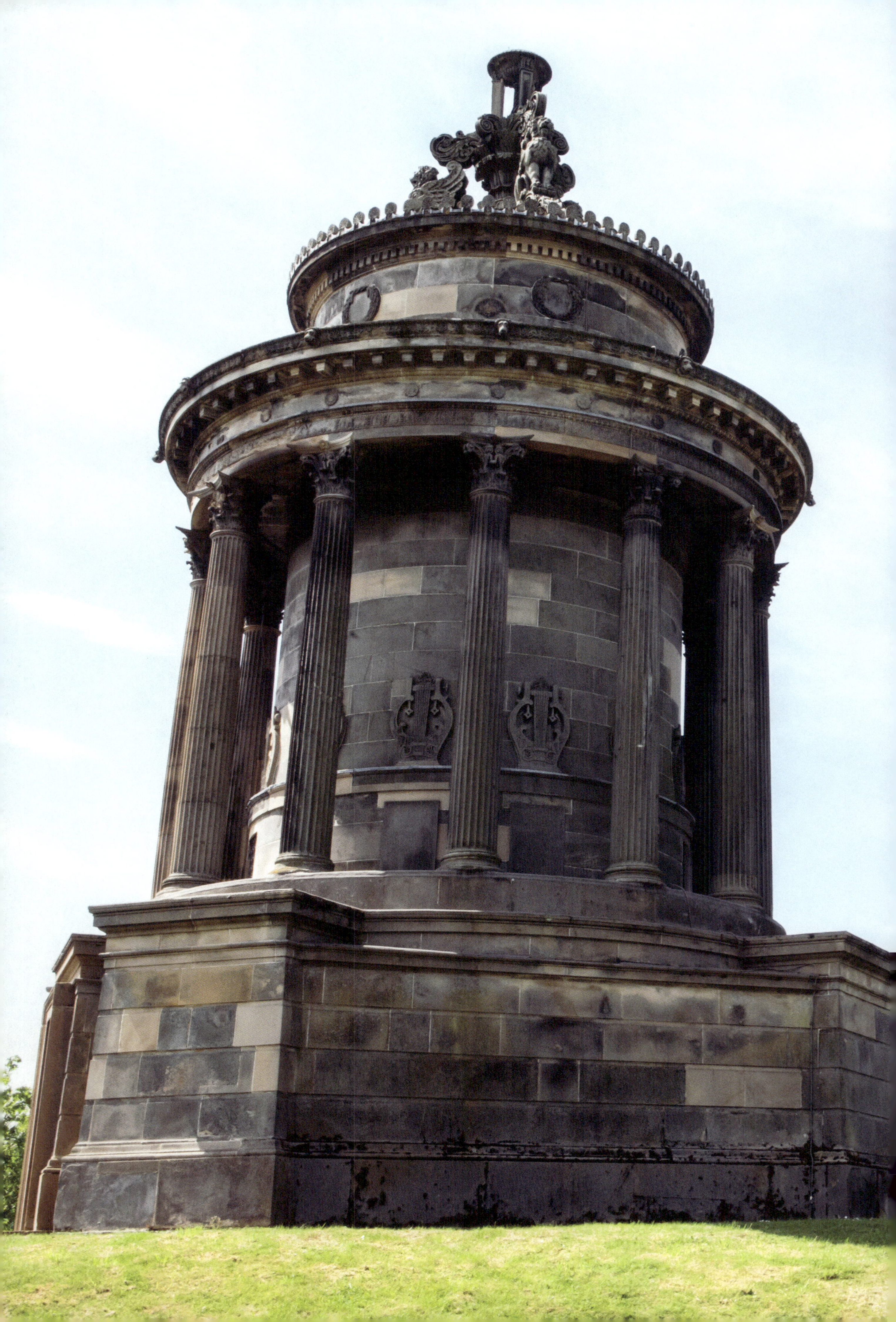

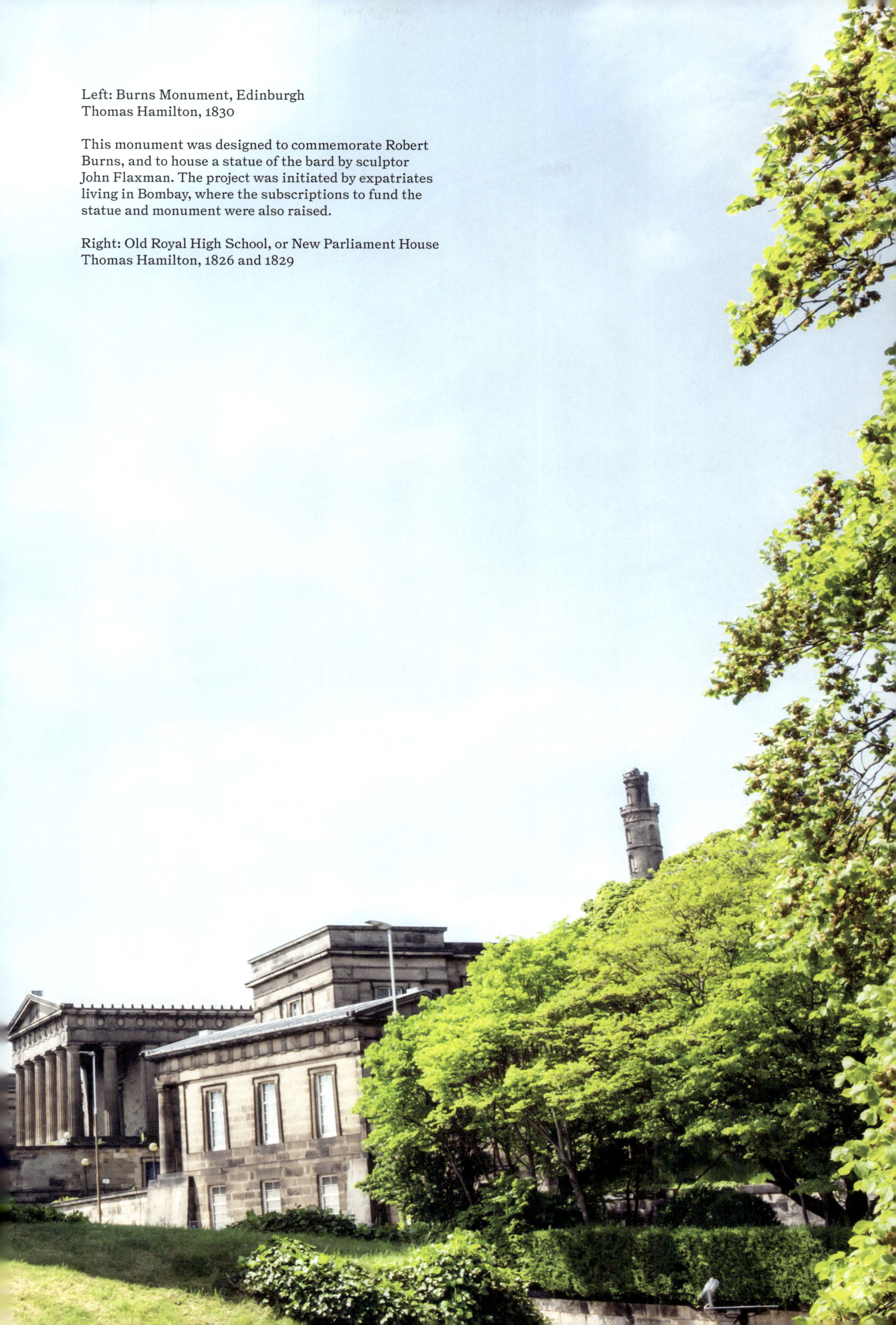

Left: Burns Monument, Edinburgh
Thomas Hamilton, 1830

This monument was designed to commemorate Robert
Burns, and to house a statue of the bard by sculptor
John Flaxman. The project was initiated by expatriates
living in Bombay, where the subscriptions to fund the
statue and monument were also raised.

Right: Old Royal High School, or New Parliament House
Thomas Hamilton, 1826 and 1829

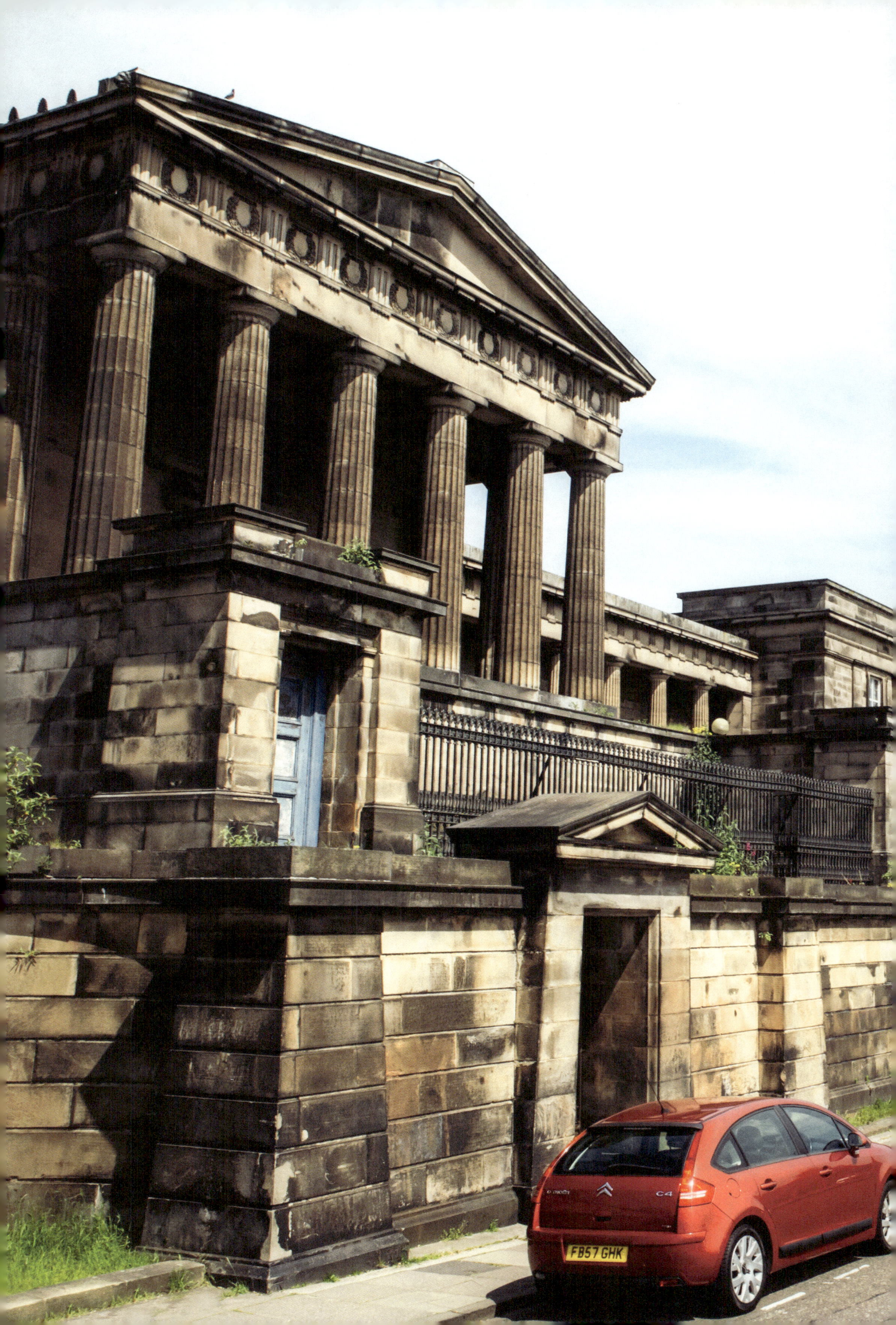

Old Royal High School, looking along Regent Road
towards Burns Monument

The nineteenth-century neoclassical building on
Calton Hill was designed in a Greek Doric style,
with Hamilton modelling the portico and Great Hall
on the Hephaisteion of Athens. Originally constructed
as the city's Royal High School, it gained its alternative
name as a result of a proposal in the 1970s for it to
house a devolved Scottish Assembly. However, the
1979 devolution referendum failed to provide sufficient
backing for a devolved assembly.

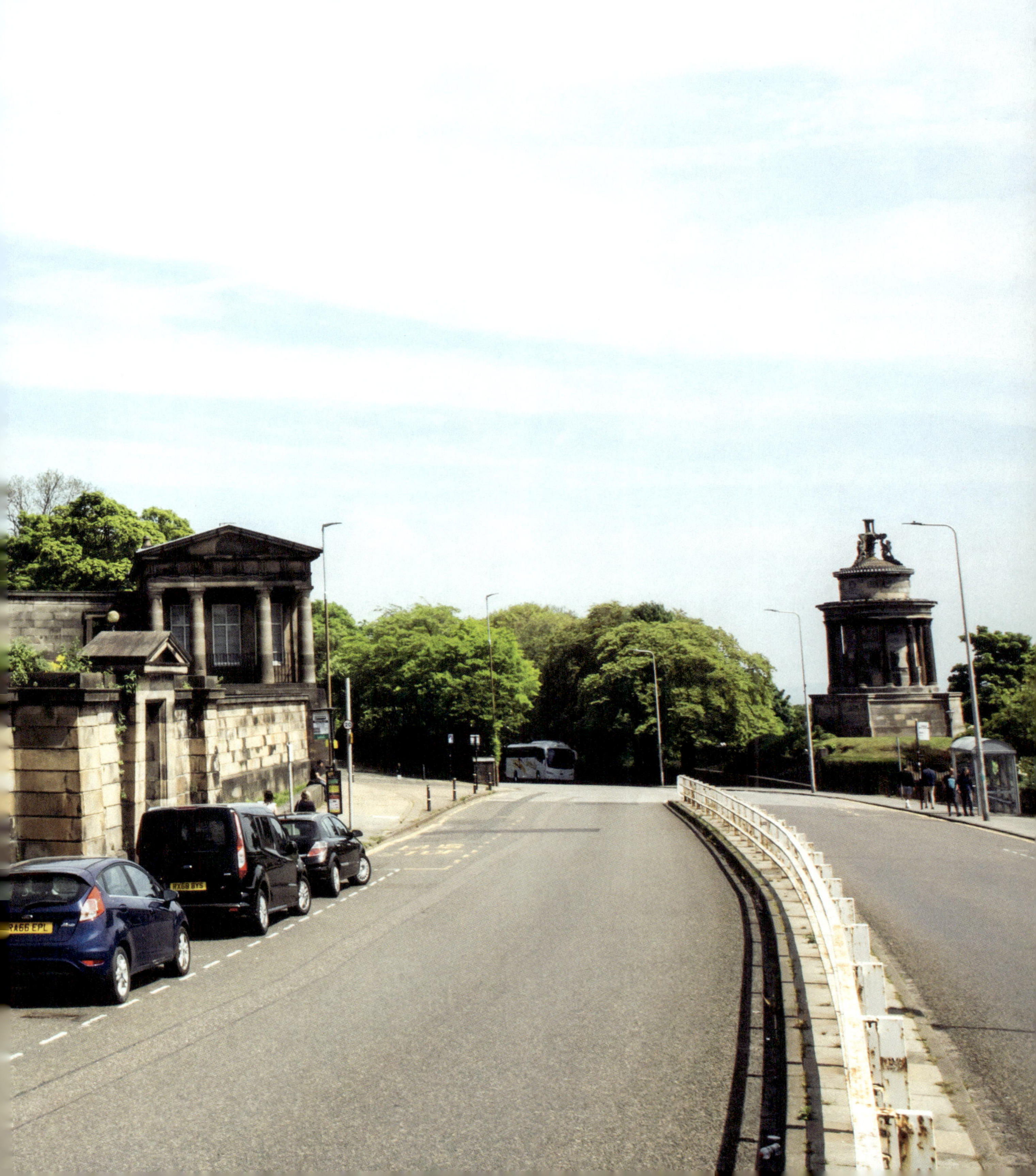

Far left: Palace of Holyroodhouse
Sir William Bruce and Robert Mylne for Charles II,
1671–1678

Centre: Scottish Parliament Building
Enric Miralles, 1999–2004

The home of the Scottish Parliament at Holyrood.
Following 292 years without a legislature of its own,
a referendum was held on 11 September 1997, which
approved the establishment of a devolved Scottish
Parliament.

In the distance: Salisbury Crags and Arthur's Seat

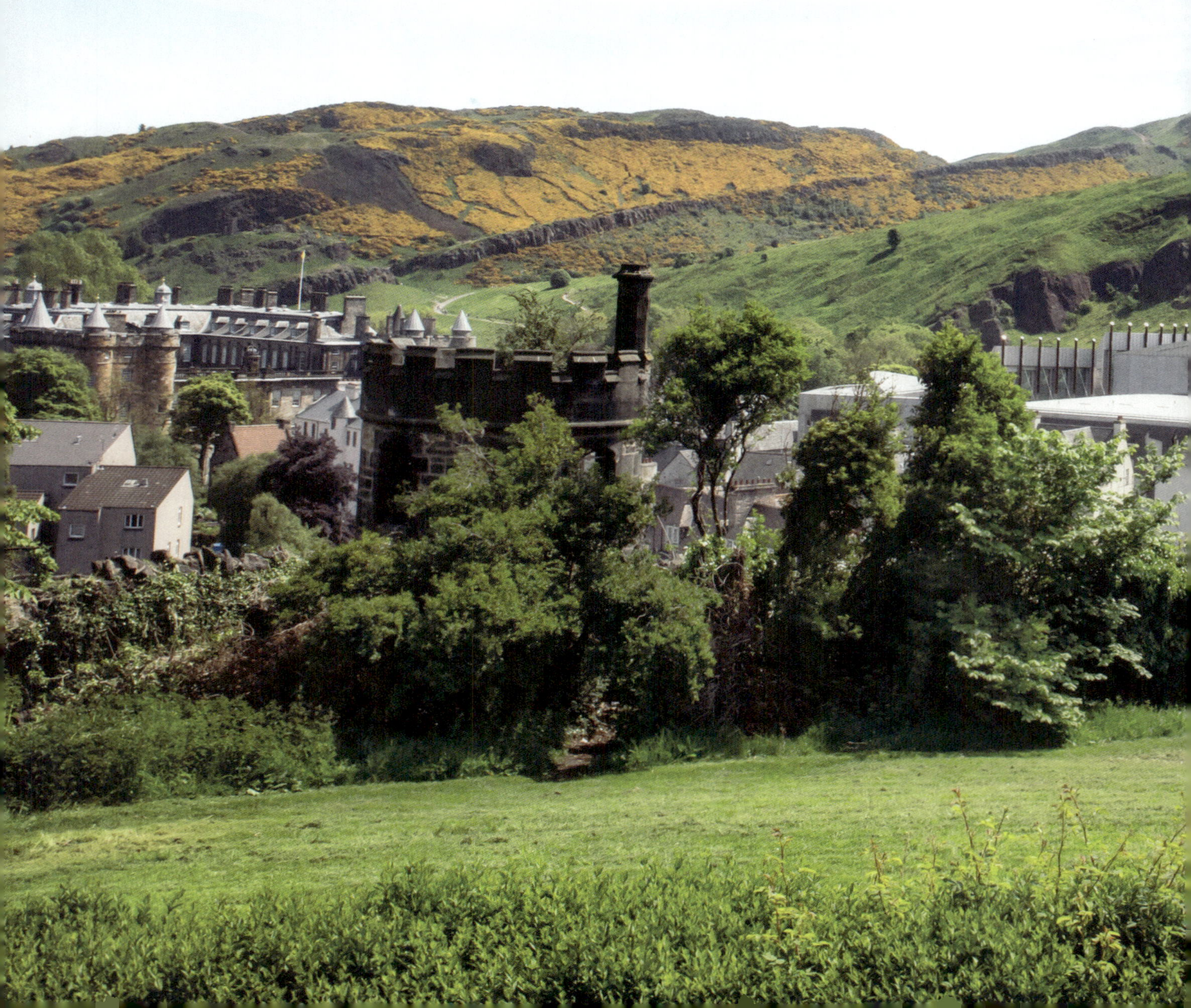

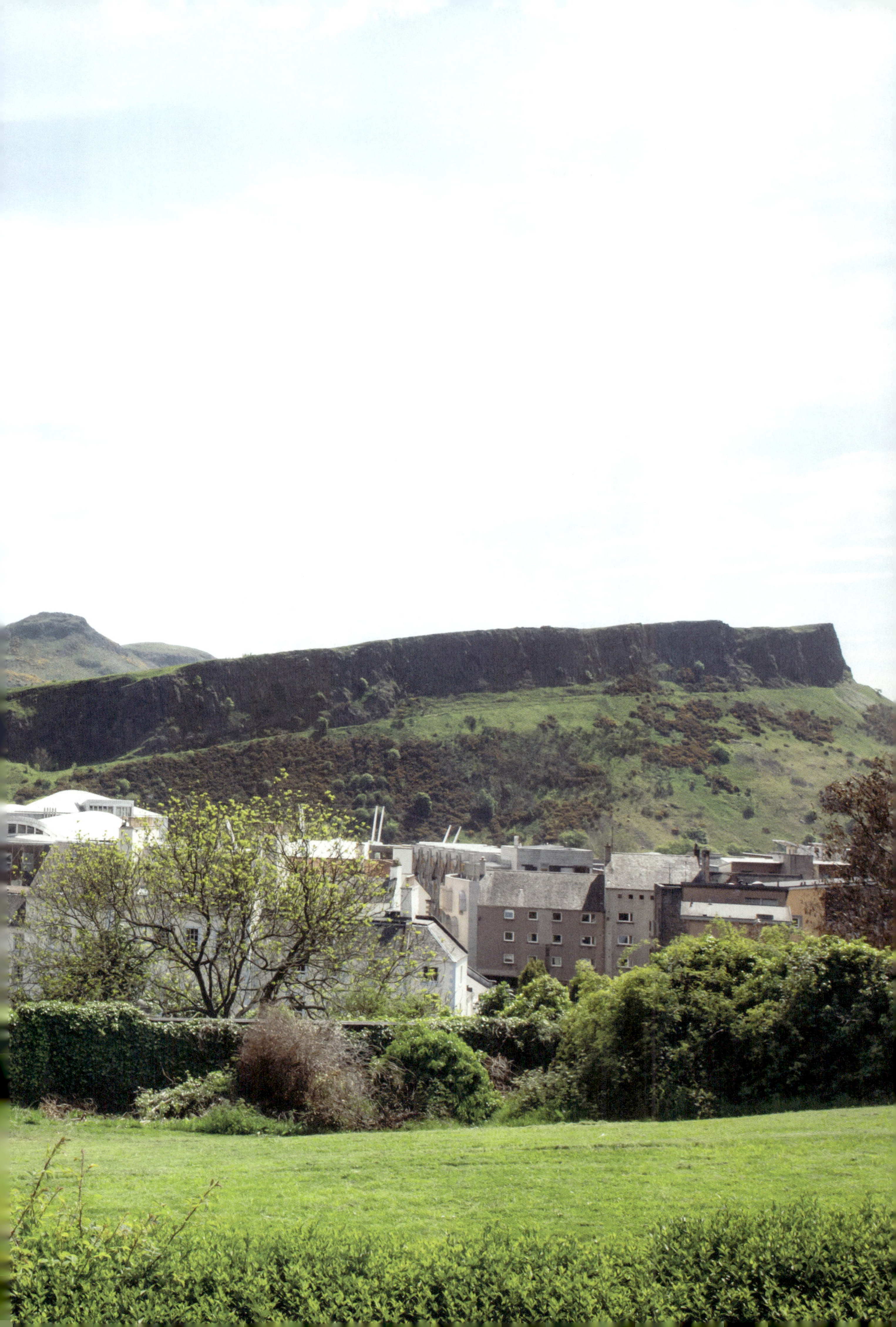

Belgium

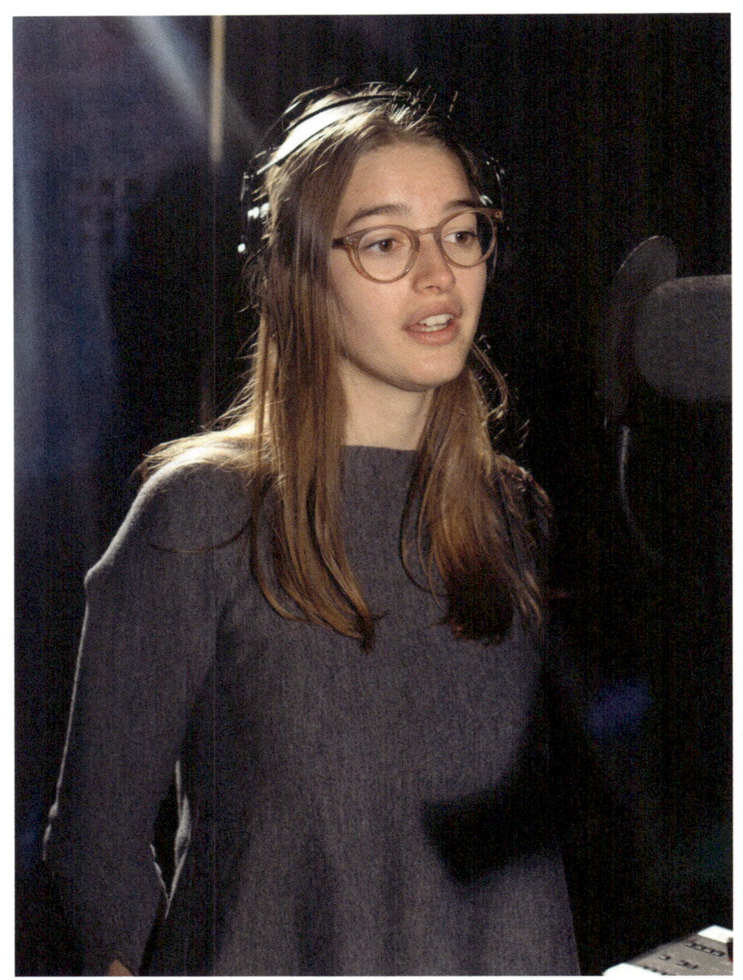

Dorothee Nys

Vervlogen Tijden

Robert Burns (1759–1796)
Translator unknown

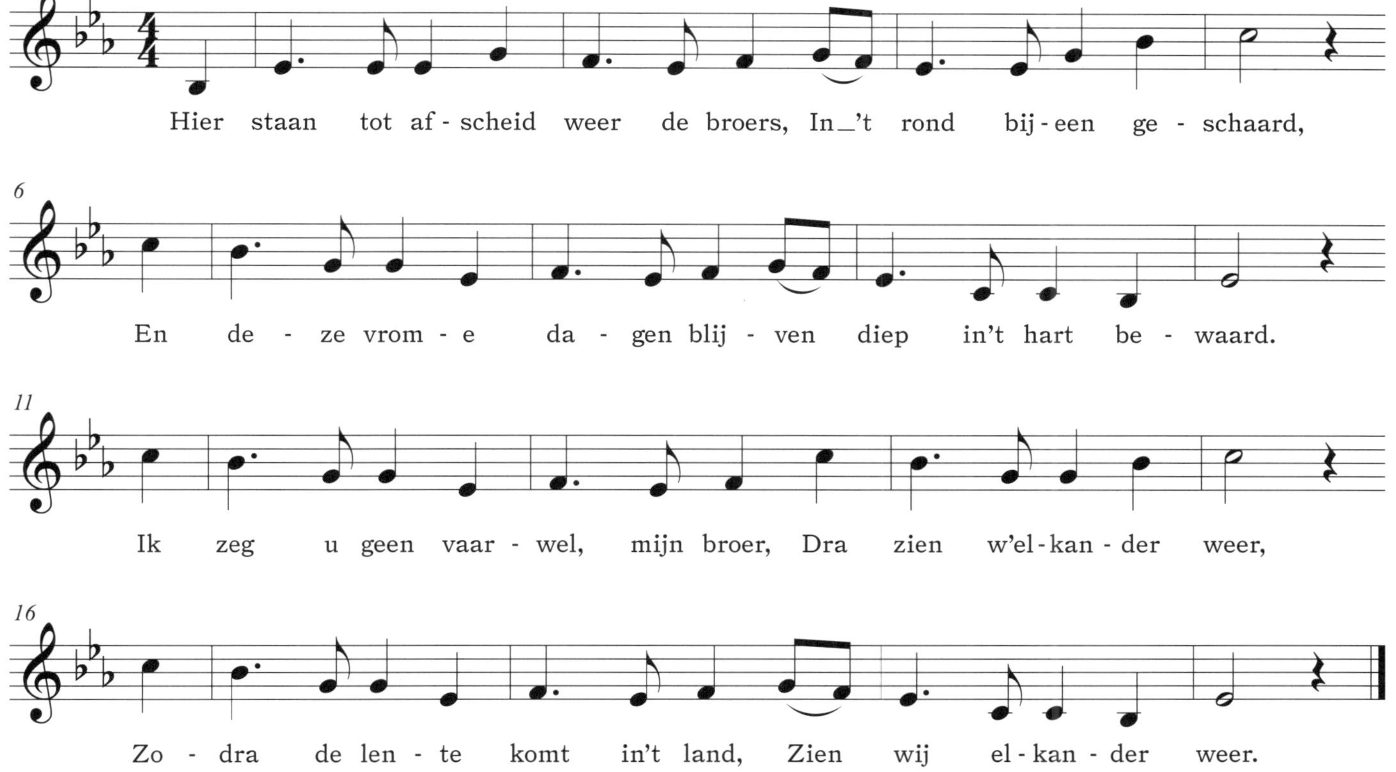

Hier staan tot afscheid weer de broers,
In't rond bijeen geschaard,
En deze vrome dagen blijven
diep in't hart bewaard.

Ik zeg u geen vaarwel, mijn broer,
Dra zien w'elkander weer,
Zodra de lente komt in't land,
Zien wij elkander weer.

France

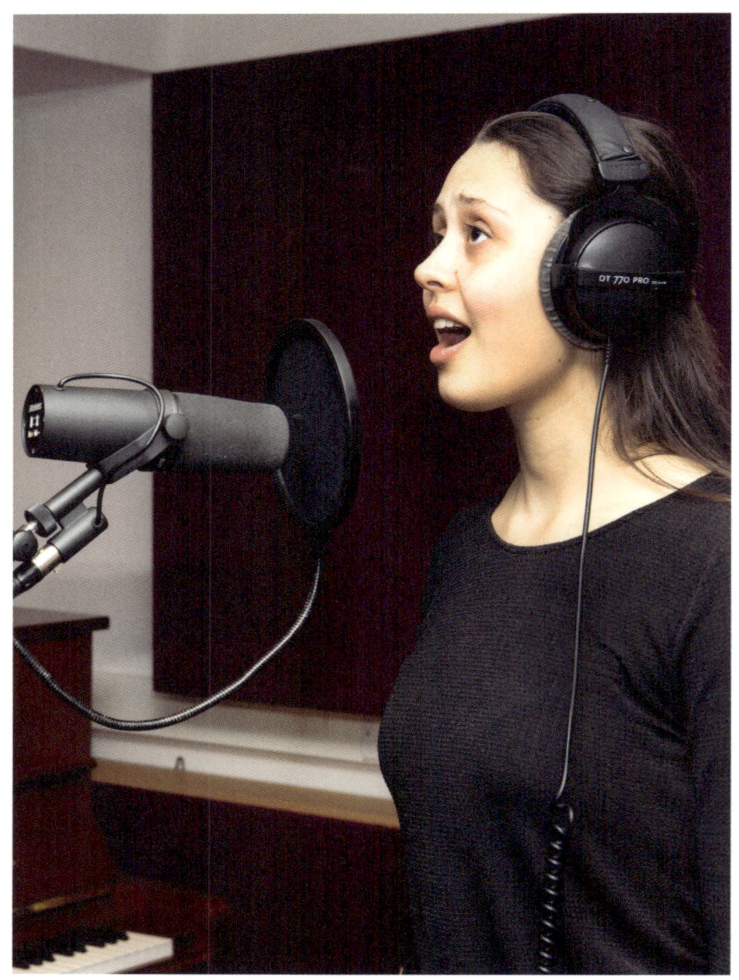

Bianca Morantin

Ce n'est qu'un au revoir

Robert Burns (1759–1796)
Translated by Jacques Sevin (1882–1951)

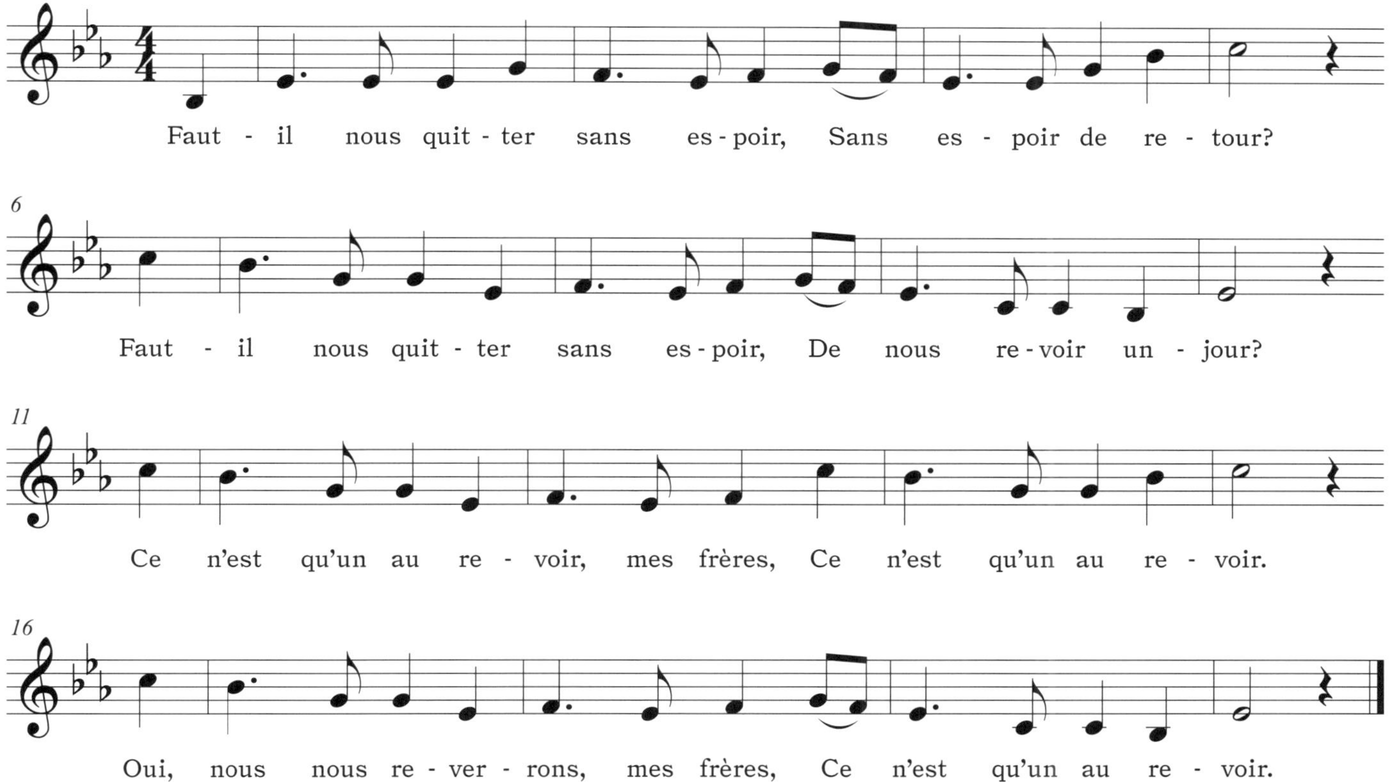

Faut-il nous quitter sans espoir,
Sans espoir de retour?
Faut-il nous quitter sans espoir,
De nous revoir un jour?

Ce n'est qu'un au revoir, mes frères,
Ce n'est qu'un au revoir.
Oui, nous nous reverrons, mes frères,
Ce n'est qu'un au revoir.

Germany

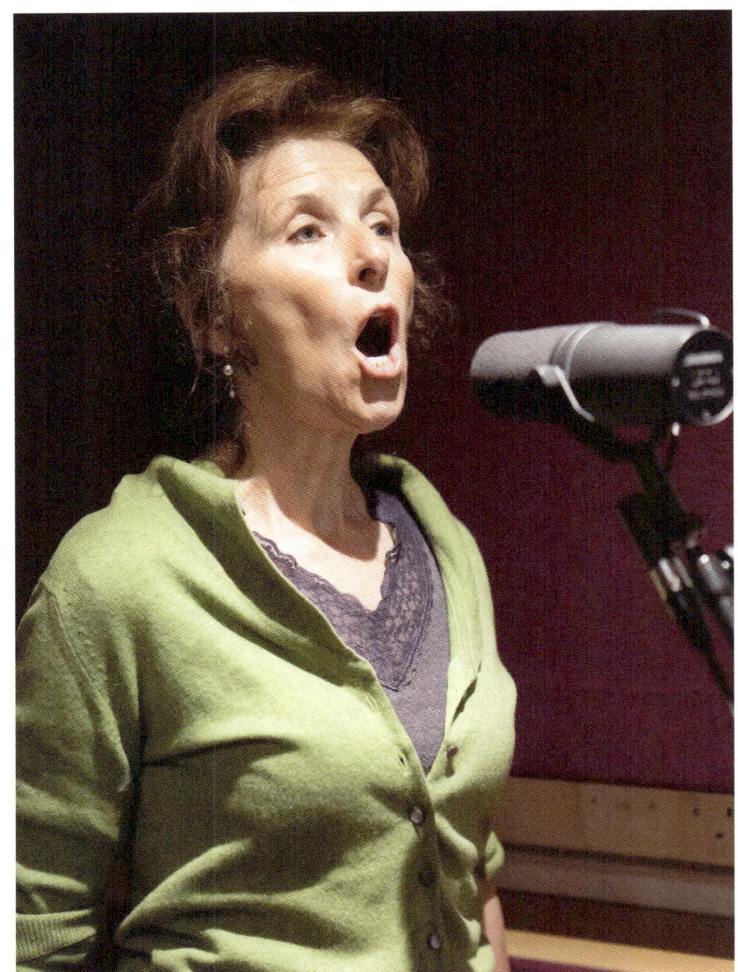

Ursula Böser

Auf gute alte Zeit

Robert Burns (1759–1796)
Translated by Karl Bartsch (1780–1858)

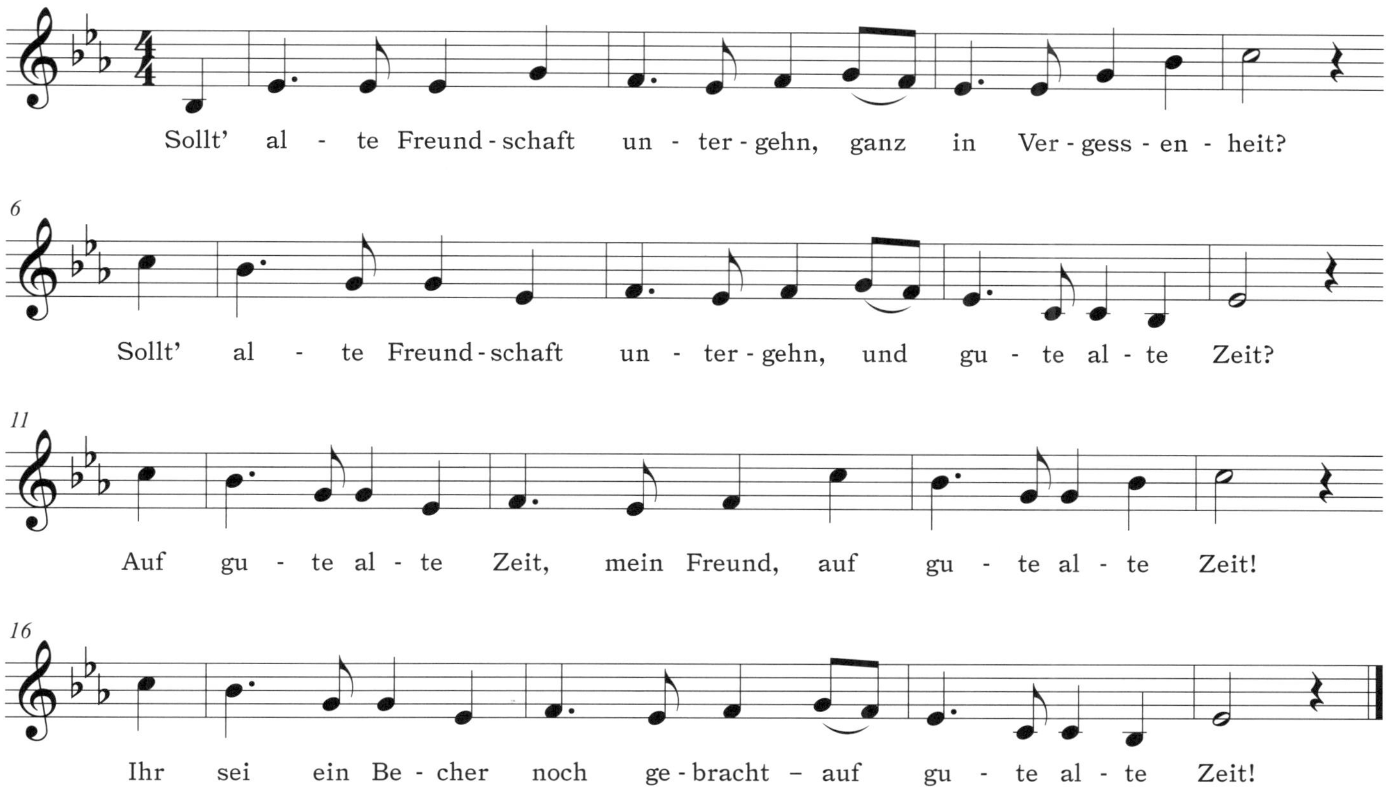

Sollt' alte Freundschaft untergehn,
Ganz in Vergessenheit?
Sollt' alte Freundschaft untergehn,
Und gute alte Zeit?

Auf gute alte Zeit, mein Freund,
Auf gute alte Zeit!
Ihr sei ein Becher noch gebracht –
Auf gute alte Zeit!

Italy

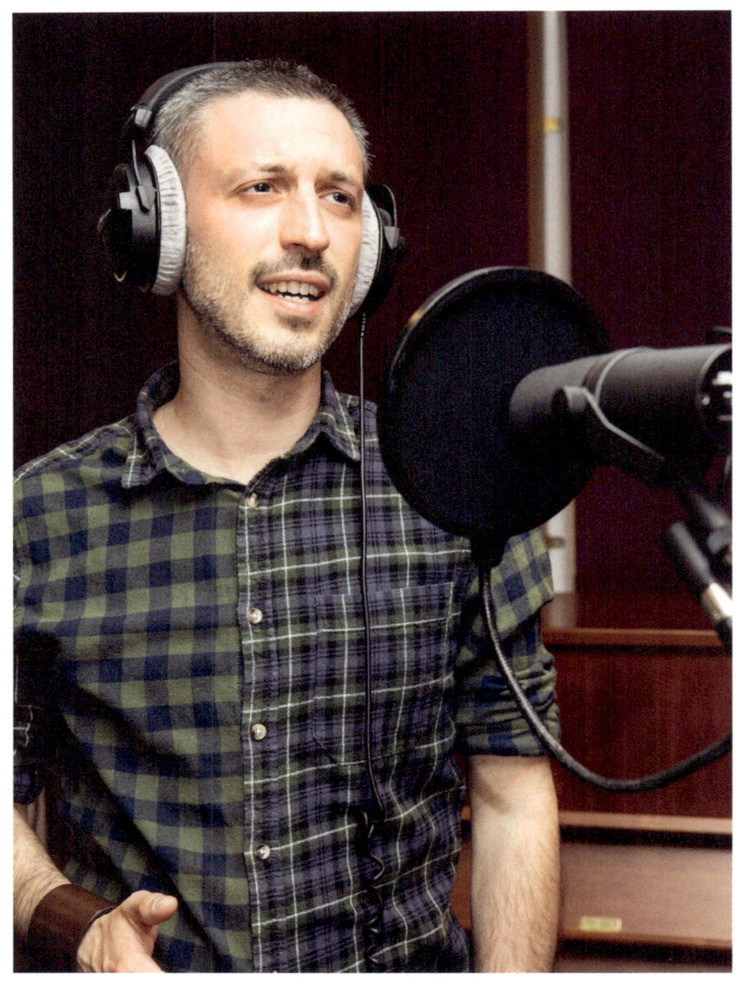

Alberto Sarti

Ai bei vecchi tempi

Robert Burns (1759–1796)
Translated by Alberto Sarti

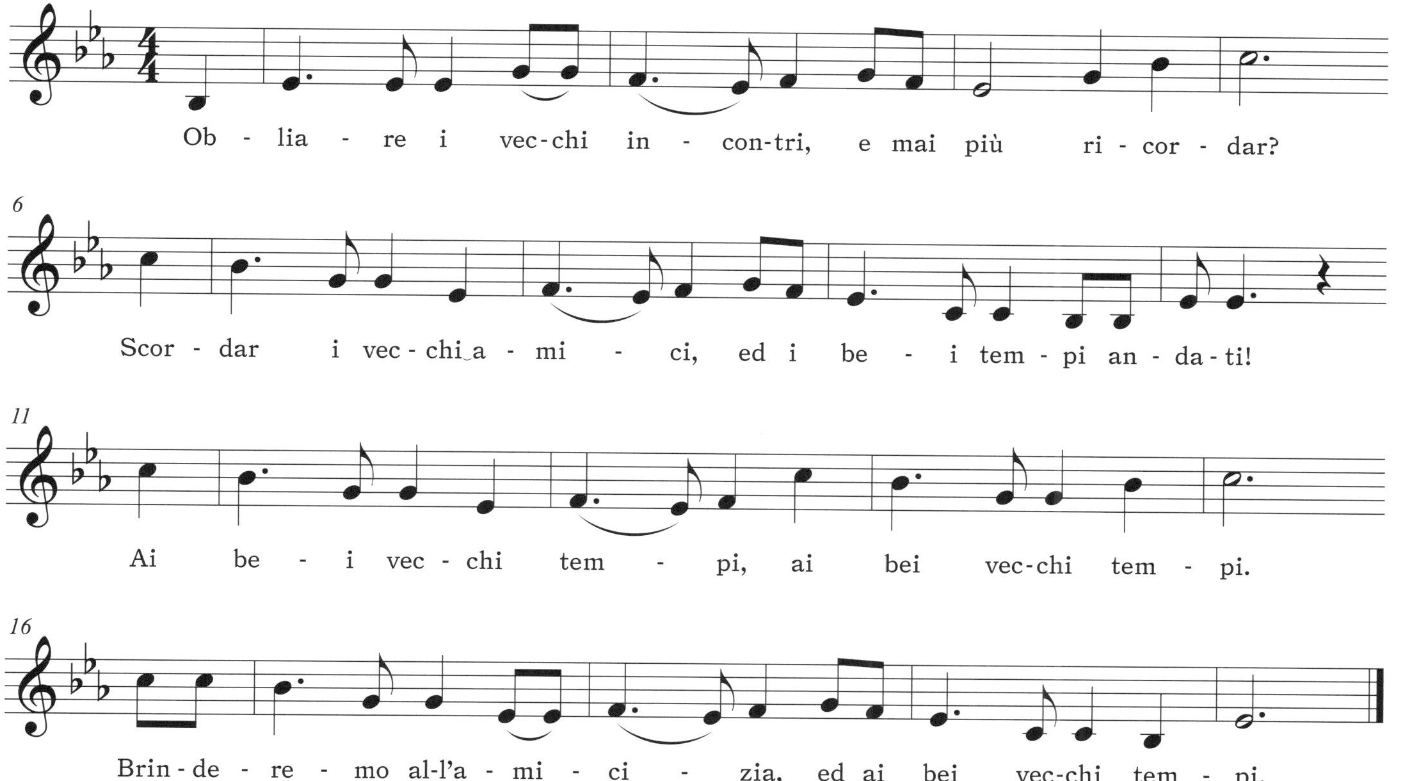

Obliare i vecchi incontri,
e mai più ricordar?
Scordar i vecchi amici,
ed i bei tempi andati!

Ai bei vecchi tempi,
ai bei vecchi tempi.
Brinderemo all'amicizia,
ed ai bei vecchi tempi.

Luxembourg

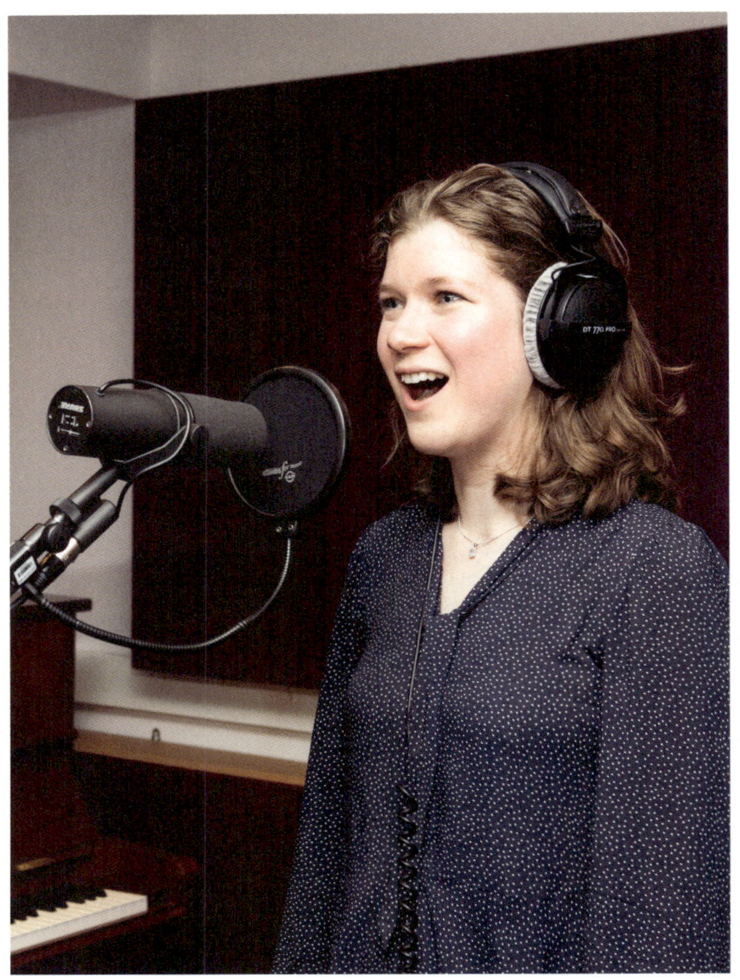

Annemarie Klein

Déi gutt al Zäit

Robert Burns (1759–1796)
Translated by Veruschka Uliczay

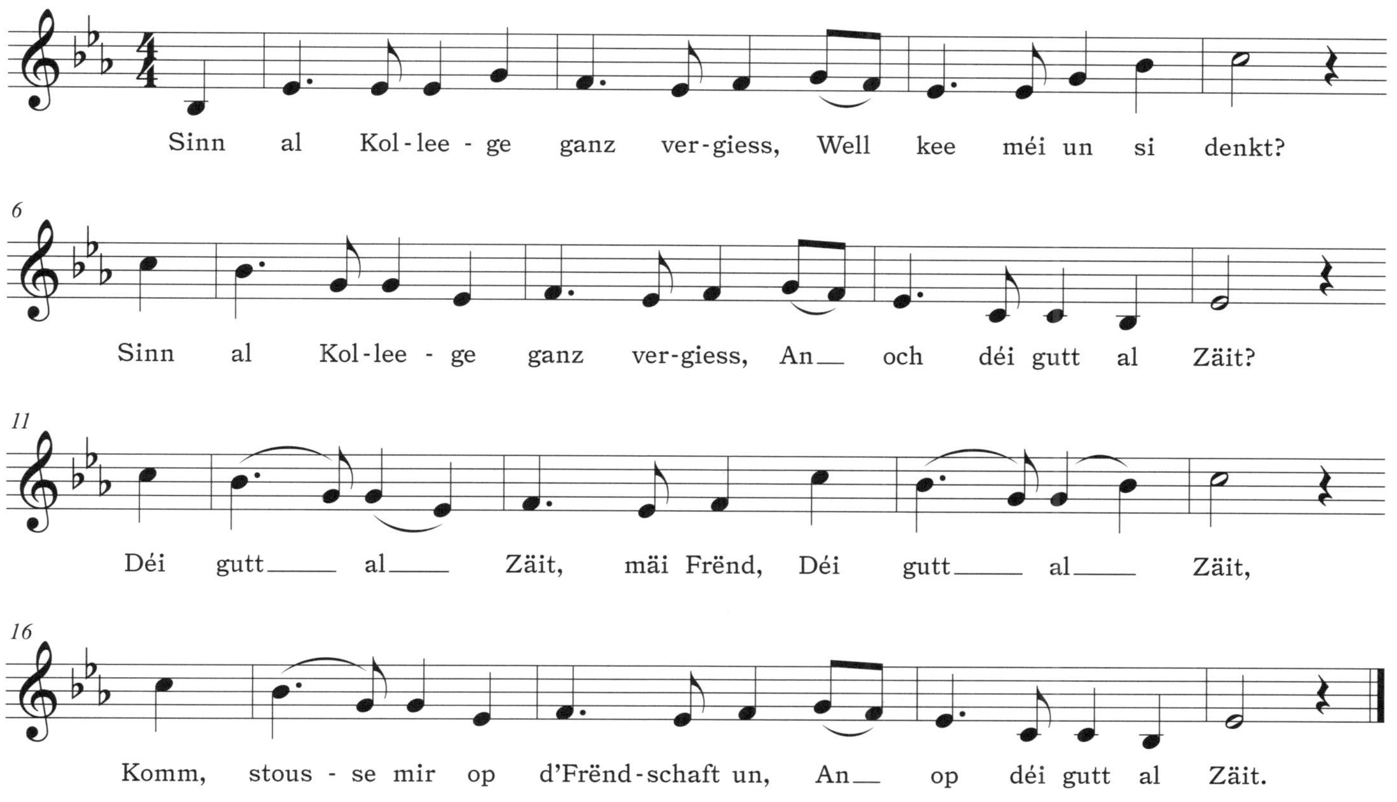

Sinn al Kolleege ganz vergiess,
Well kee méi un si denkt?
Sinn al Kolleege ganz vergiess,
An och déi gutt al Zäit?

Déi gutt al Zäit, mäi Frënd,
Déi gutt al Zäit,
Komm, stousse mir op d'Frëndschaft un,
An op déi gutt al Zäit.

Netherlands

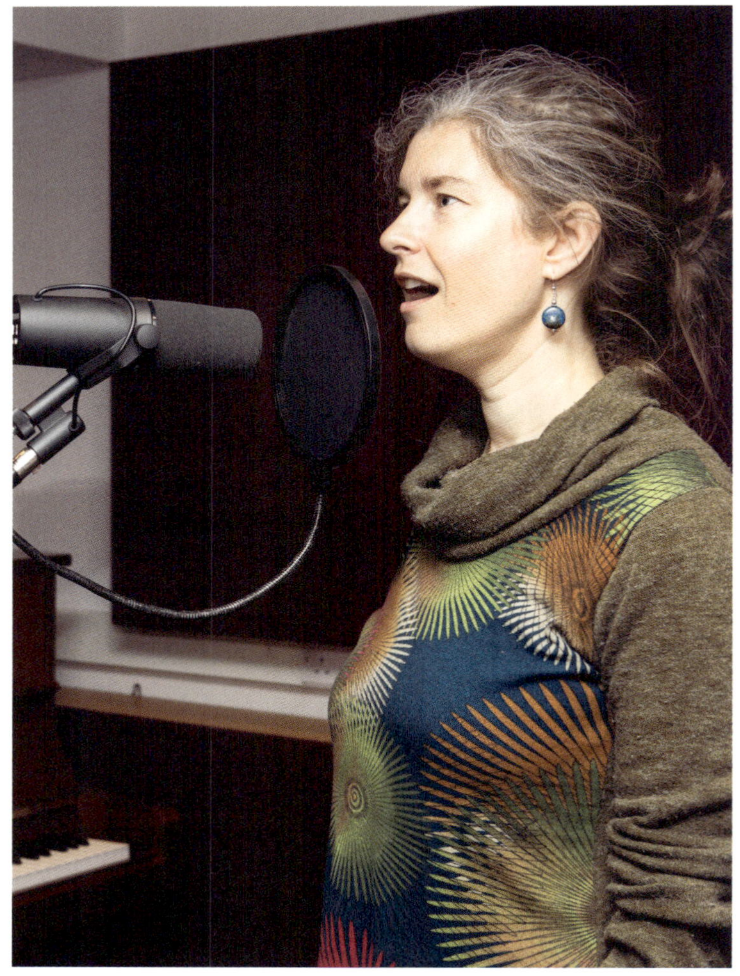

Kristine Mackenzie-Janson

Goede, oude tijd

Robert Burns (1759–1796)
Translated by Juliette Van Gurp

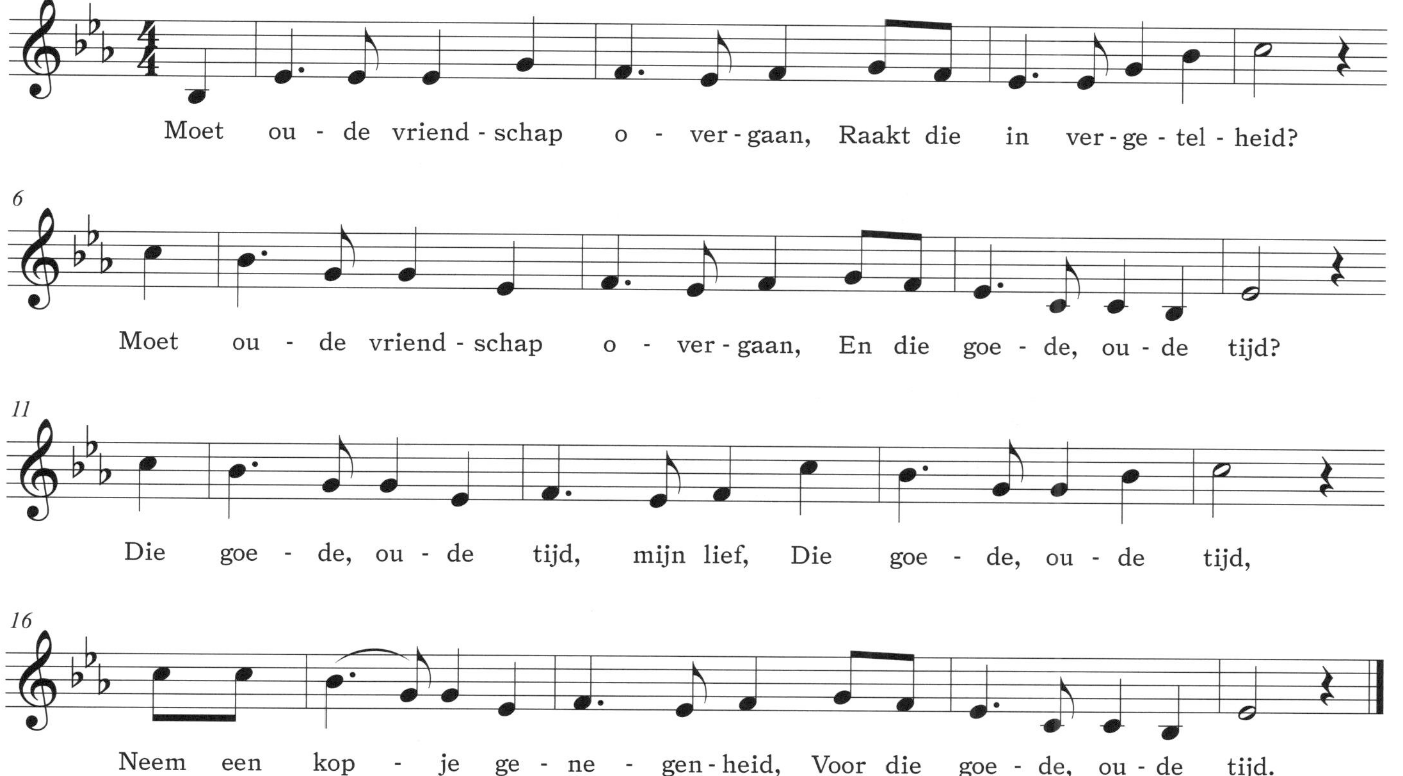

Moet oude vriendschap overgaan,
Raakt die in vergetelheid?
Moet oude vriendschap overgaan,
En die goede, oude tijd?

Die goede, oude tijd, mijn lief,
Die goede, oude tijd,
Neem een kopje genegenheid,
Voor die goede, oude tijd.

Denmark

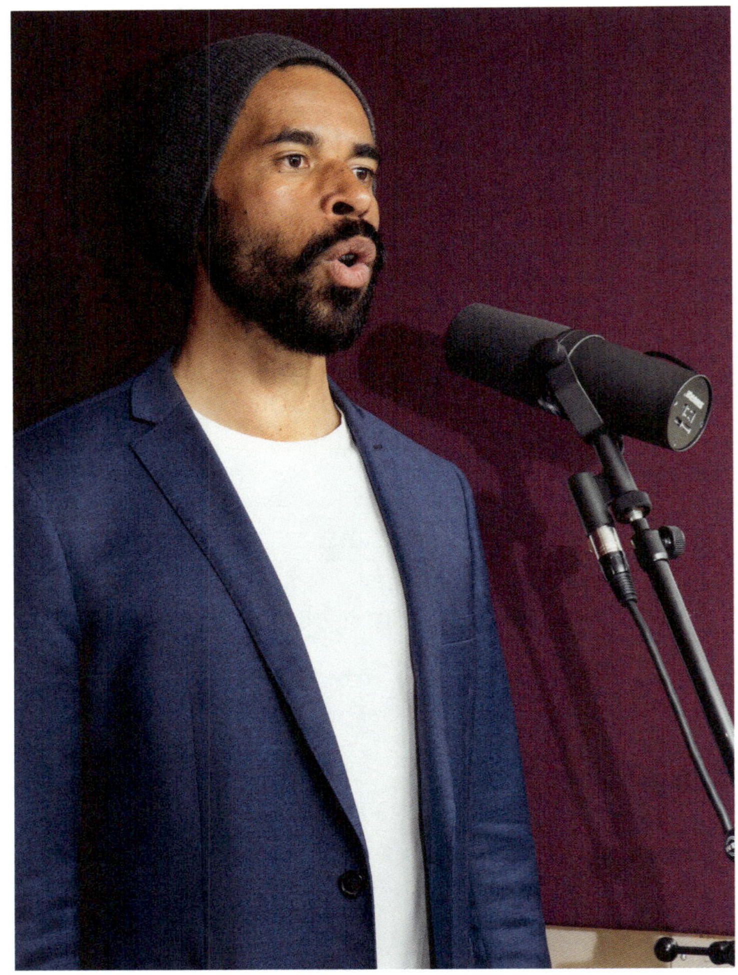

René Sommer Lindsay

Skuld Gammel Venskab

Robert Burns (1759–1796)
Translated by Jeppe Aakjær (1866–1930)

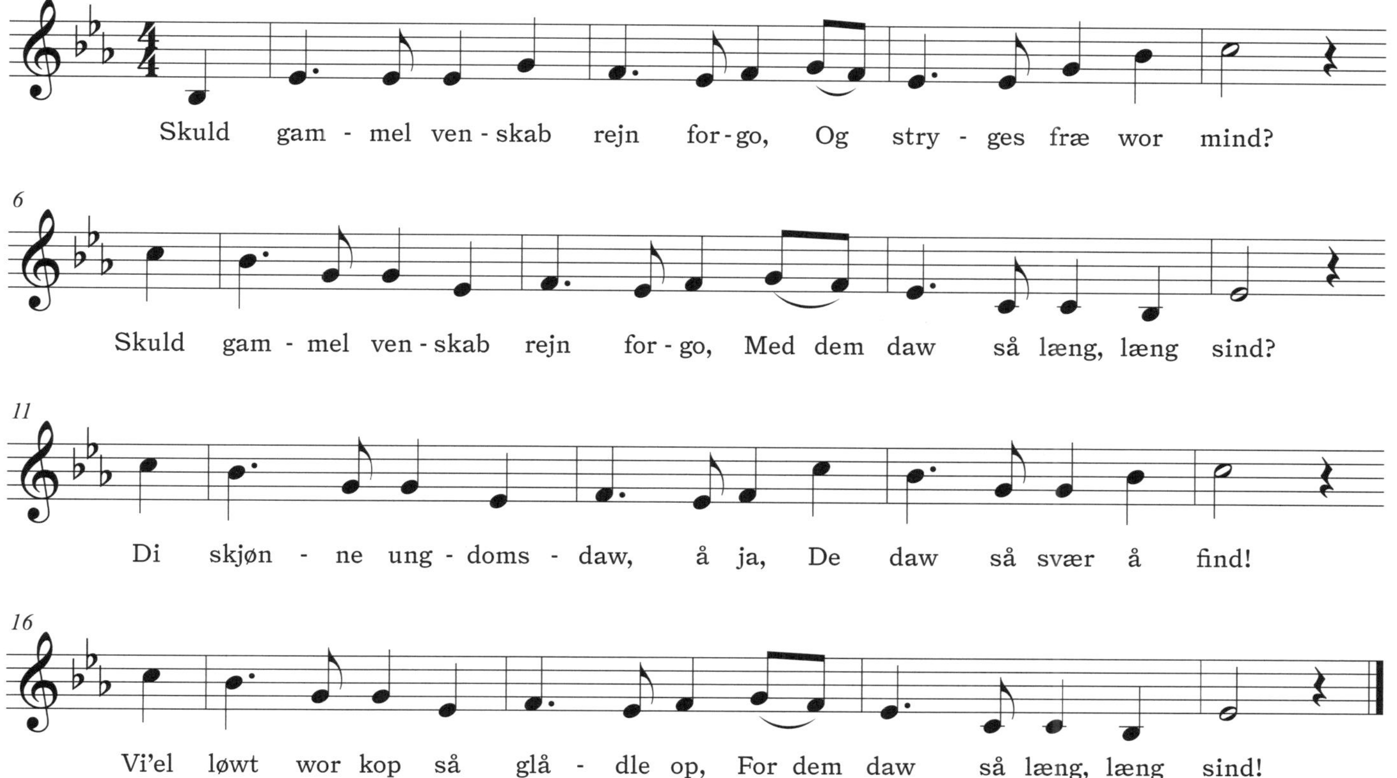

Skuld gammel venskab rejn forgo,
Og stryges fræ wor mind?
Skuld gammel venskab rejn forgo,
Med dem daw så læng, læng sind?

Di skjønne ungdomsdaw, å ja,
De daw så svær å find!
Vi'el løwt wor kop så glådle op,
For dem daw så læng, læng sind!

Ireland

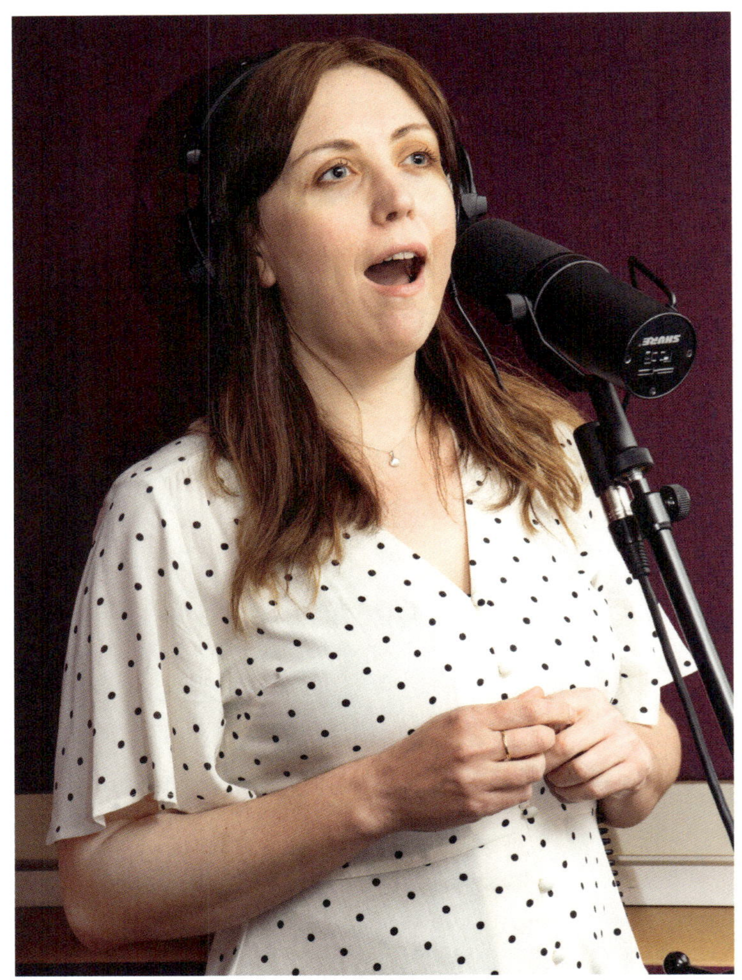

Lori Sky

Na Laethanta Fada Ó Shin

Robert Burns (1759–1796)
Translation by The Translation Room Ltd

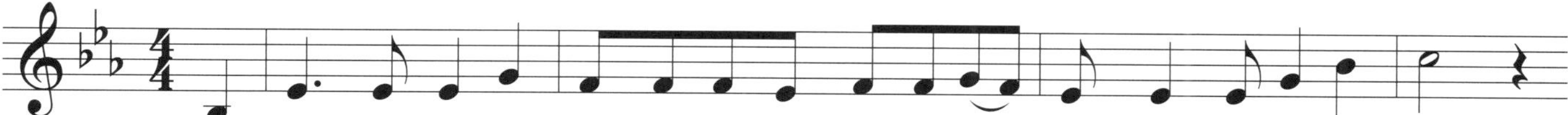

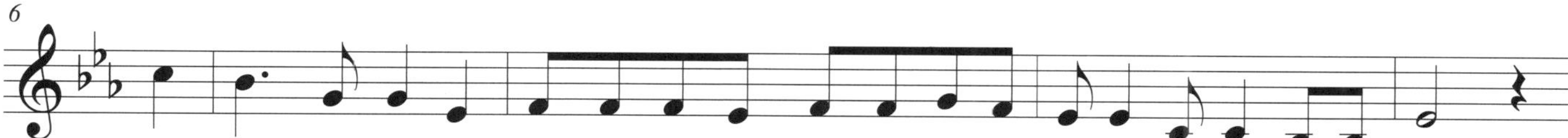

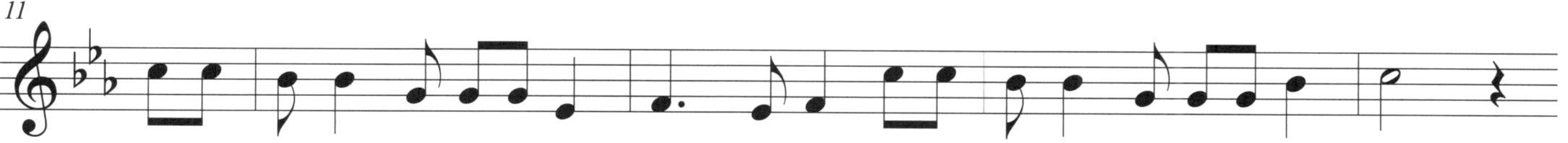

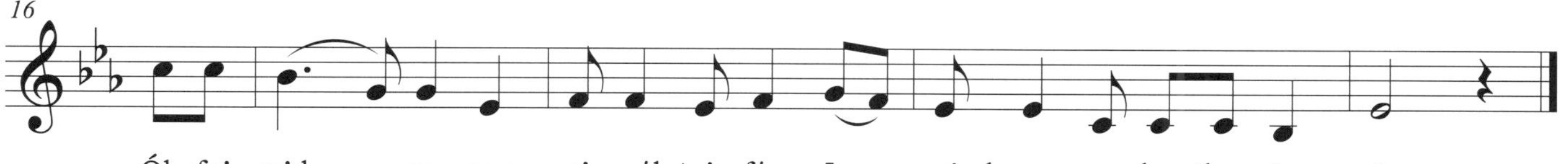

Ar cheart dearmad a dhéanamh ar sheanchairde,
Gan smaoineamh orthu go deo?
Ar cheart dearmad a dhéanamh ar sheanchairde,
Is ar na laethe a bhí againn leo?

Do na laethanta fada ó shin, a stór,
Do na laethanta fada ó shin,
Ólfaimid cupan cineáltais fós,
I gcuimhne na laethanta sin.

United Kingdom

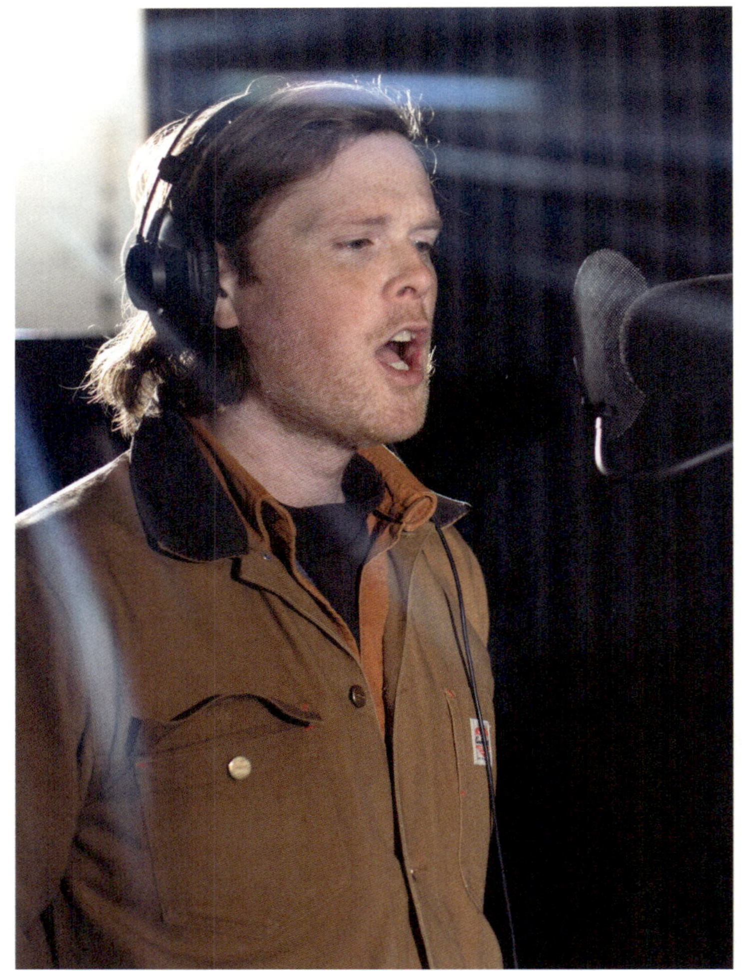

Rory Haye

Auld Lang Syne

Robert Burns (1759–1796)
Published in *Select Collection of Original Scottish Airs* by George Thomson, 1799

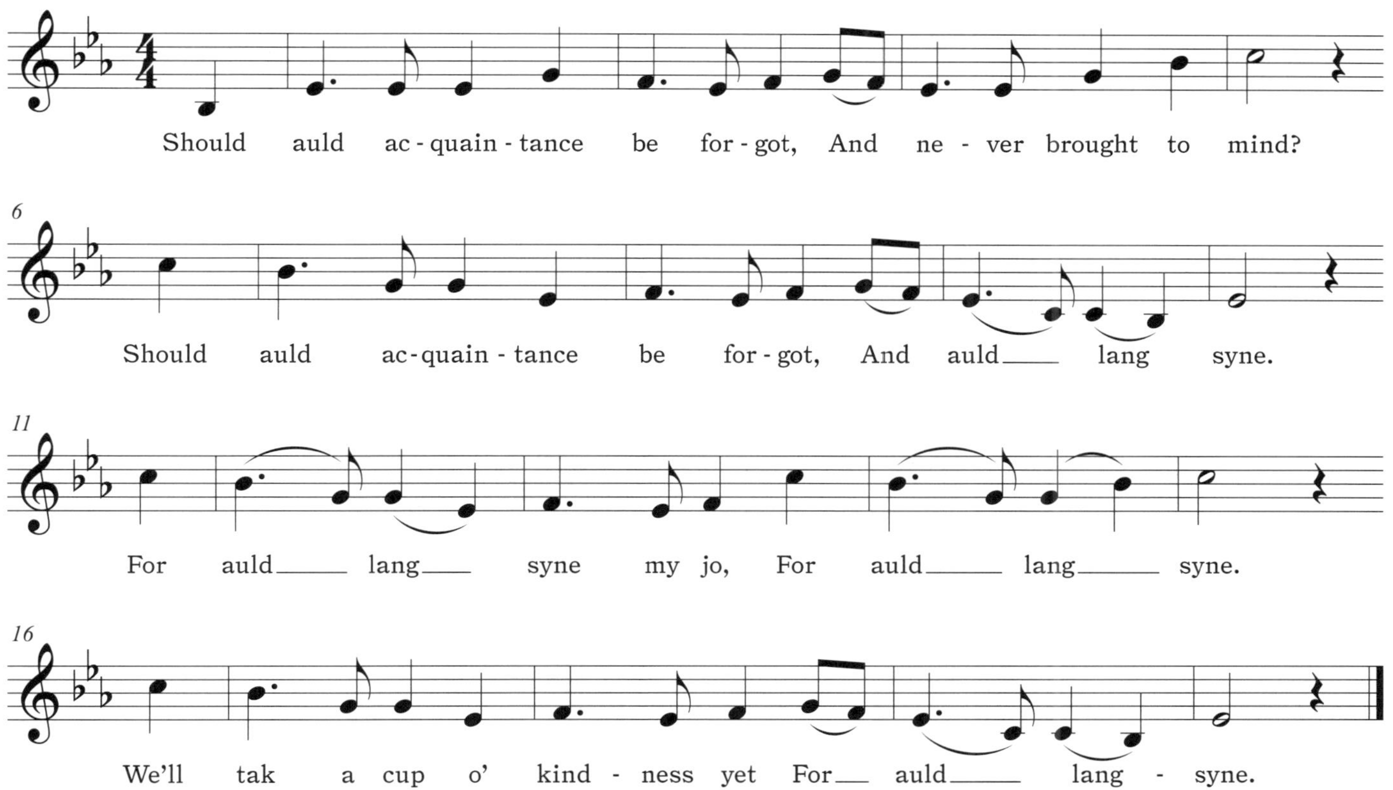

Should auld acquaintance be forgot,
And never brought to mind?
Should auld acquaintance be forgot,
And auld lang syne.

For auld lang syne my jo,
For auld lang syne.
We'll tak a cup o' kindness yet,
For auld lang syne.

Greece

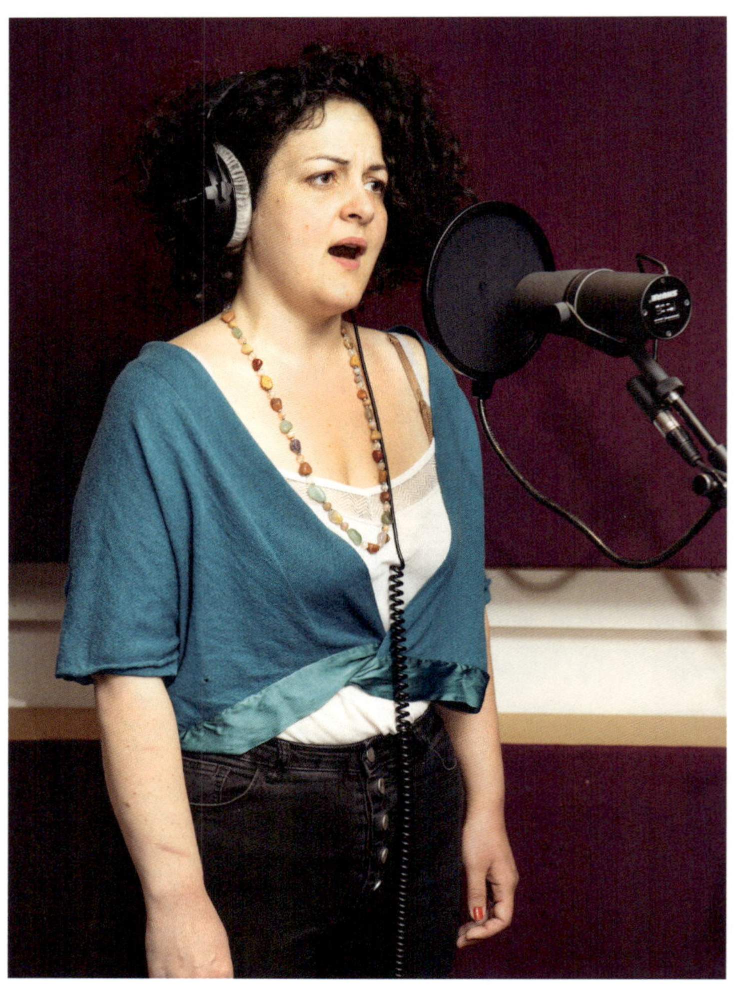

Isidora Bouziouri

Όχι, δεν χωριζόμαστε

Robert Burns (1759–1796)
Greek Boy Scouts song based on 'Auld Lang Syne'

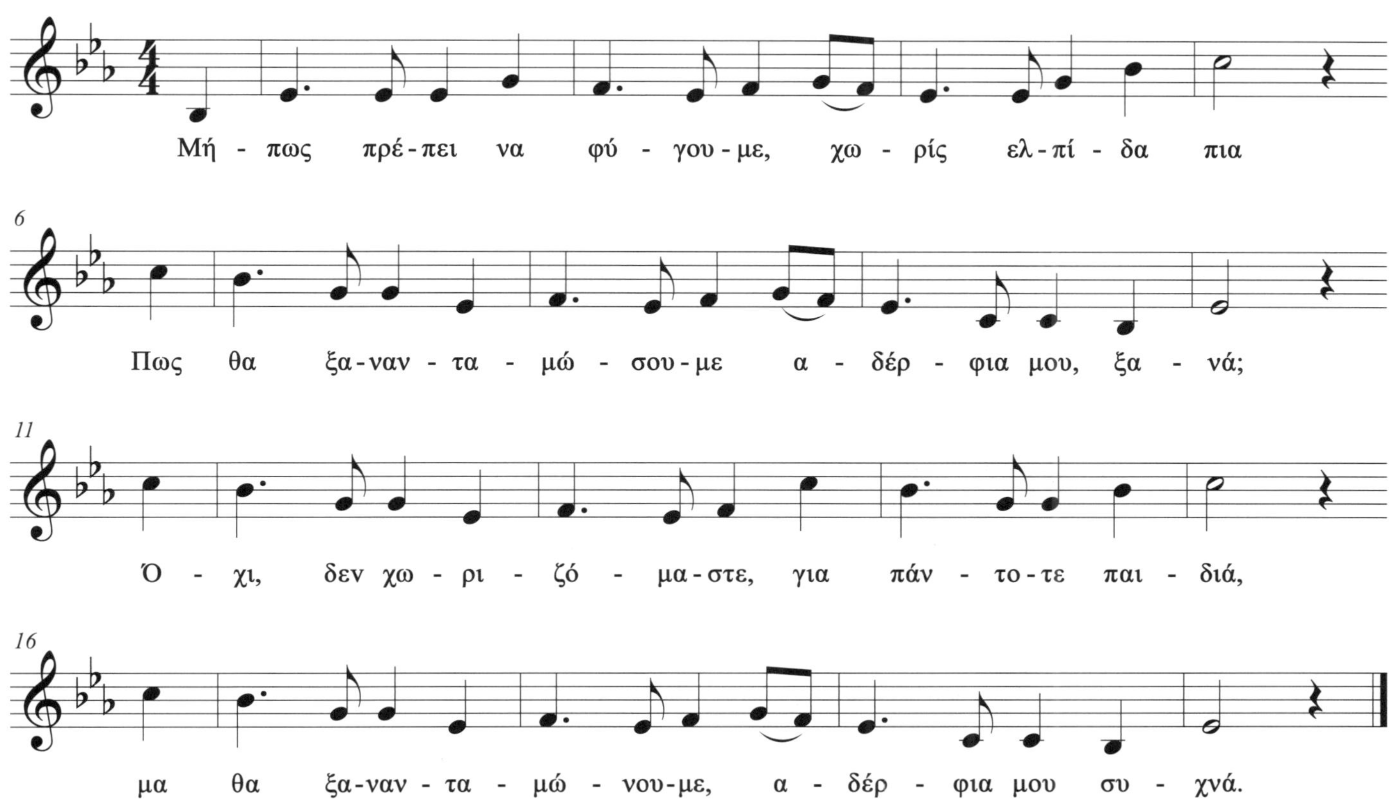

Μήπως πρέπει να φύγουμε,
χωρίς ελπίδα πια,
πως θα ξανανταμώσουμε,
αδέρφια μου ξανά;

Όχι δεν χωριζόμαστε,
για πάντοτε παιδιά,
μα θα ξανανταμώνουμε,
αδέρφια μου συχνά.

Portugal

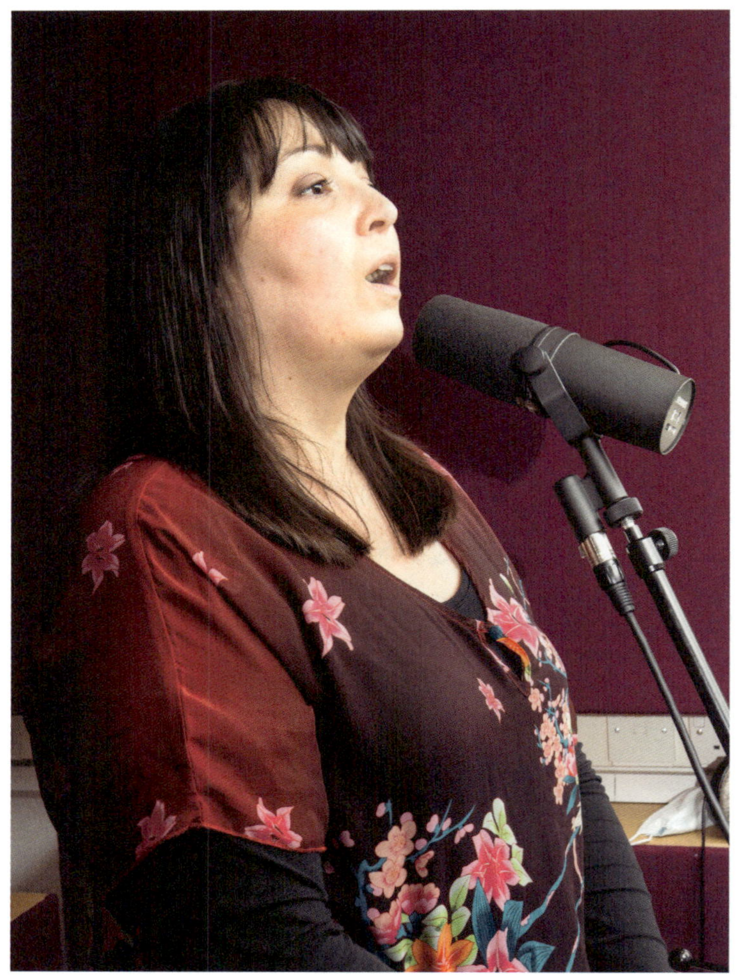

Carla Mendonça Ward

Tão bons os tempos idos

Robert Burns (1759–1796)
Translated by Ana Vozone

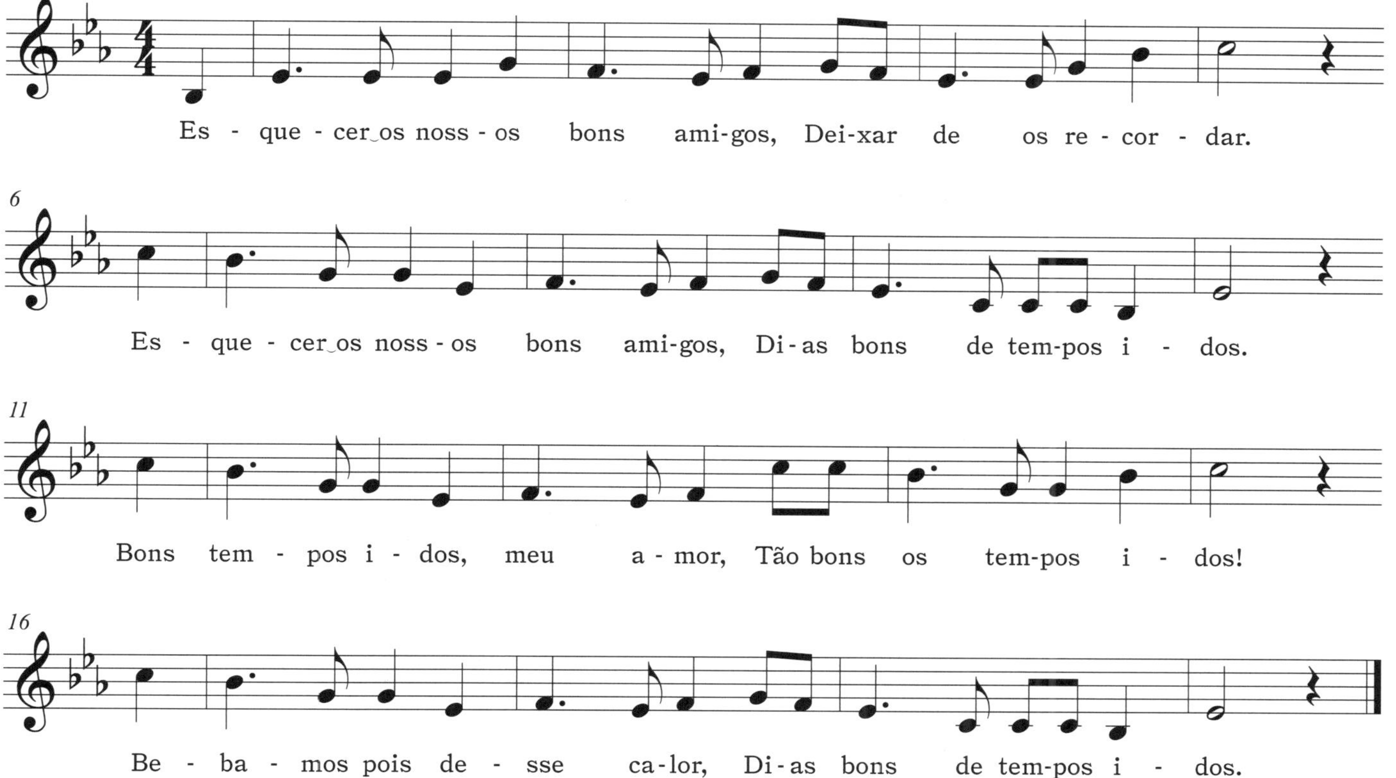

Esquecer os nossos bons amigos,
Deixar de os recordar.
Esquecer os nossos bons amigos,
Dias bons de tempos idos.

Bons tempos idos, meu amor,
Tão bons os tempos idos!
Bebamos pois desse calor,
Dias bons de tempos idos.

Spain

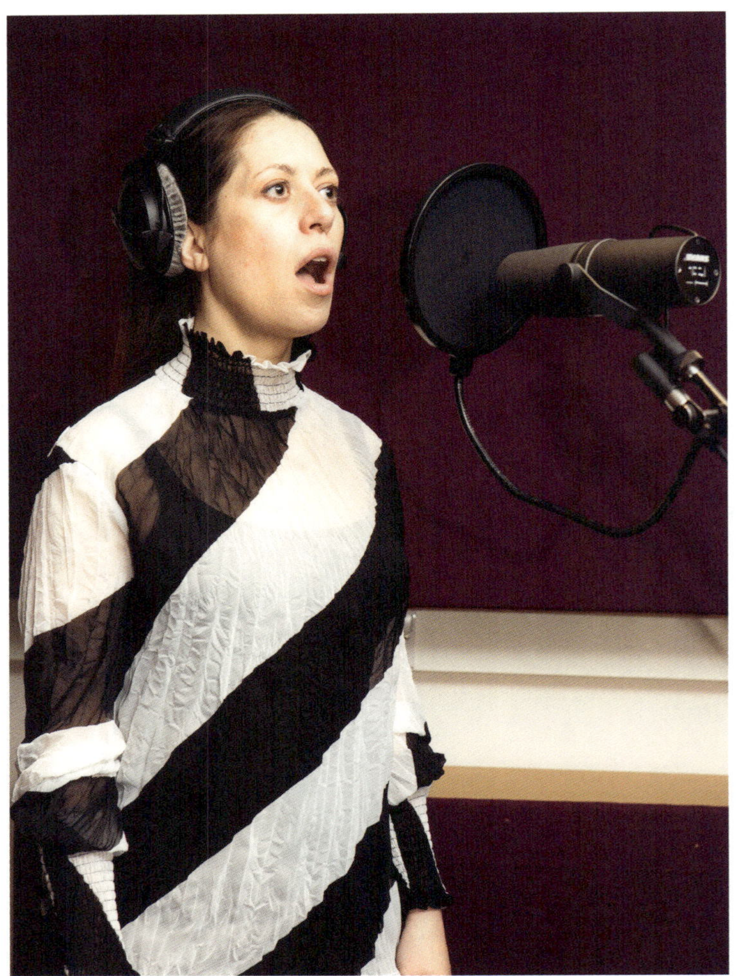

Amaya López-Carromero

Aunque lejos estés

Robert Burns (1759–1796)
Translation from the Centre for Robert Burns Studies

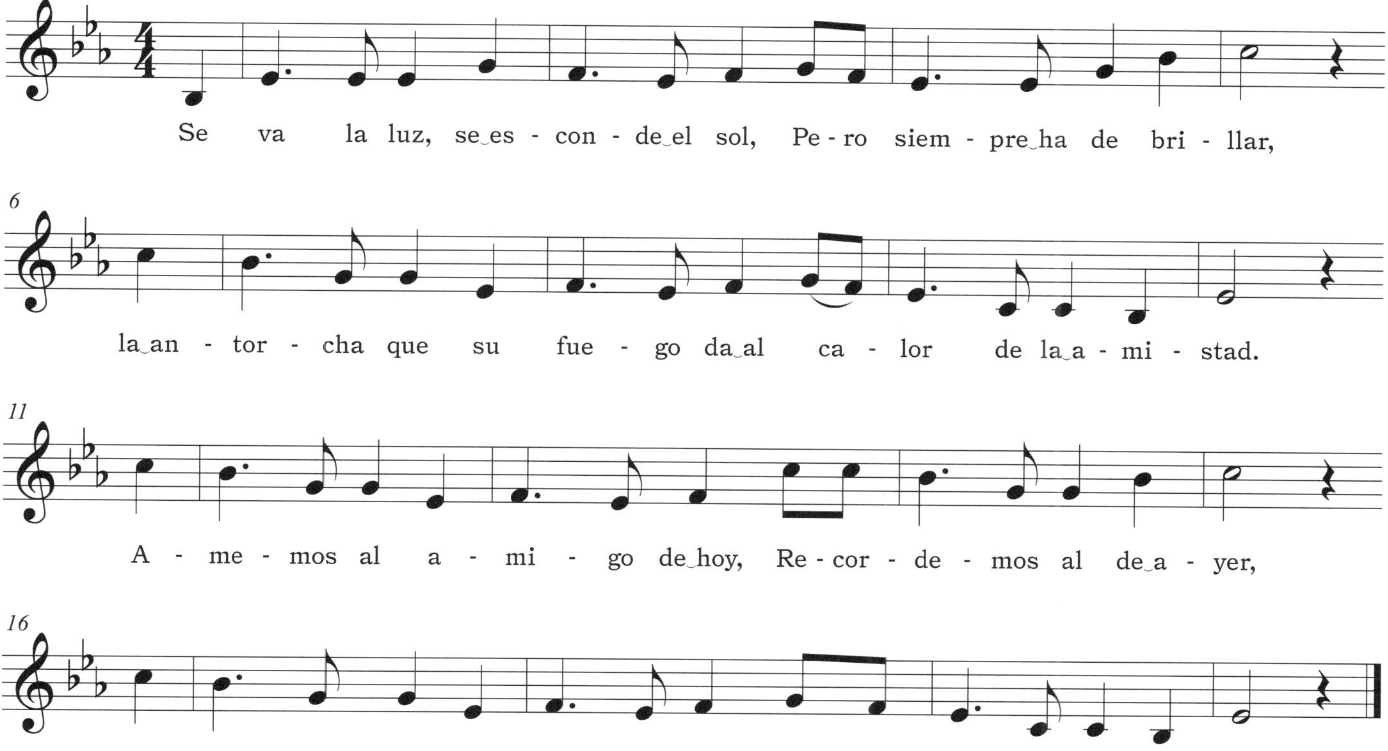

Se va la luz, se esconde el sol,
pero siempre ha de brillar,
la antorcha que su fuego da,
al calor de la amistad.

Amemos al amigo de hoy,
recordemos al de ayer,
Amigo, aunque lejos estés,
siempre amigo has de ser.

Austria

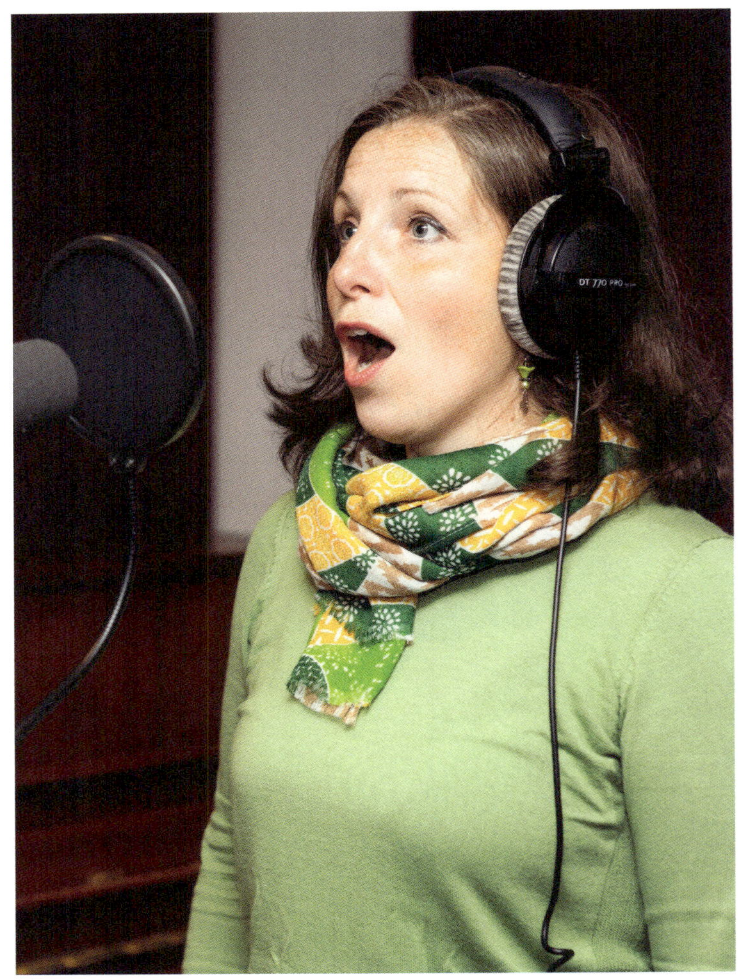

Ulrike Wutscher

An die vergang'ne Zeit

Robert Burns (1759–1796)
Translated by Ulrike Wutscher

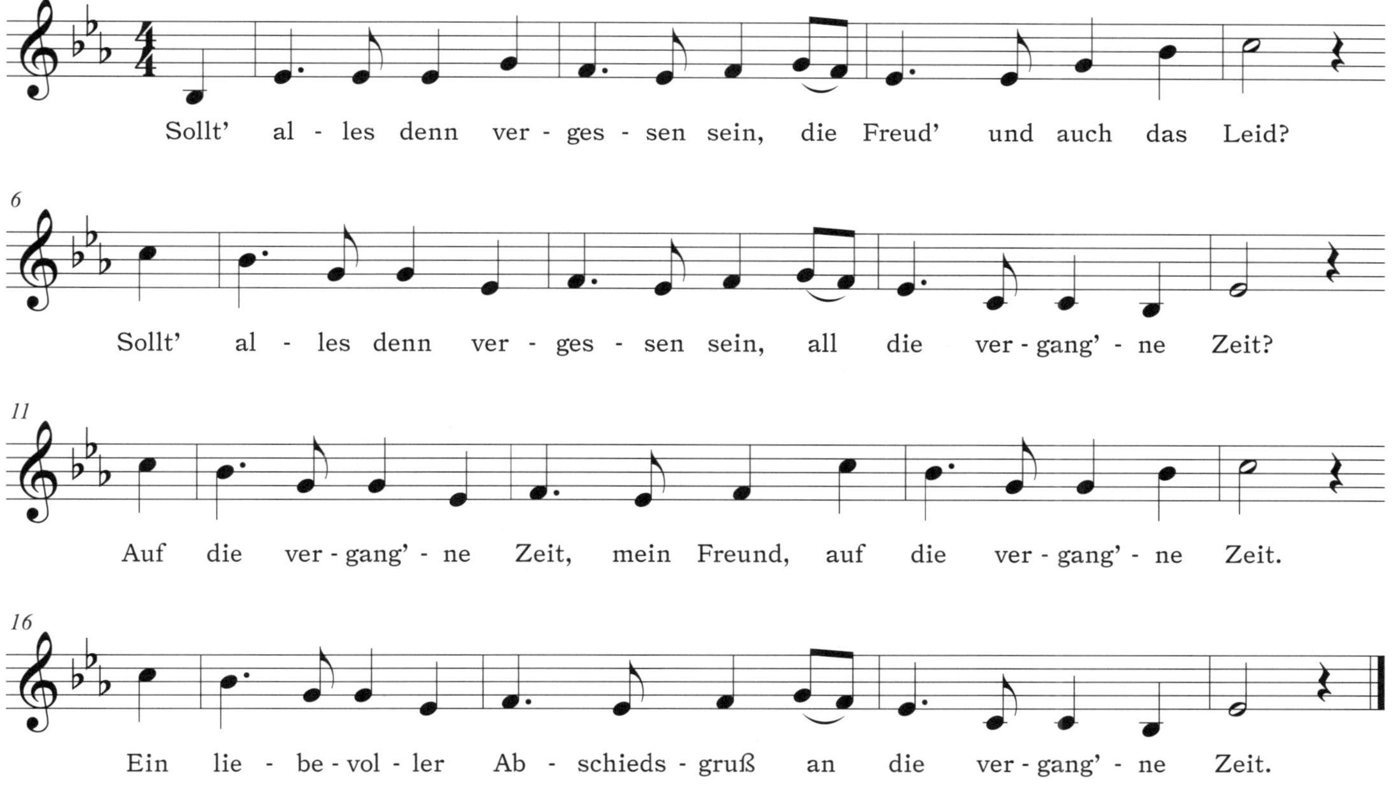

Sollt' alles denn vergessen sein,
die Freud' und auch das Leid?
Sollt' alles denn vergessen sein,
all die vergang'ne Zeit?

Auf die vergang'ne Zeit, mein Freund,
auf die vergang'ne Zeit.
Ein liebevoller Abschiedsgruß
an die vergang'ne Zeit.

Finland

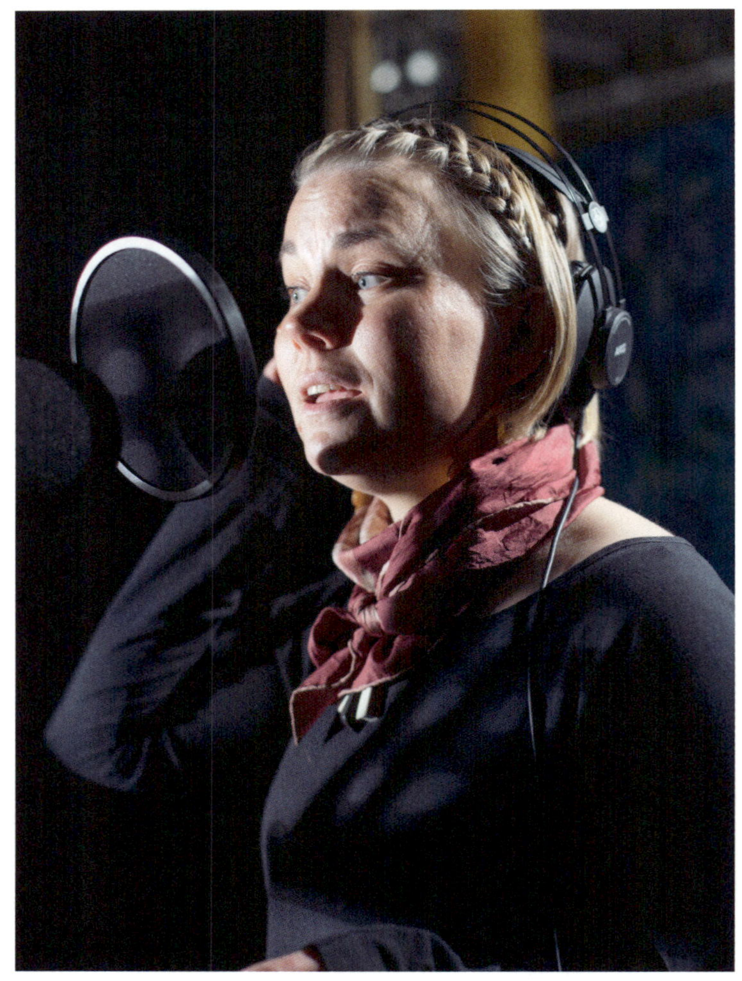

Outi Smith

Tää ystävyys ei raukene

Robert Burns (1759–1796)
Translator unknown

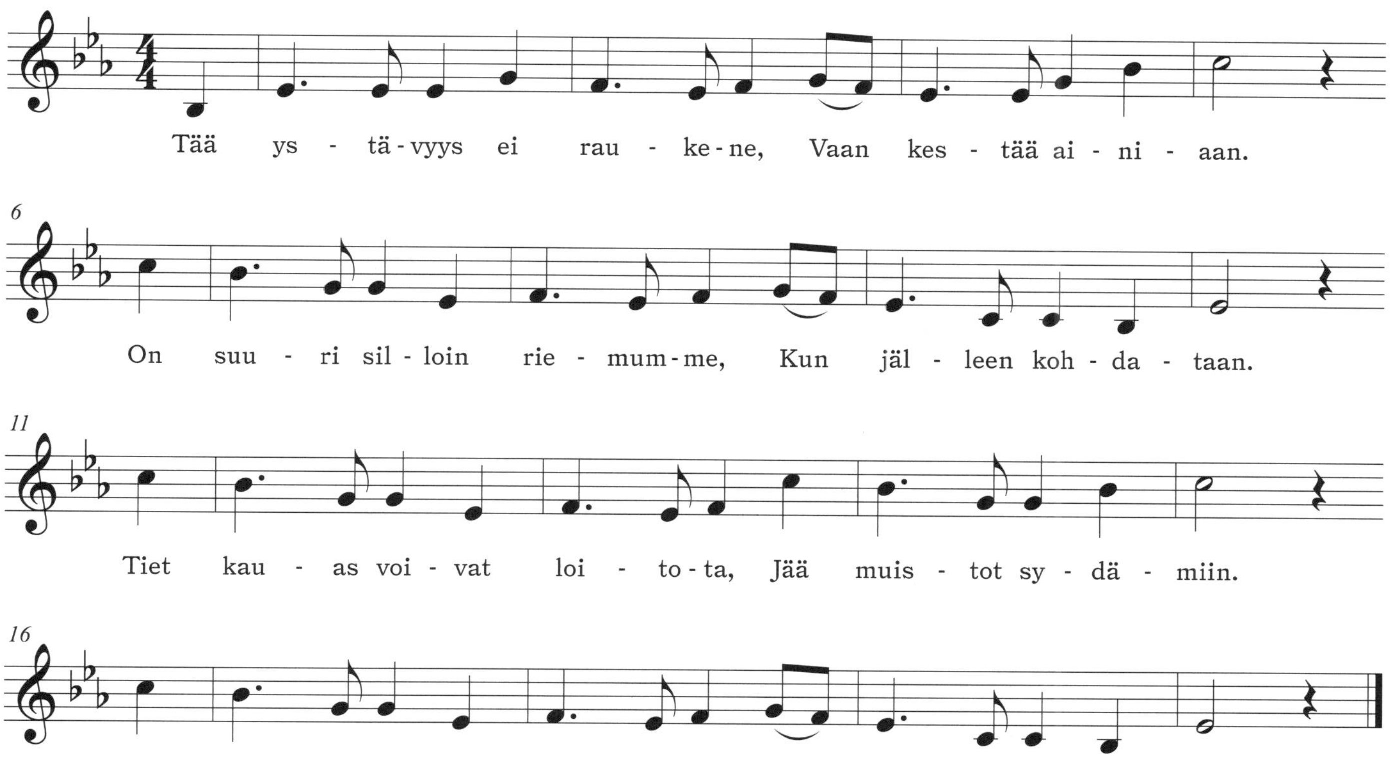

Tää ystävyys ei raukene,
Vaan kestää ainiaan.
On suuri silloin riemumme,
Kun jälleen kohdataan.

Tiet kauas voivat loitota,
Jää muistot sydämiin.
Siis vielä kiitos kaikesta,
Ja terve, näkemiin.

Sweden

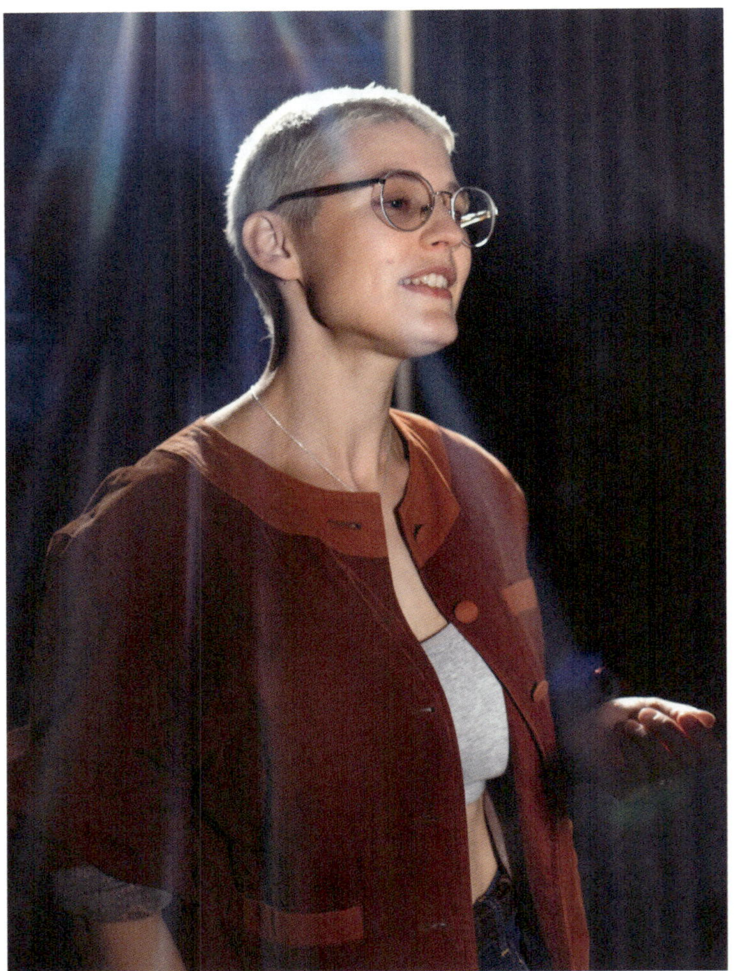

Tova Svanfeldt

Skall gammal vänskap glömmas bort

Robert Burns (1759–1796)
Translated by Magnus Gustaf Retzius (1842–1919)

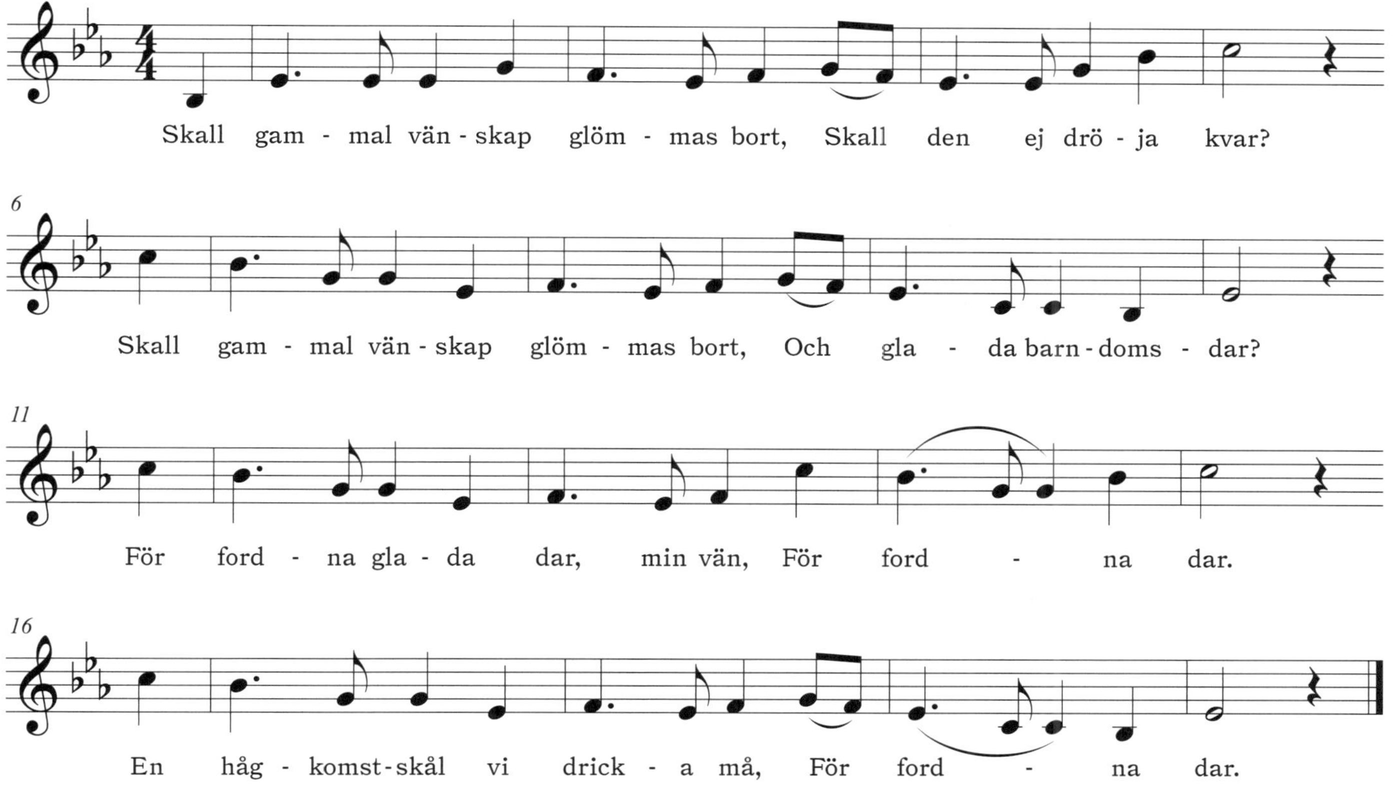

Skall gammal vänskap glömmas bort,
Skall den ej dröja kvar?
Skall gammal vänskap glömmas bort,
Och glada barndomsdar?

För fordna glada dar, min vän,
För fordna dar.
En hågkomstskål vi dricka må,
För fordna dar.

Cyprus

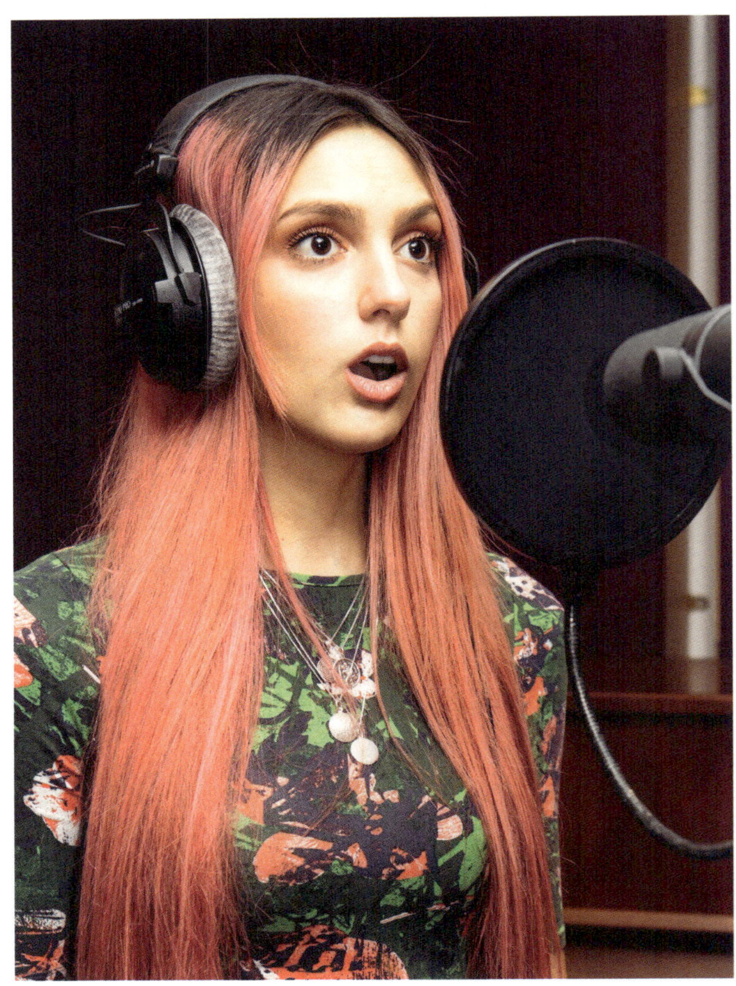

Crystalla Lola Serghiou

θα Ξανανταμώσουμε

Robert Burns (1759–1796)
Greek Boy Scouts song based on 'Auld Lang Syne'

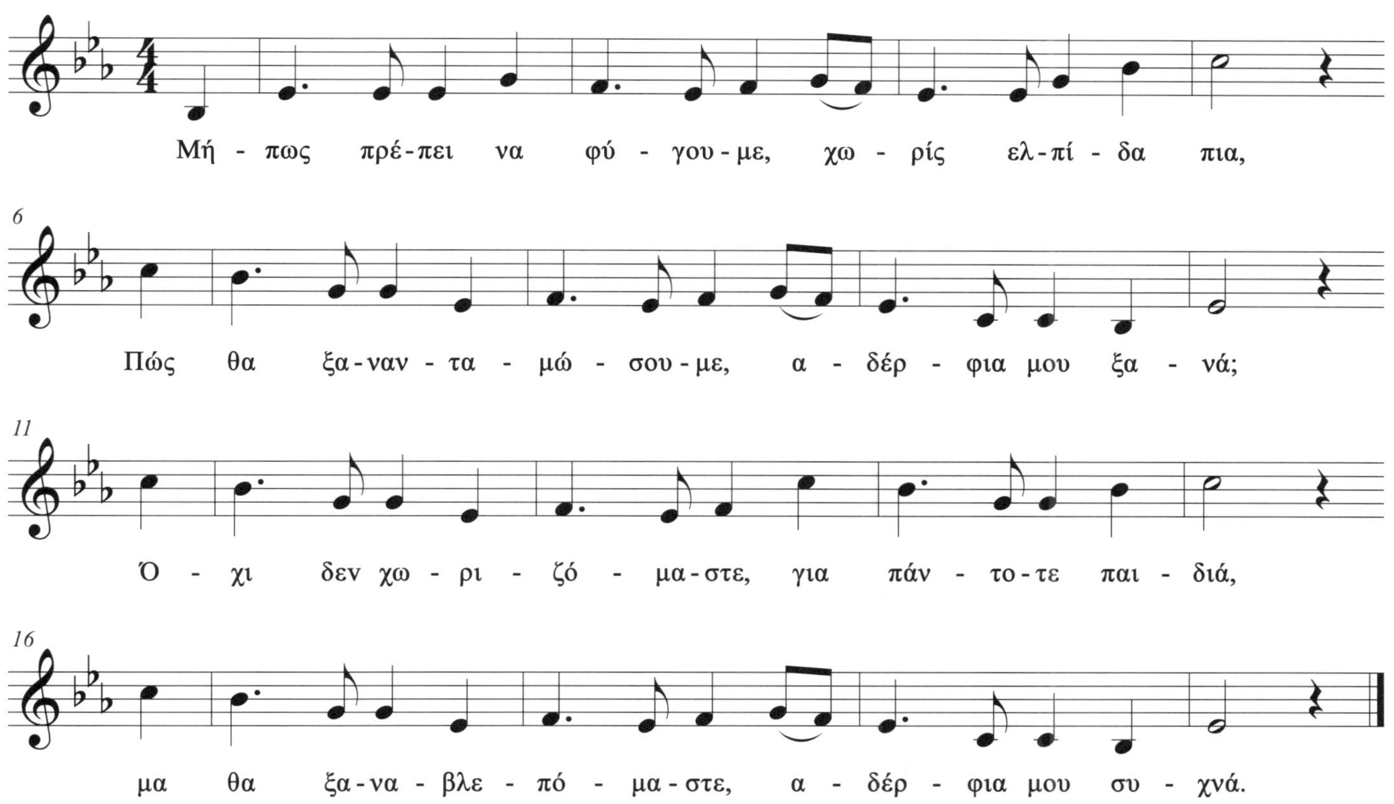

Μήπως πρέπει να φύγουμε,
χωρίς ελπίδα πια,
πώς θα ξανανταμώσουμε,
αδέρφια μου ξανά;

Όχι δεν χωριζόμαστε,
για πάντοτε παιδιά,
μα θα ξαναβλεπόμαστε,
αδέρφια μου συχνά.

Czech Republic

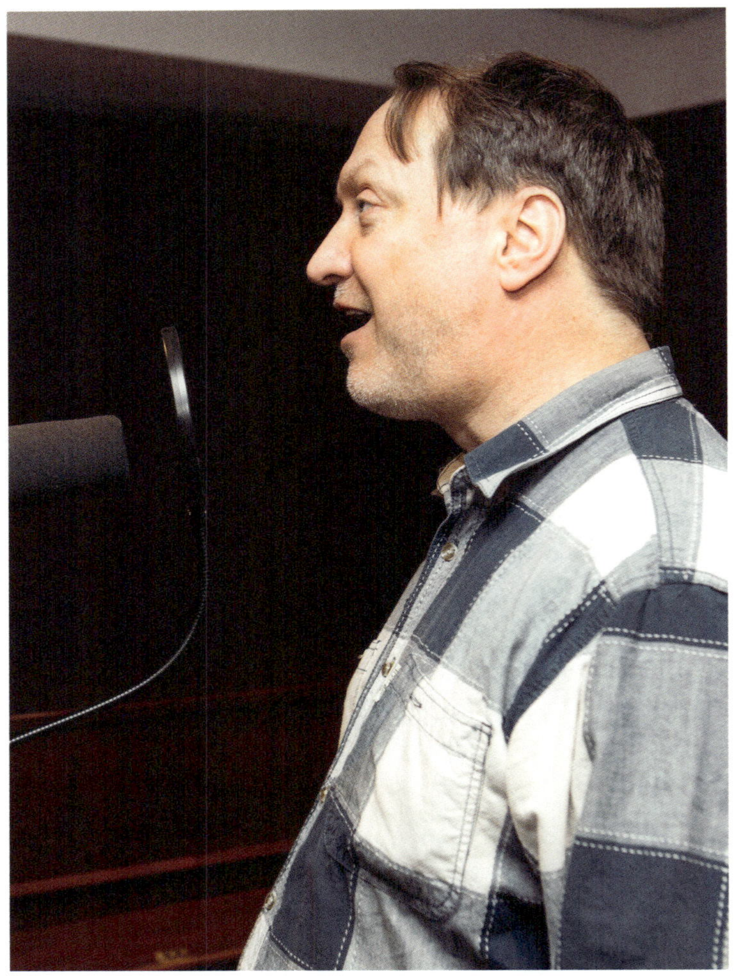

Štěpán Janča

Dávno již

Robert Burns (1759–1796)
Translated by Josef Václav Sládek (1845–1912)

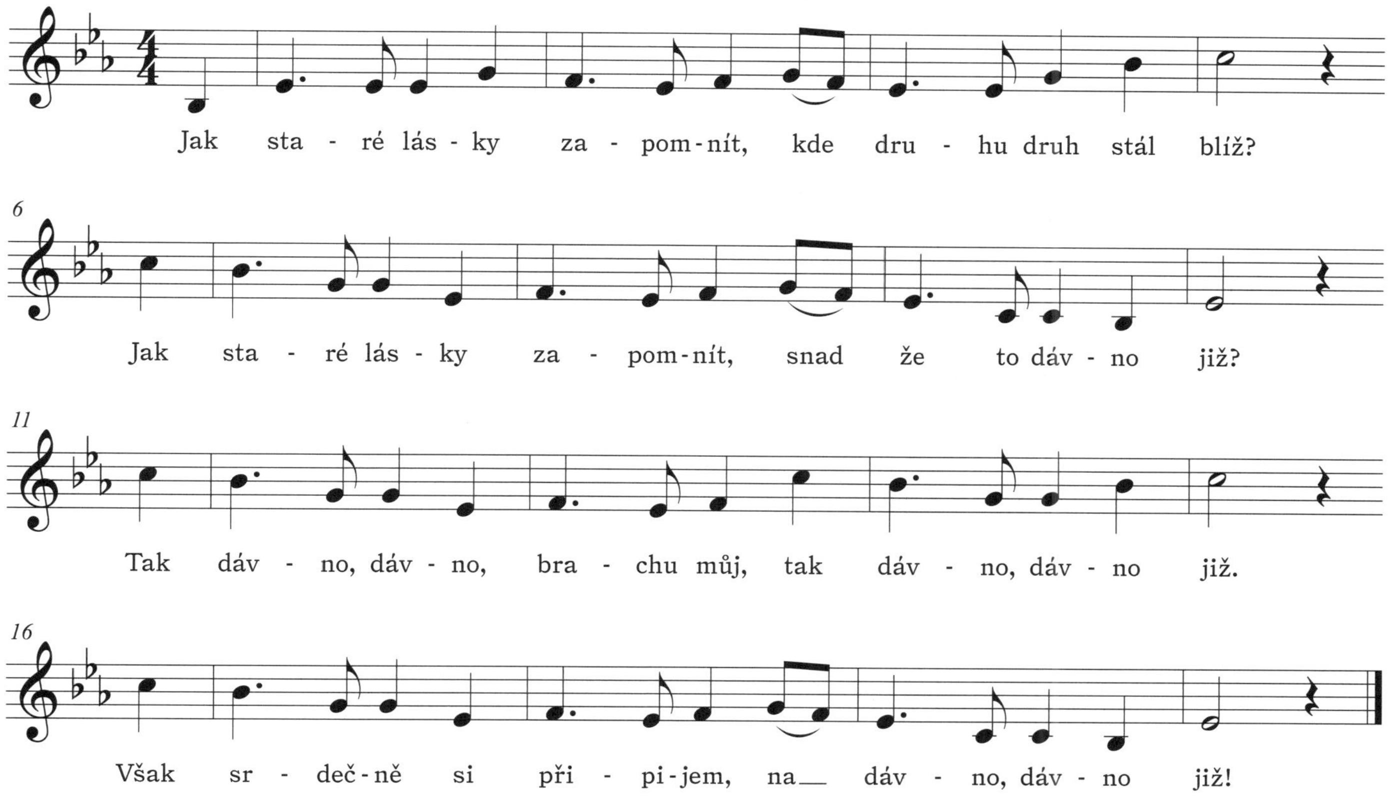

Jak staré lásky zapomnít,
kde druhu druh stál blíž?
Jak staré lásky zapomnít,
snad že to dávno již?

Tak dávno, dávno, brachu můj,
tak dávno, dávno již.
Však srdečně si připijem,
na dávno, dávno již!

Estonia

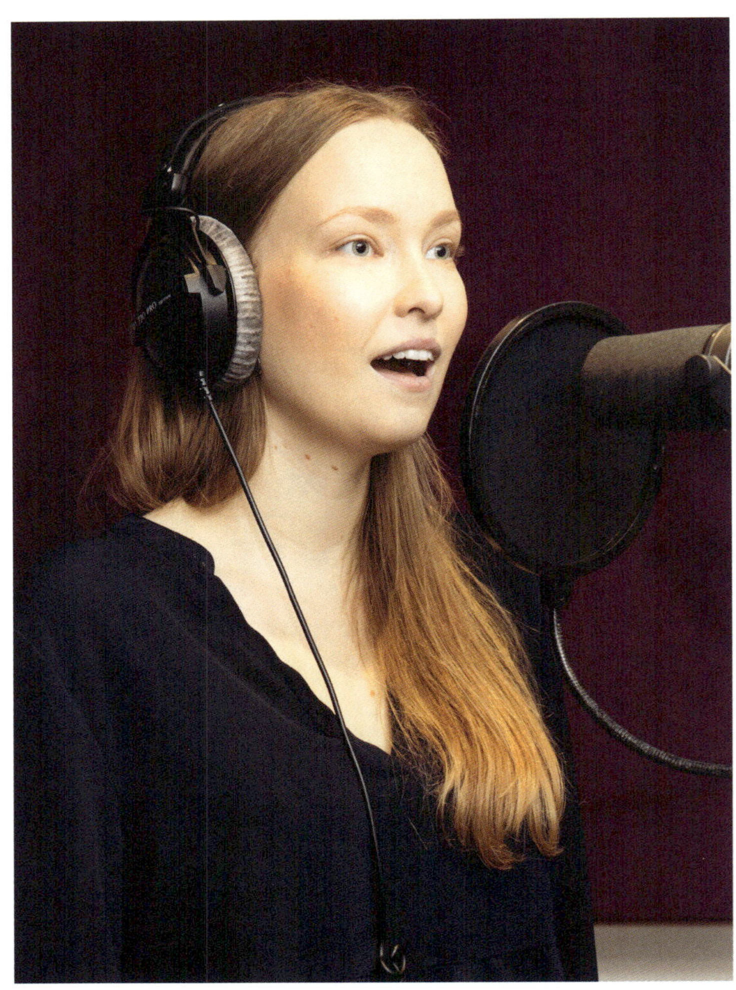

Greteliis Kattus

Ajad ammused

Robert Burns (1759–1796)
Translated by Ivi Leiar

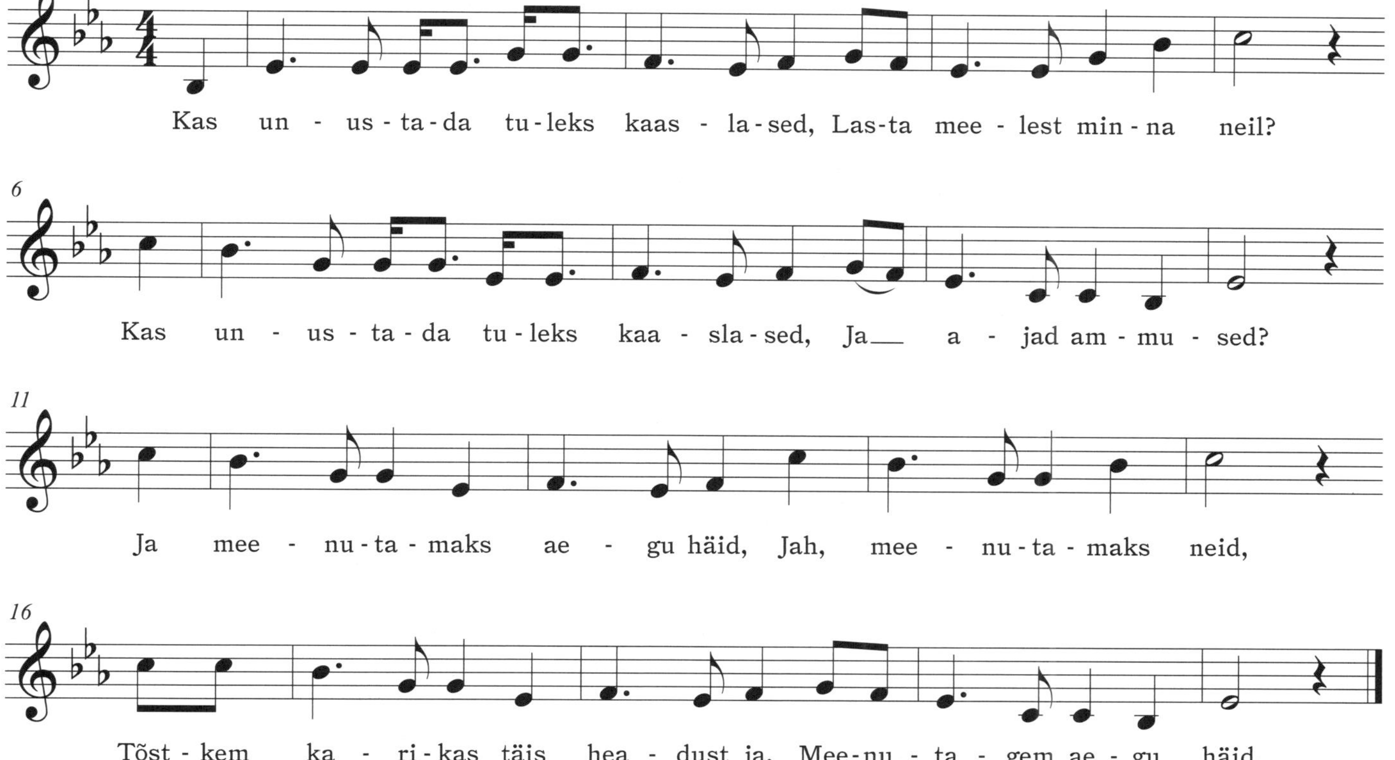

Kas unustada tuleks kaaslased,
Lasta meelest minna neil?
Kas unustada tuleks kaaslased,
Ja ajad ammused?

Ja meenutamaks aegu häid,
Jah, meenutamaks neid,
Tõstkem karikas täis headust ja,
Meenutagem aegu häid.

Hungary

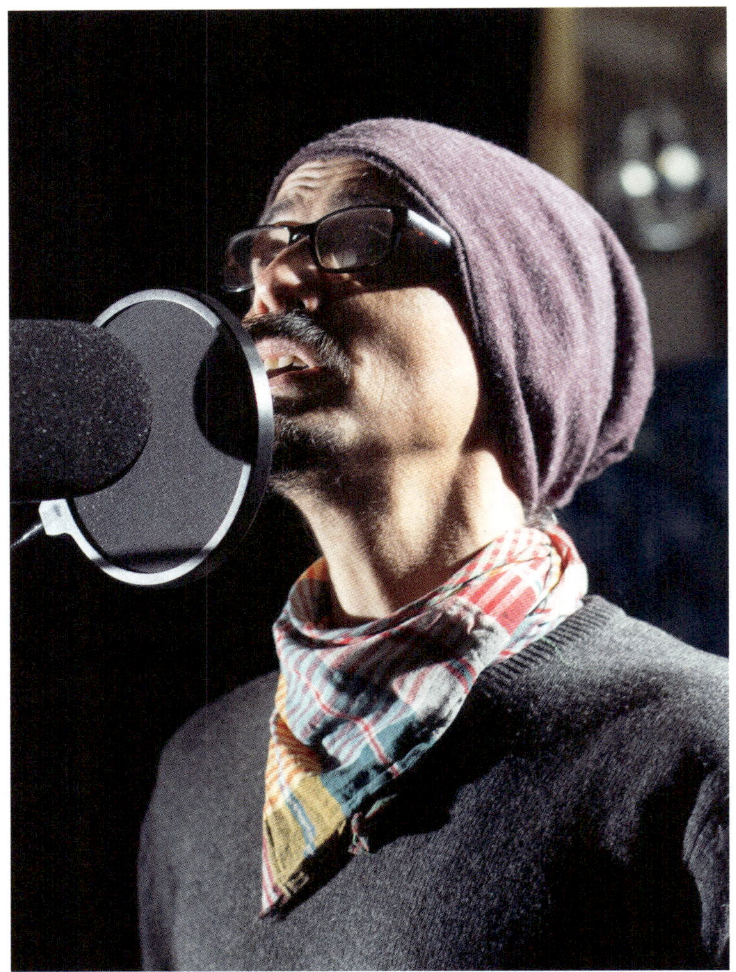

Bado Réti

Régmúlt idők

Robert Burns (1759–1796)
Translated by Bado Réti

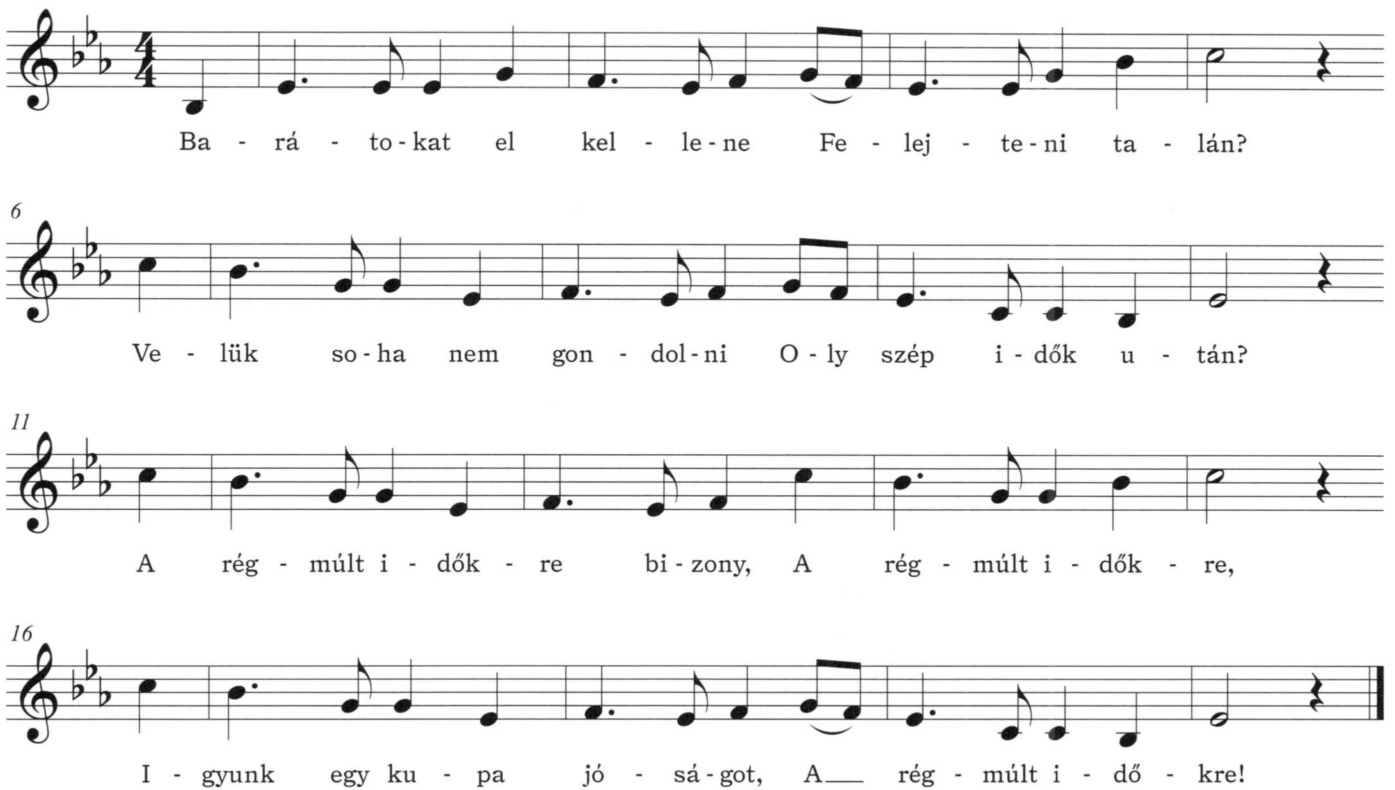

Barátokat el kellene
Felejteni talán?
Velük soha nem gondolni
Oly szép idők után?

A régmúlt időkre bizony,
A régmúlt időkre,
Igyunk egy kupa jóságot,
A régmúlt időkre!

Latvia

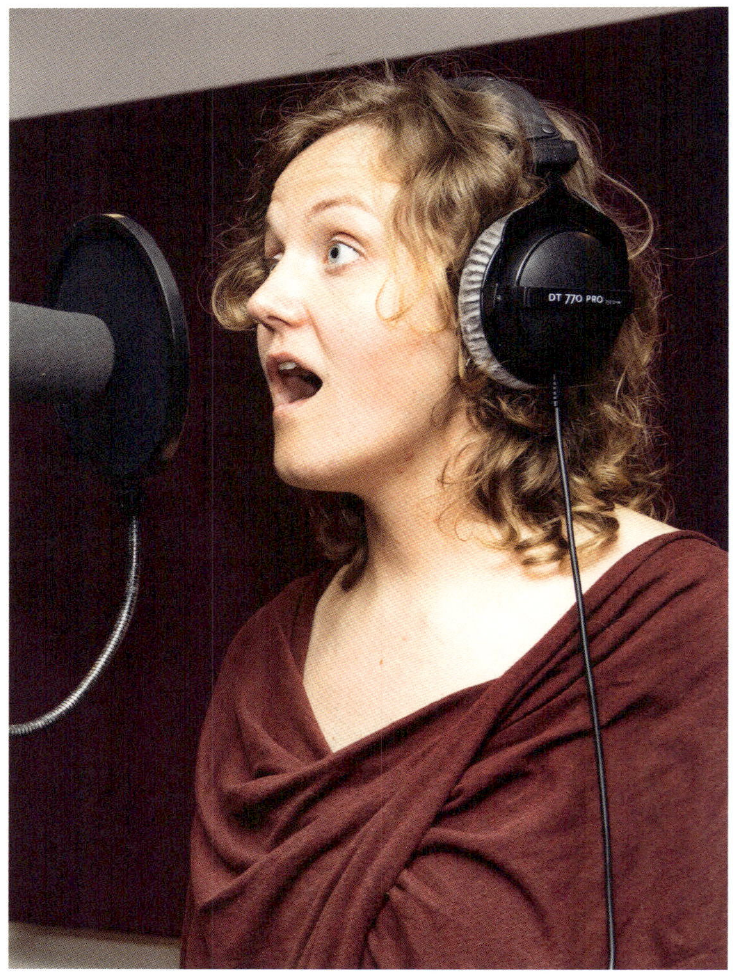

Anna Marta Šveisberga

To Labo Laiku Dēļ

Robert Burns (1759–1796)
Translated by Kitty Brige

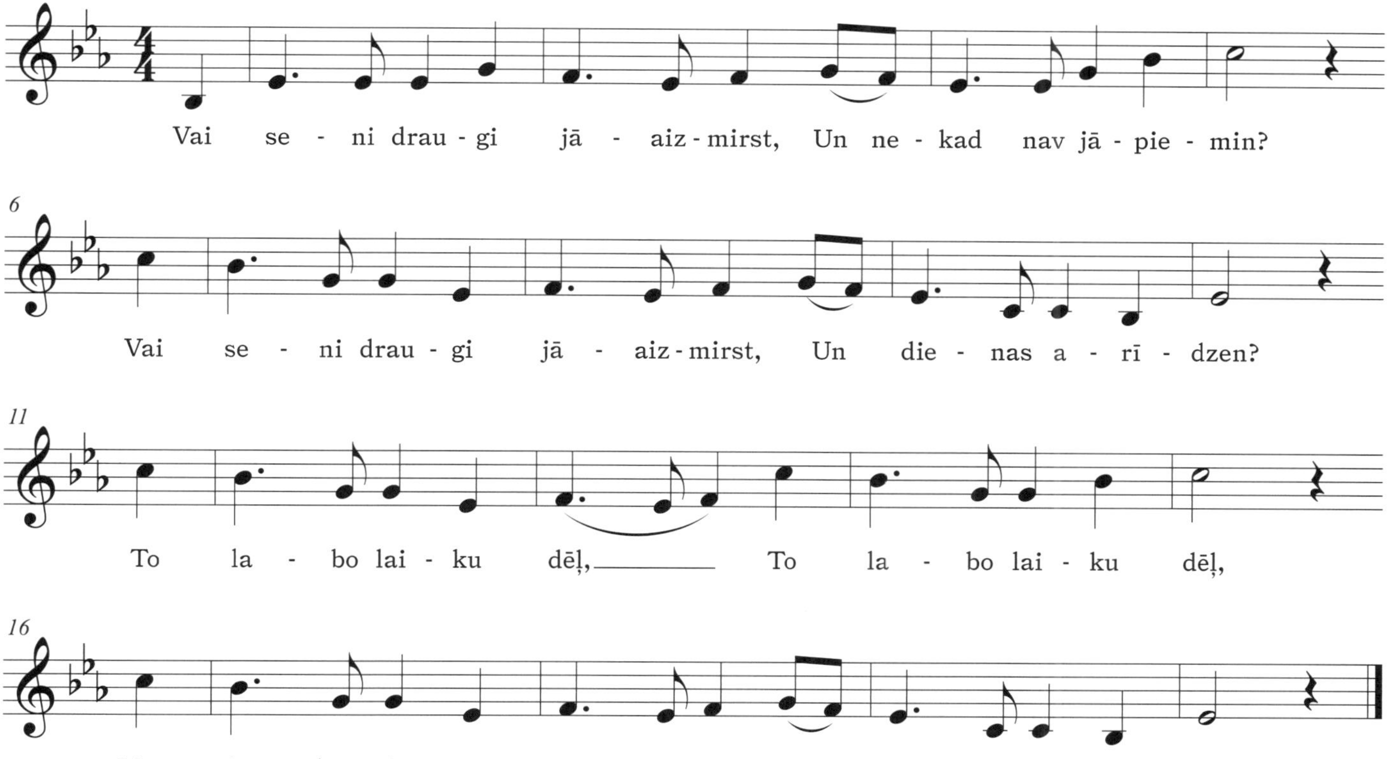

Vai seni draugi jāaizmirst,
Un nekad nav jāpiemin?
Vai seni draugi jāaizmirst,
Un dienas arīdzen?

To labo laiku dēļ,
To labo laiku dēļ,
Mēs iedzersim un svinēsim,
To labo laiku dēļ.

Lithuania

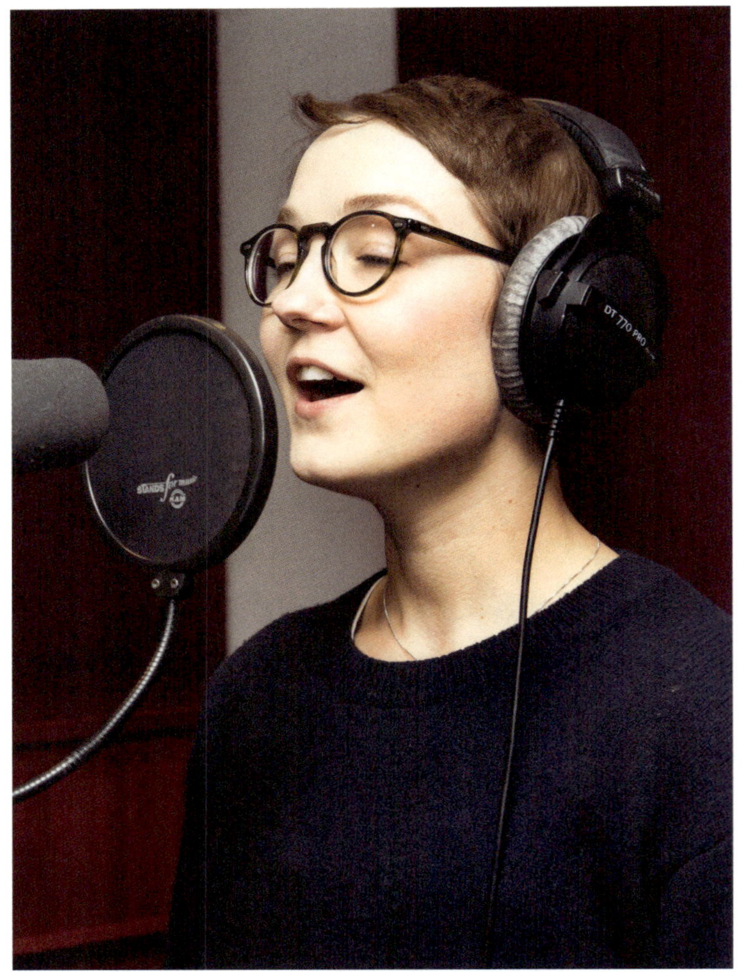

Julija Straizyte

Prabėgusios Dienos

Robert Burns (1759–1796)
Translation from Centre for Robert Burns Studies

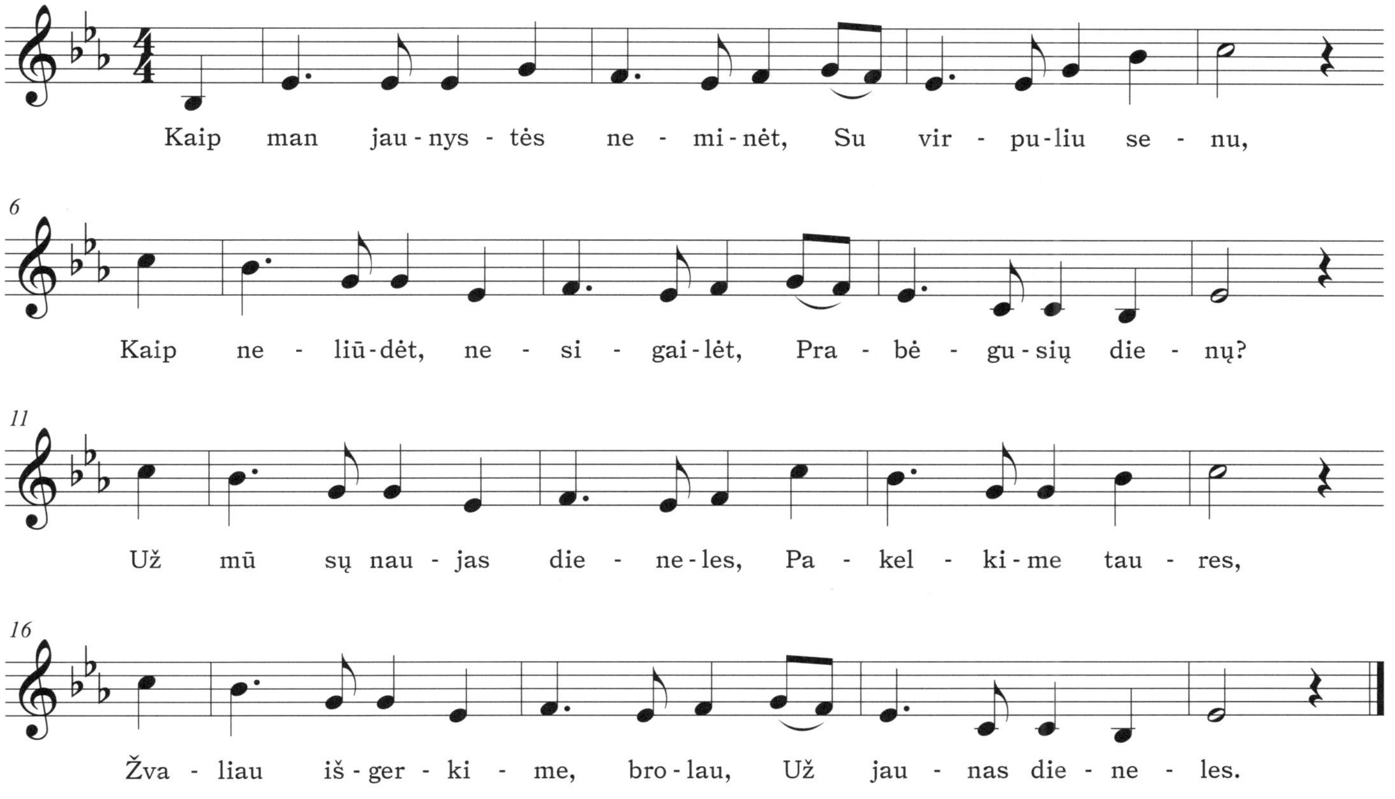

Kaip man jaunystės neminėt,
Su virpuliu senu,
Kaip neliūdėt, nesigailėt,
Prabėgusių dienų?

Už mūsų naujas dieneles,
Pakelkime taures,
Žvaliau išgerkime, brolau,
Už jaunas dieneles.

Malta

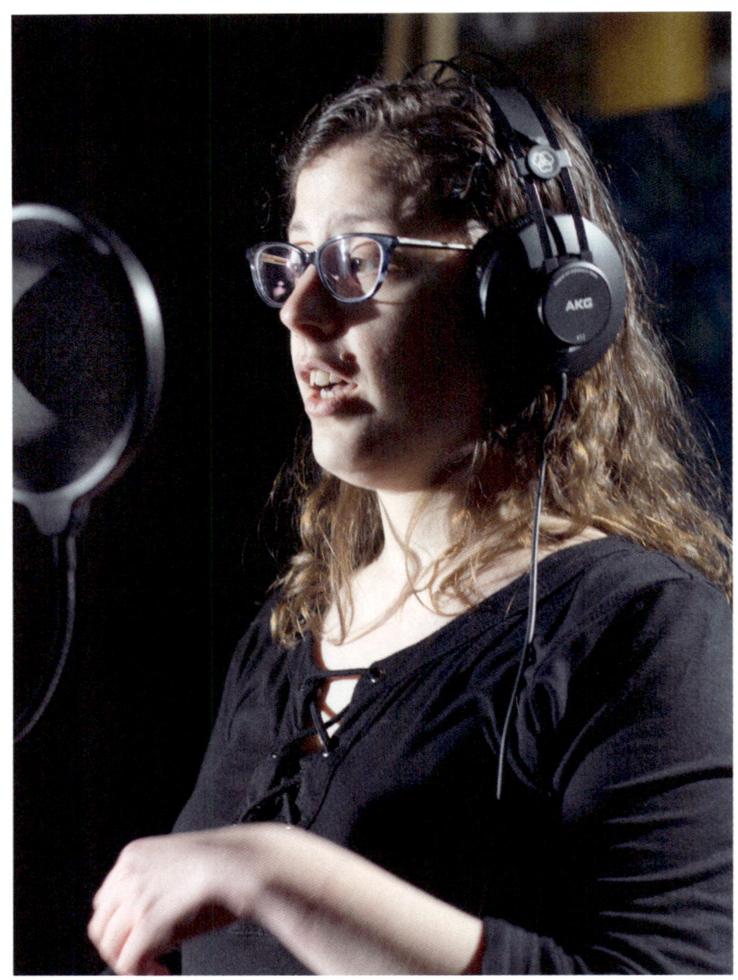

Laura Cioffi

Għaż-Żminijiet l'Għaddew

Robert Burns (1759–1796)
Translated by Christopher Bezzina

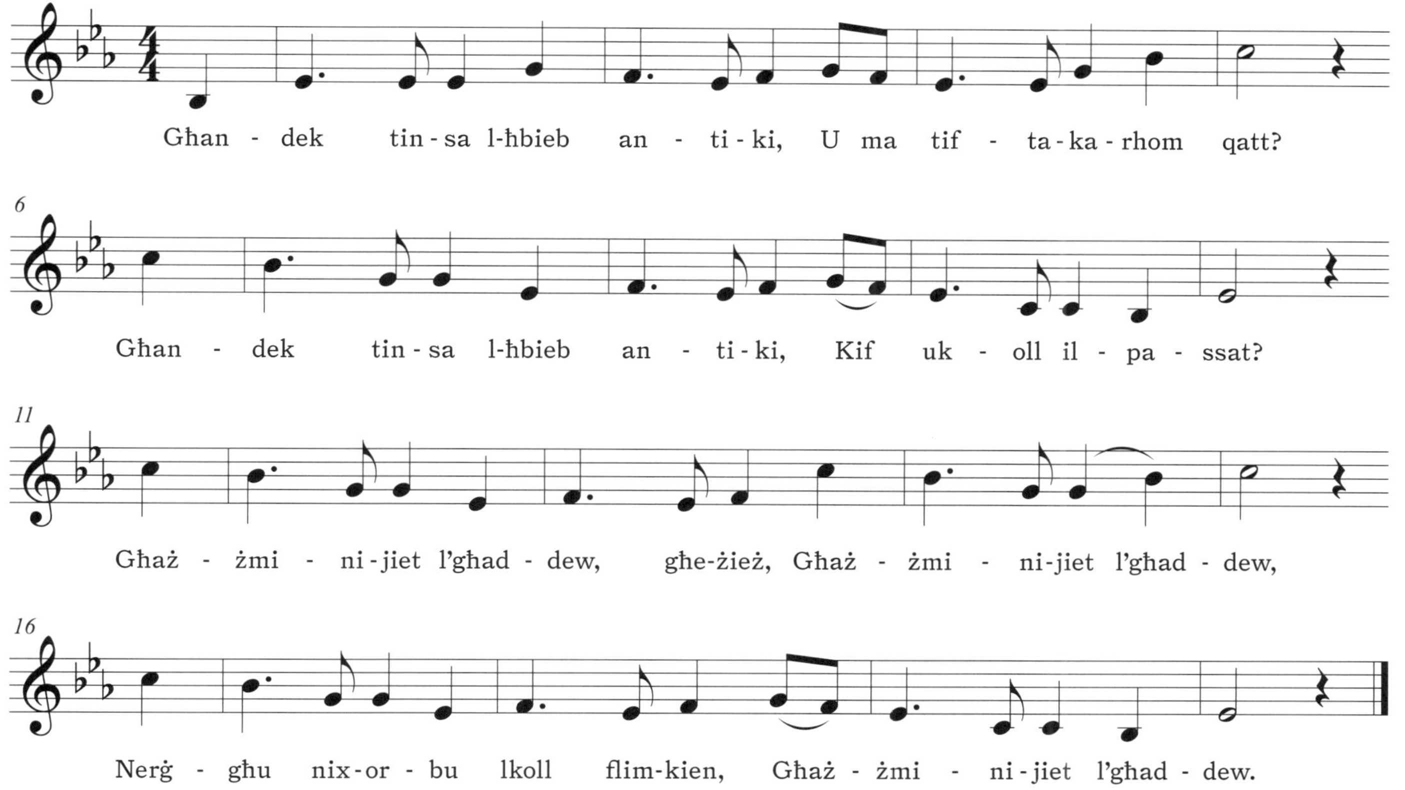

Għandek tinsa l-ħbieb antiki,
U ma tiftakarhom qatt?
Għandek tinsa l-ħbieb antiki,
Kif ukoll il-passat?

Għaż-żminijiet l'għaddew, għeżież,
Għaż-żminijiet l'għaddew,
Nerġgħu nixorbu lkoll flimkien,
Għaż-żminijiet l'għaddew.

Poland

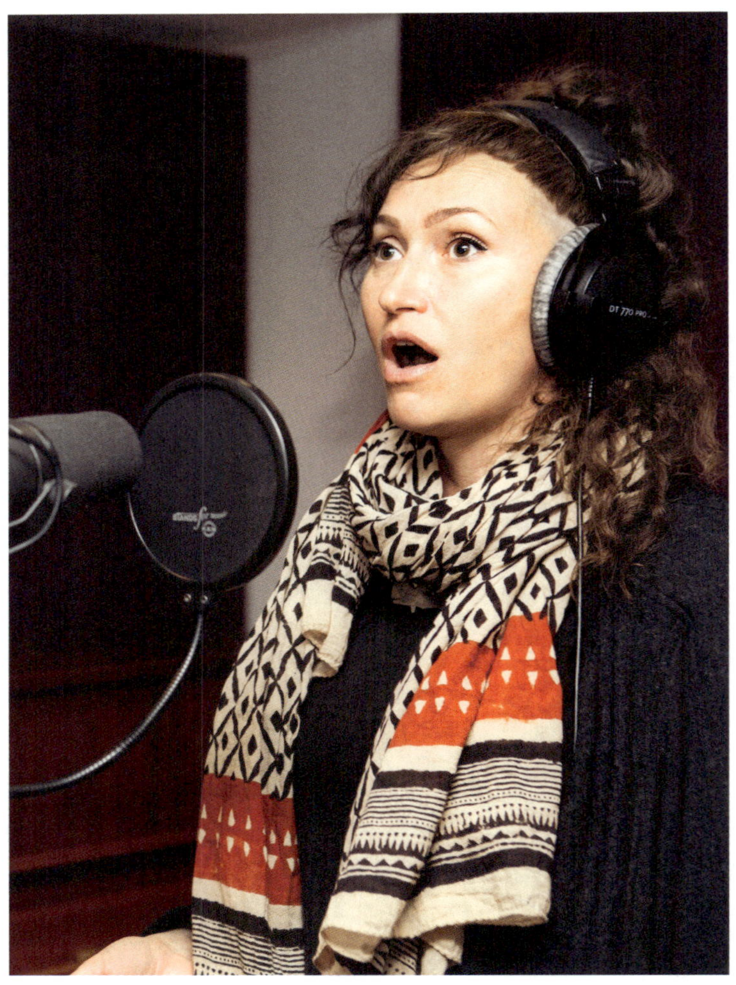

Monika Niemczynowicz

Dawno Minione Dni

Robert Burns (1759–1796)
Translated by Jadwiga Ruchlewska

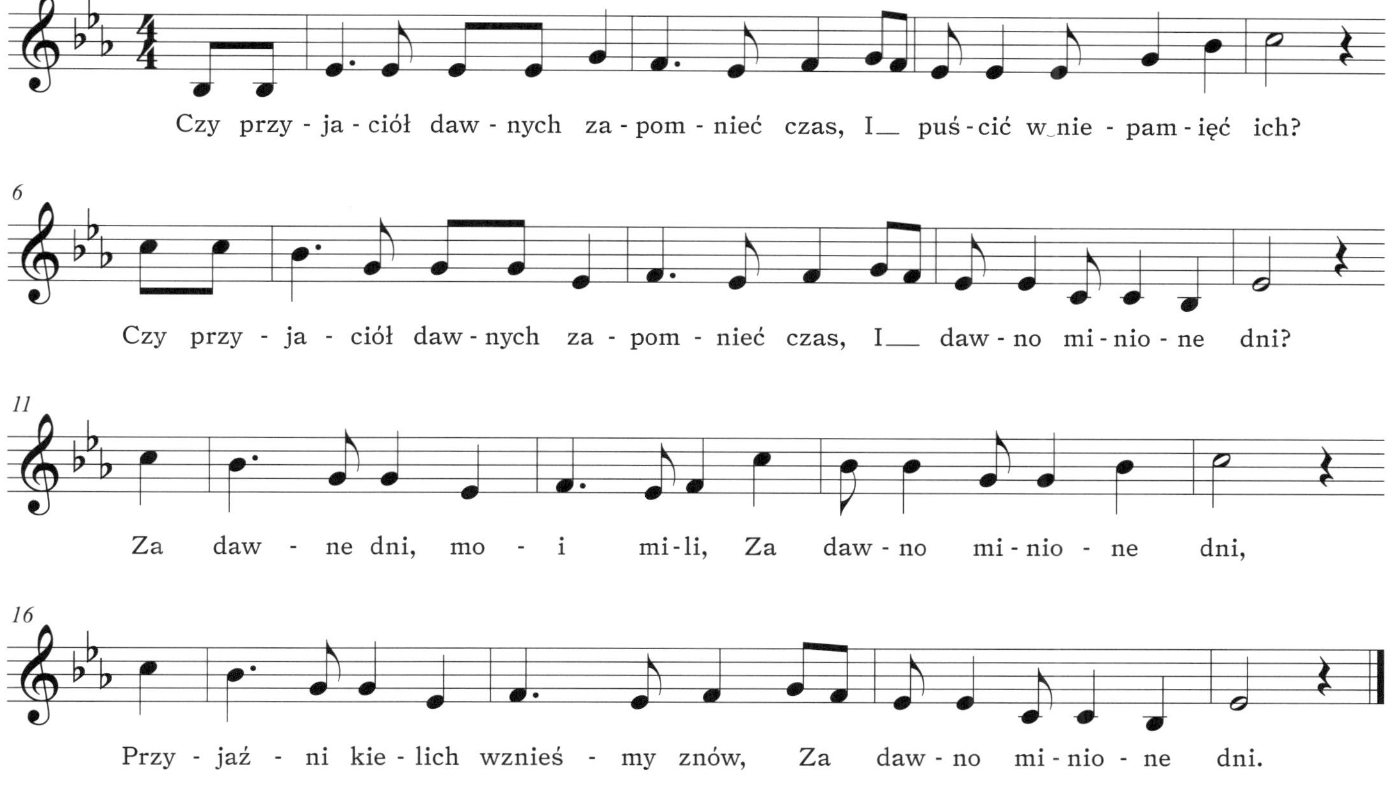

Czy przyjaciół dawnych zapomnieć czas,
I puścić w niepamięć ich?
Czy przyjaciół dawnych zapomnieć czas,
I dawno minione dni?

Za dawne dni, moi mili,
Za dawno minione dni,
Przyjaźni kielich wznieśmy znów,
Za dawno minione dni.

Slovakia

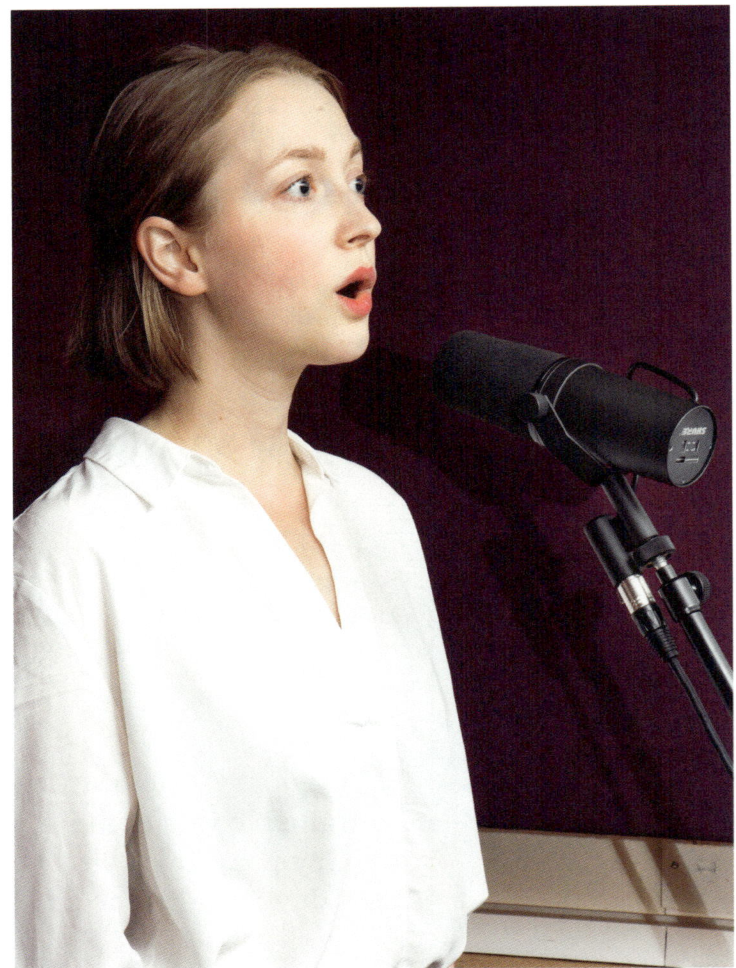

Lucia Šmatláková

Zašlý čas

Robert Burns (1759–1796)
Translated by Lucia Šmatláková

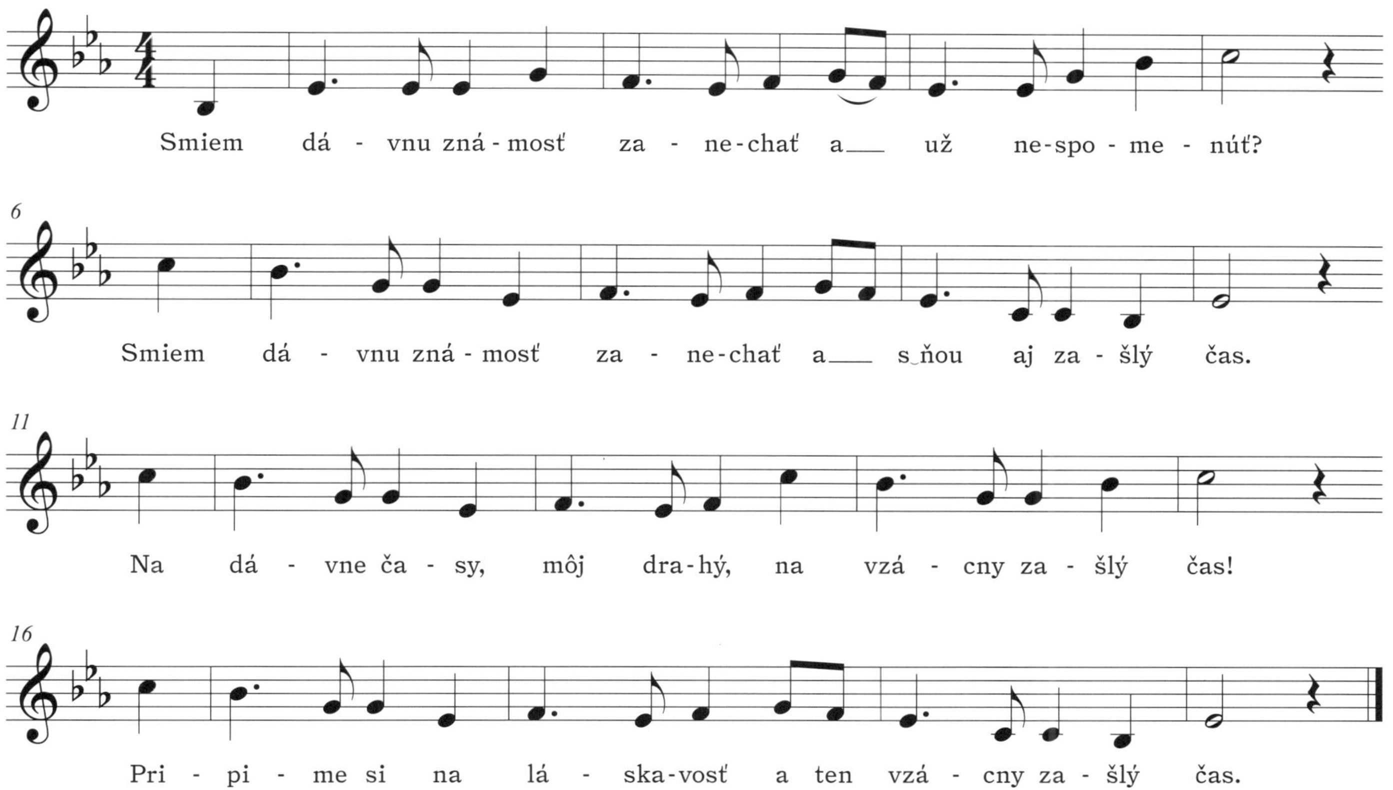

Smiem dávnu známosť zanechať
a už nespomenúť?
Smiem dávnu známosť zanechať
a s ňou aj zašlý čas.

Na dávne časy, môj drahý,
na vzácny zašlý čas!
Pripime si na láskavosť
a ten vzácny zašlý čas.

Slovenia

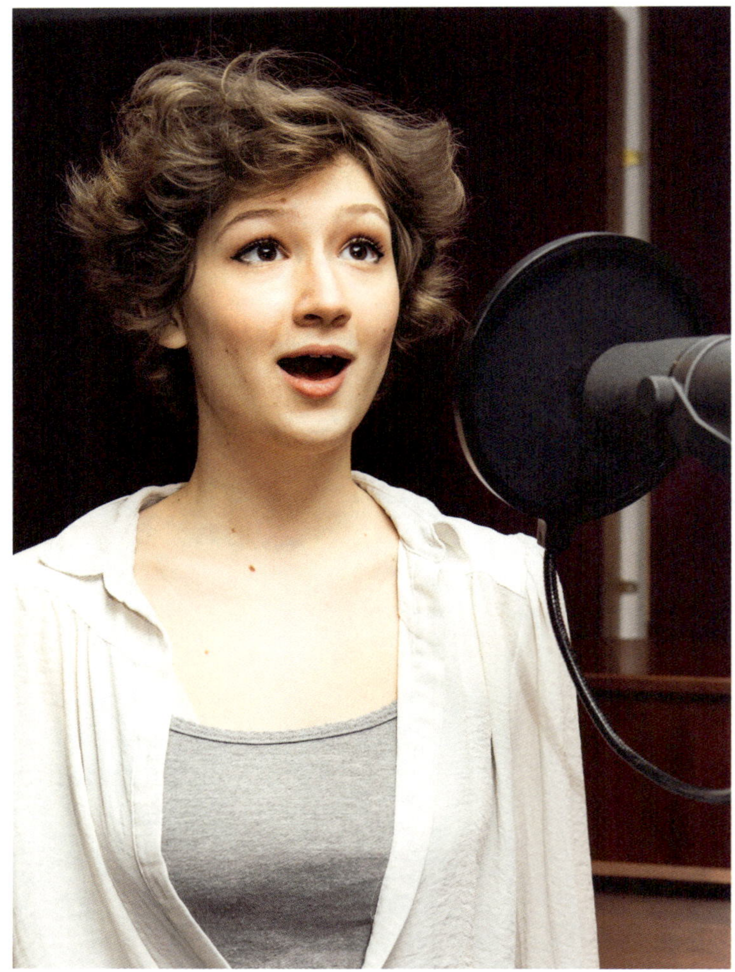

Rahela Horvat Toš

Na vse minule dni

Robert Burns (1759–1796)
Translated by Tomi Dobaj

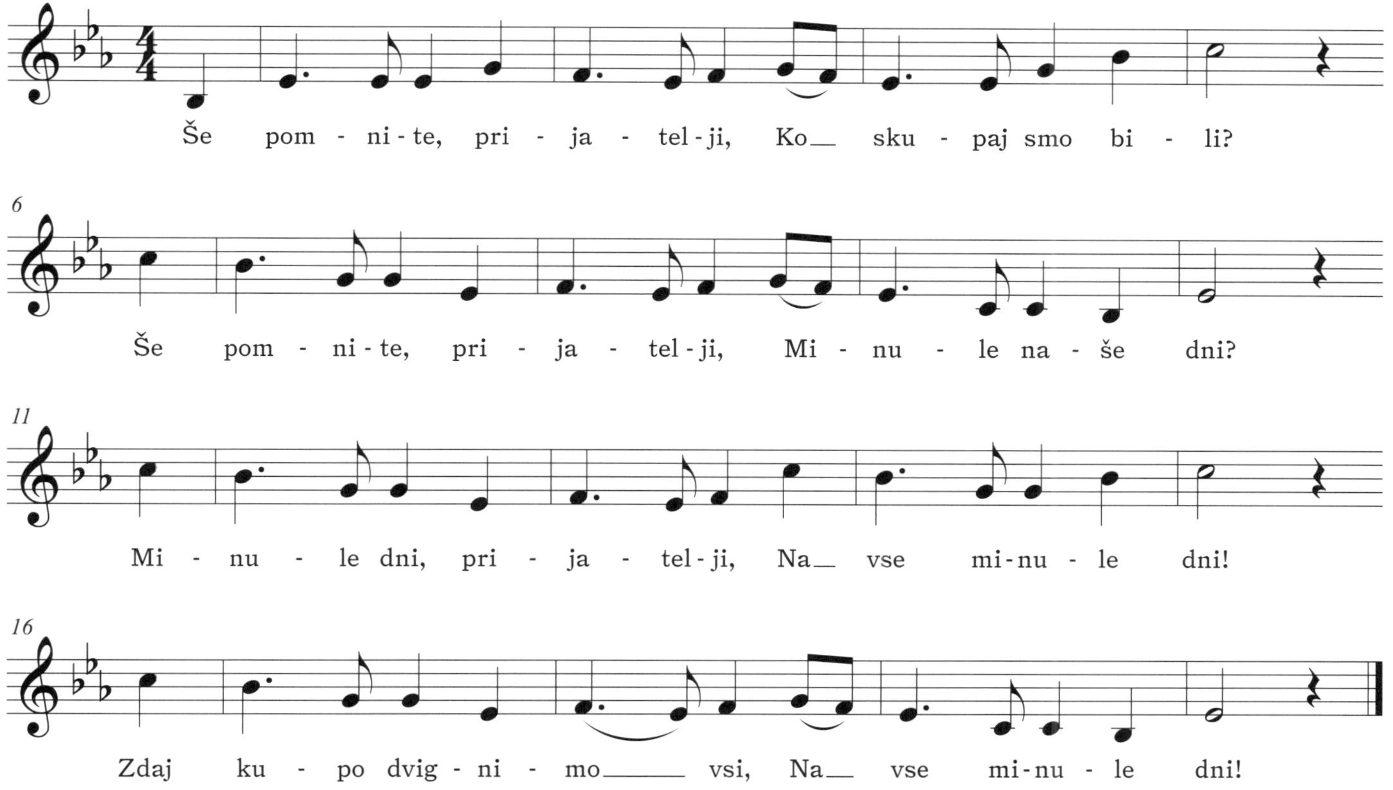

Še pomnite, prijatelji,
Ko skupaj smo bili?
Še pomnite, prijatelji,
Minule naše dni?

Minule dni, prijatelji,
Na vse minule dni!
Zdaj kupo dvignimo vsi,
Na vse minule dni!

Bulgaria

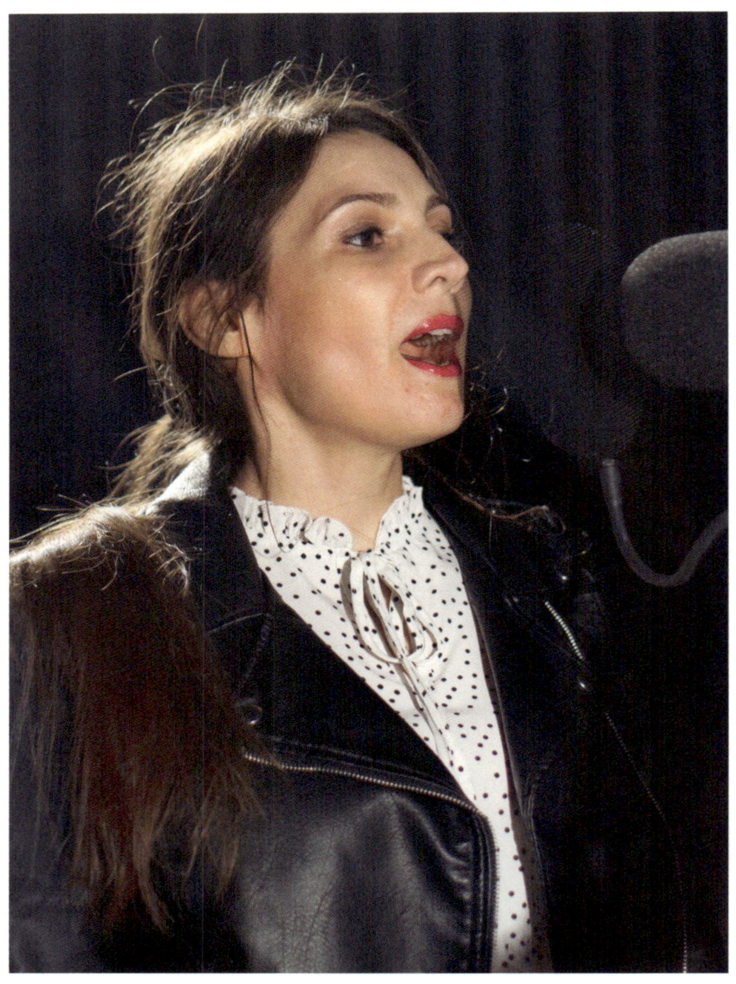

Gergana Vasileva

Старата дружба

Robert Burns (1759–1796)
Translated by Nataliya Nedkova

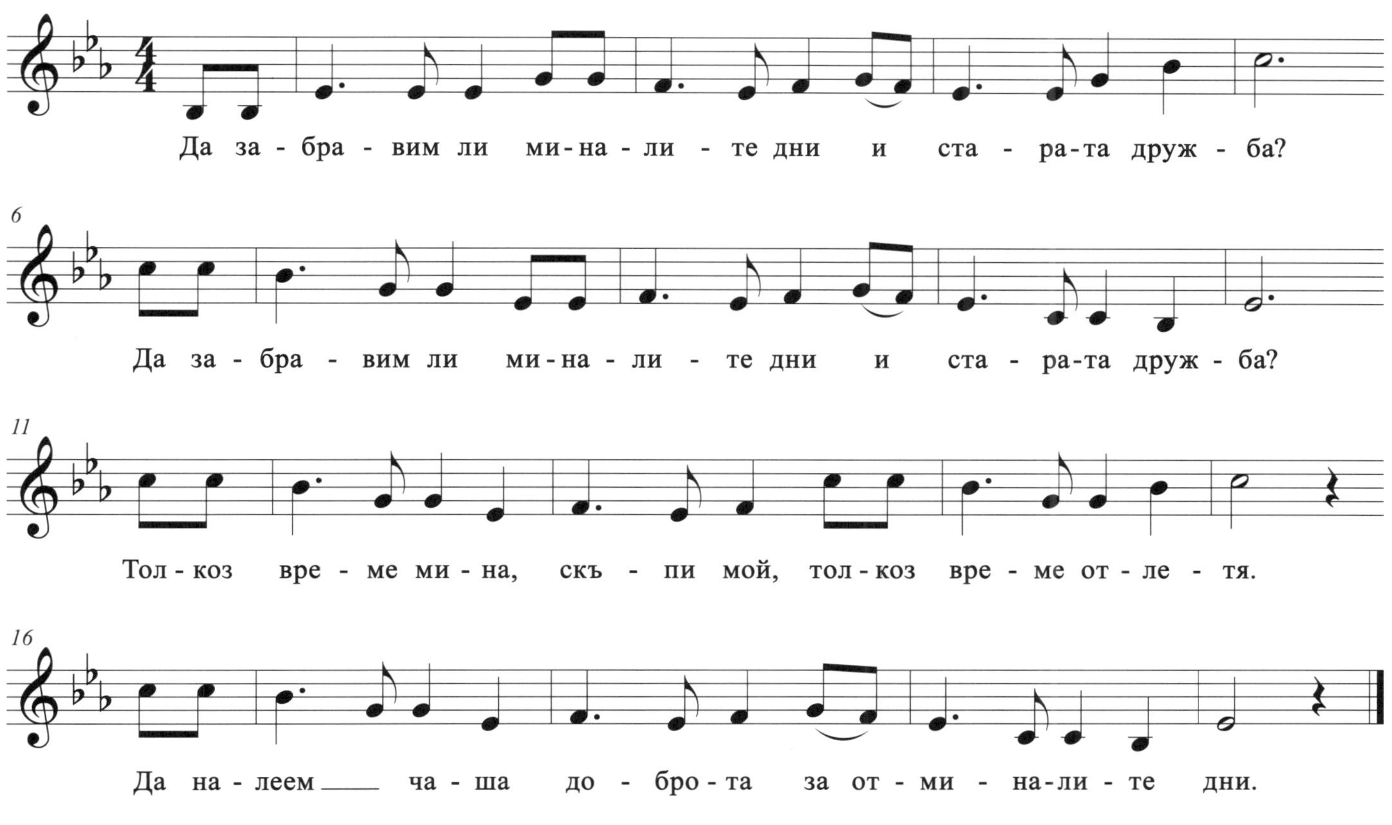

Да забравим ли миналите дни
и старта дружба?
Да забравим ли миналите дни
и старта дружба?

Толкоз време мина, скъпи мой,
толкоз време отлетя.
Да налеем чаша доброта
за отминалите дни.

Romania

76

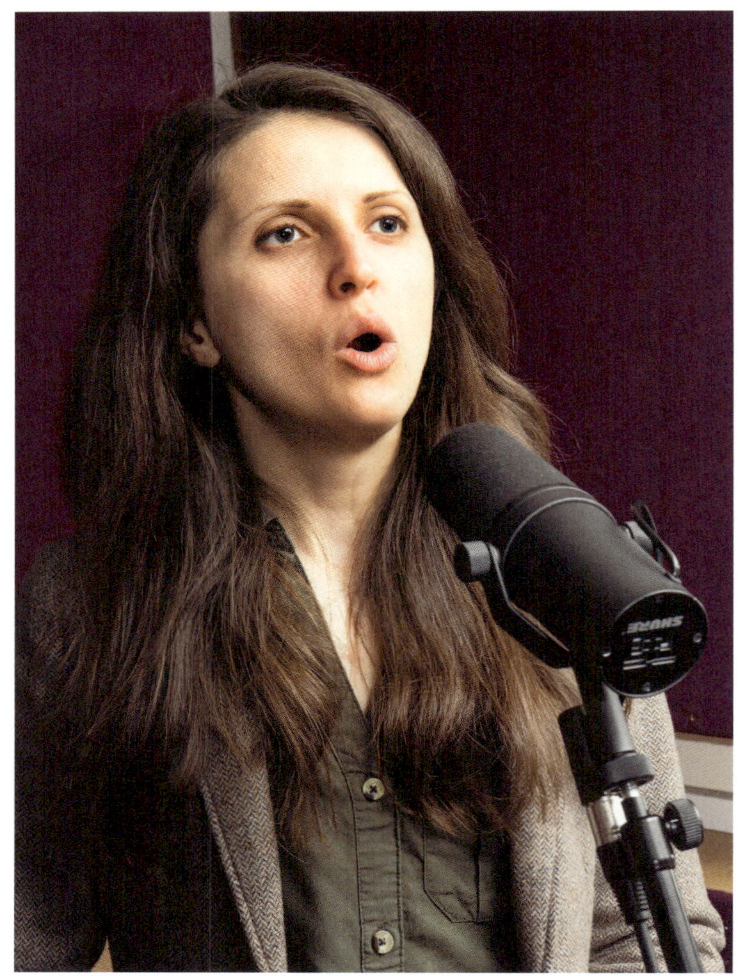

Alexandra Dodu

Pentru timpul de-altădat'

Robert Burns (1759–1796)
Translated by Alexandra Dodu

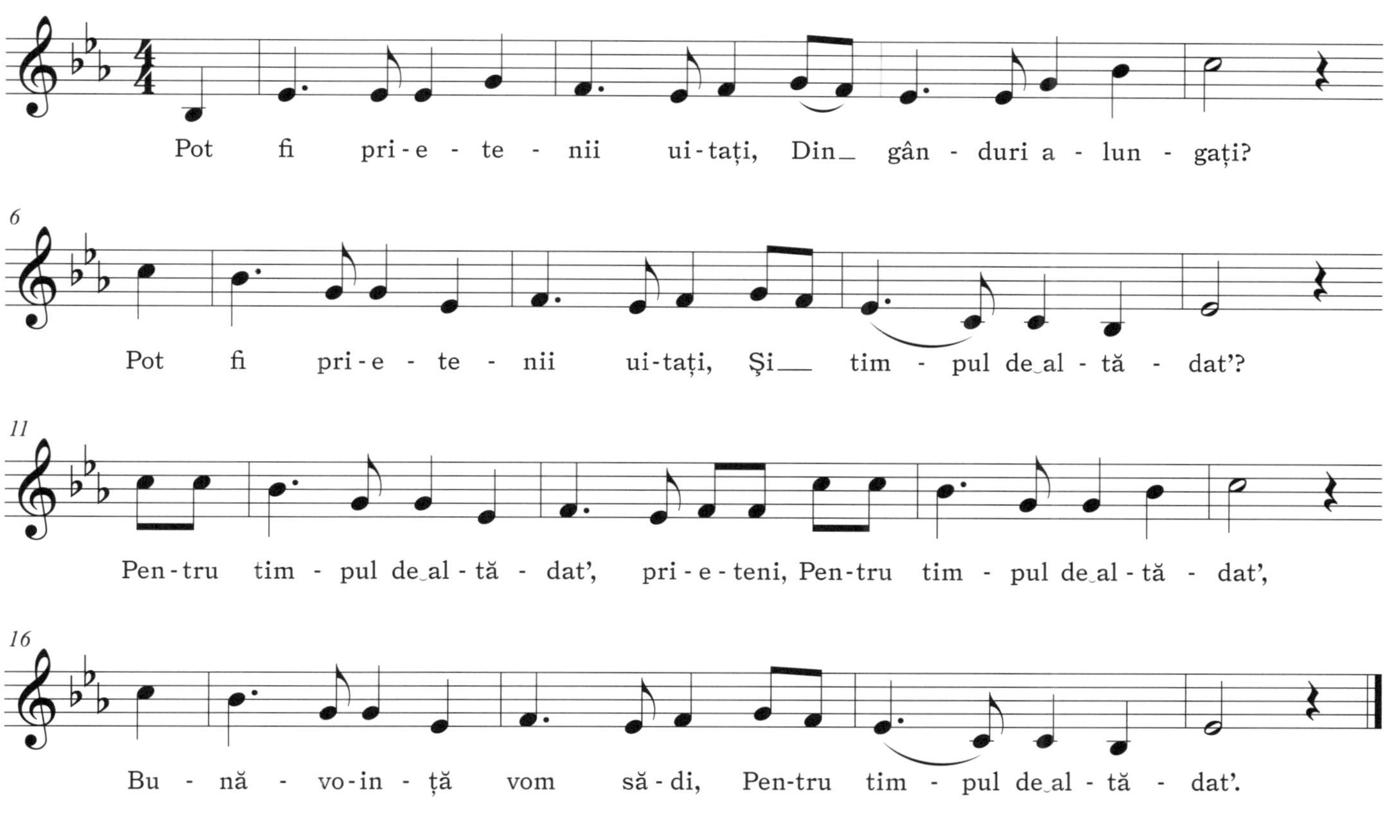

Pot fi prietenii uitați,
Din gânduri alungați?
Pot fi prietenii uitați,
Și timpul de-altădat'?

Pentru timpul de-altădat', prieteni,
Pentru timpul de-altădat',
Bunăvoință vom sădi,
Pentru timpul de-altădat'.

Croatia

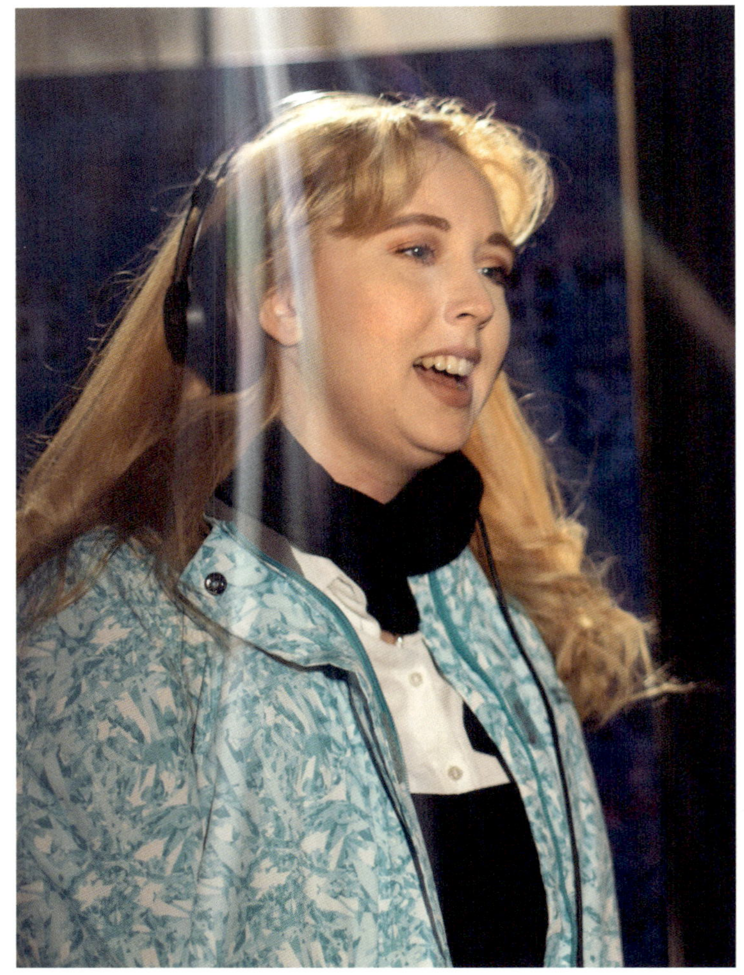

Elizabeth Malnar

Za dobra stara vremena

Robert Burns (1759–1796)
Translated by Fedja Imamovic

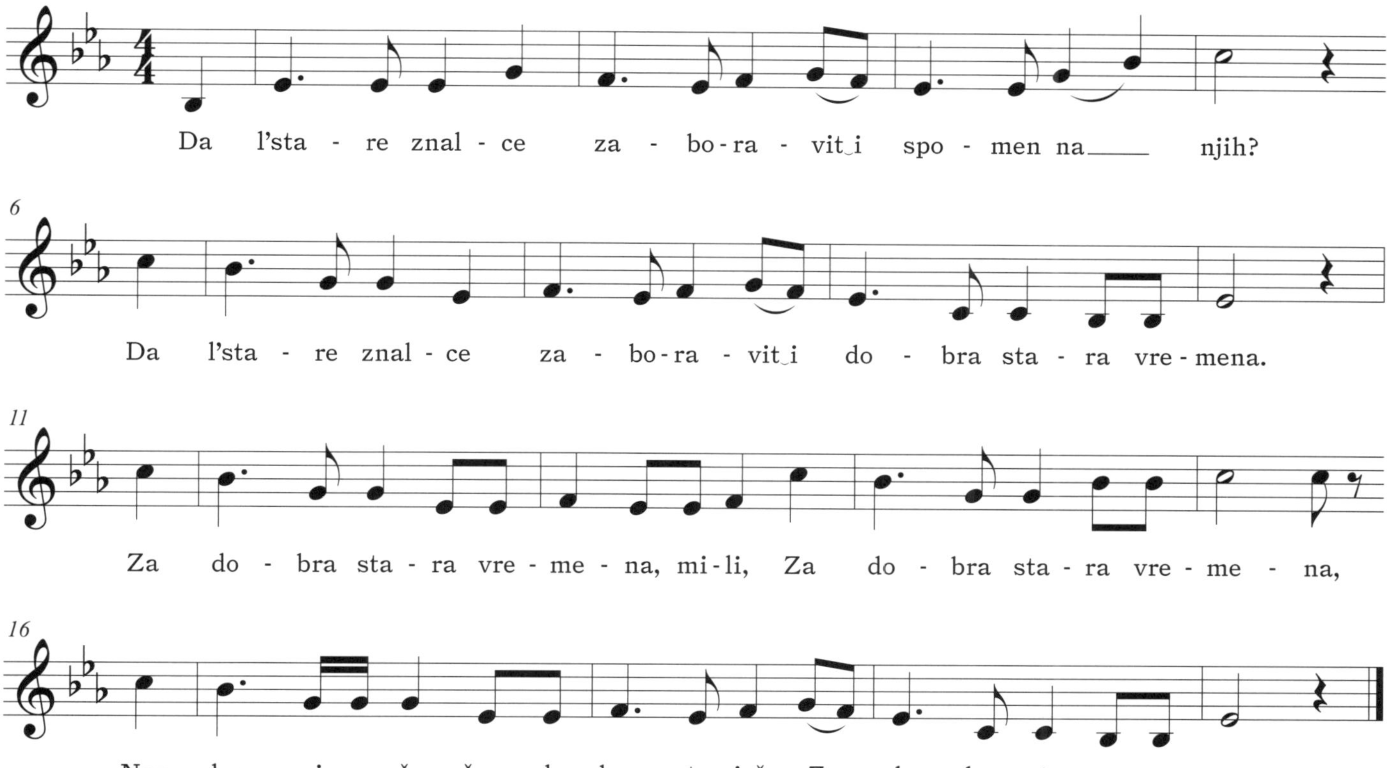

Da l'stare znalce zaboravit
I spomen na njih?
Da l'stare znalce zaboravit
I dobra stara vremena.

Za dobra stara vremena, mili,
Za dobra stara vremena,
Nazdravimo čašom dobrote još,
Za dobra stara vremena.

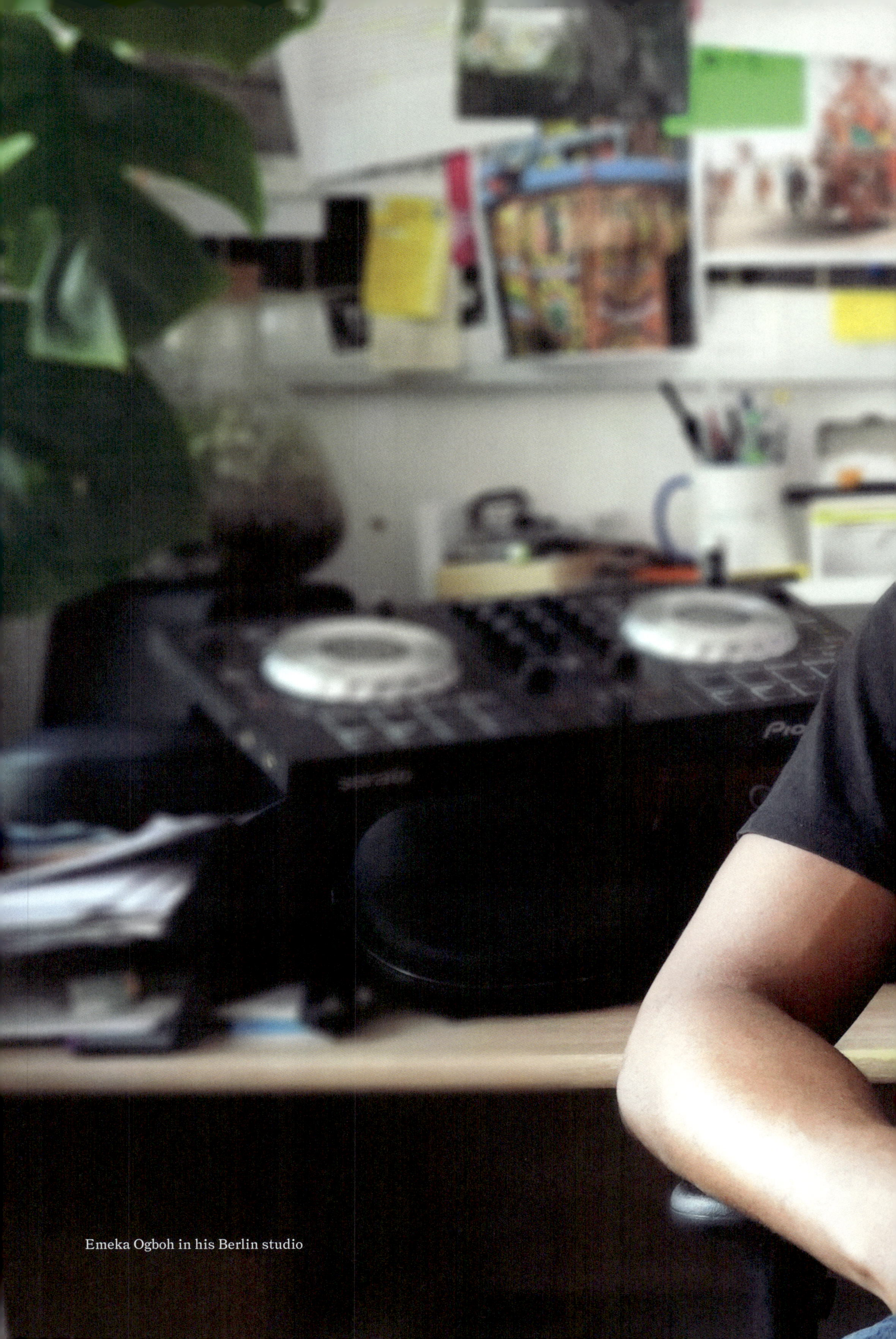

Emeka Ogboh in his Berlin studio

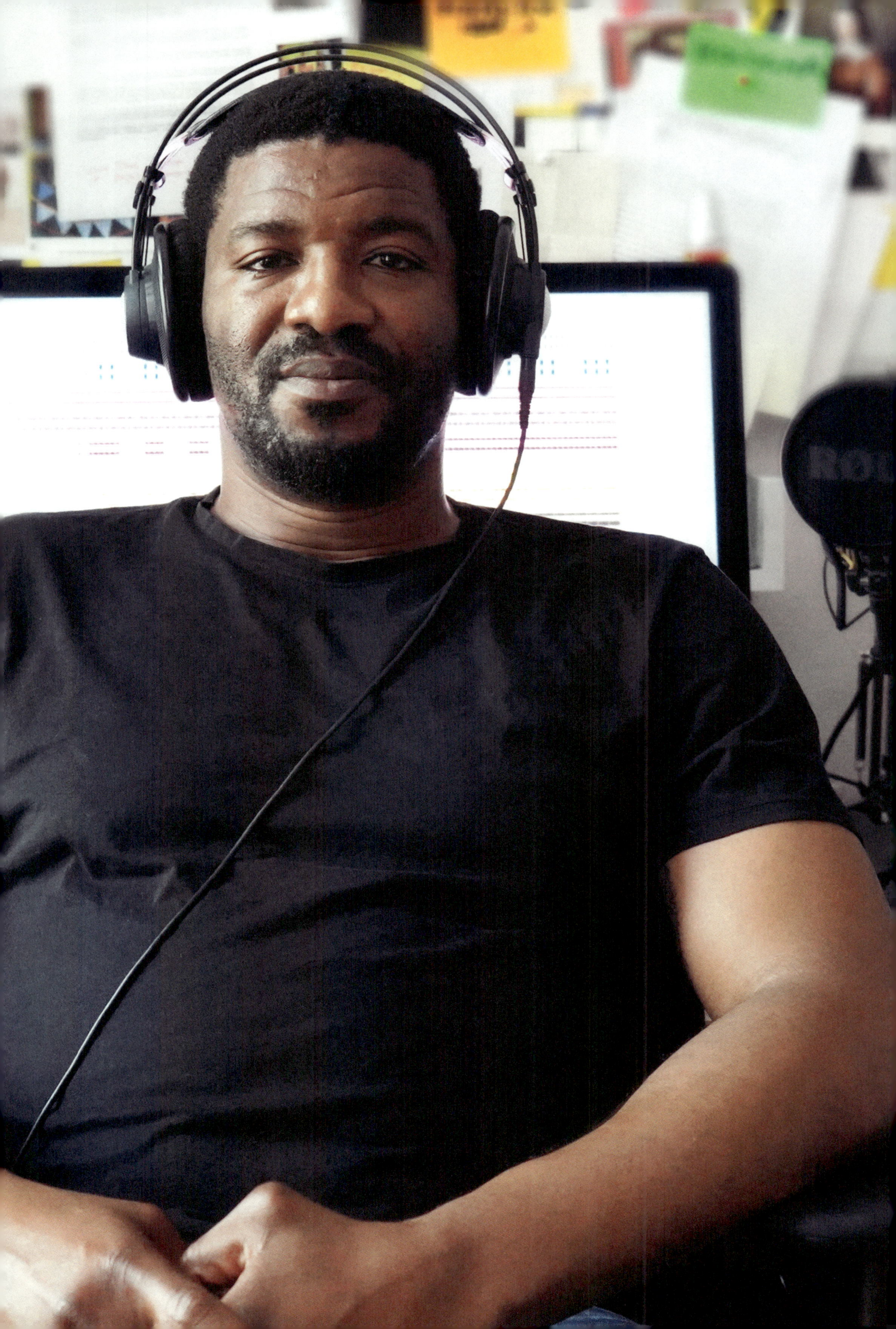

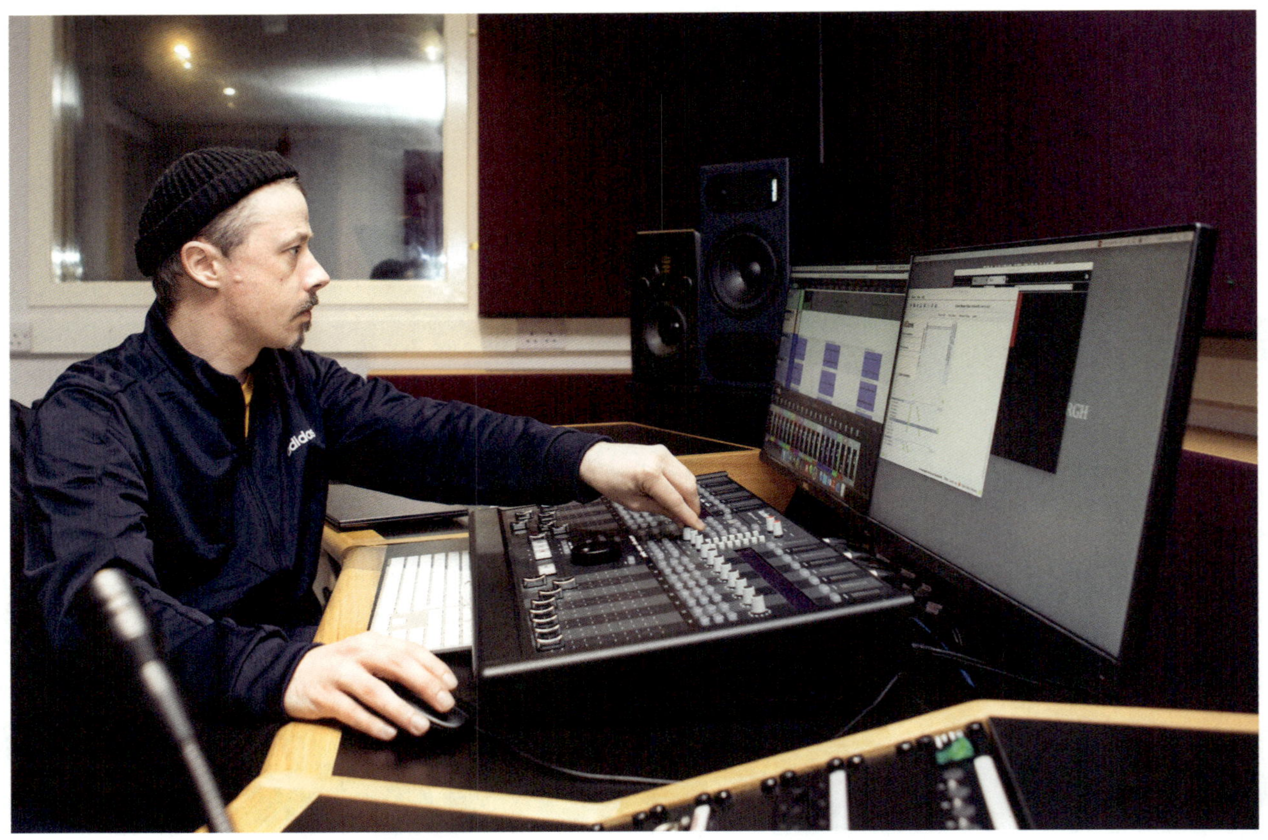

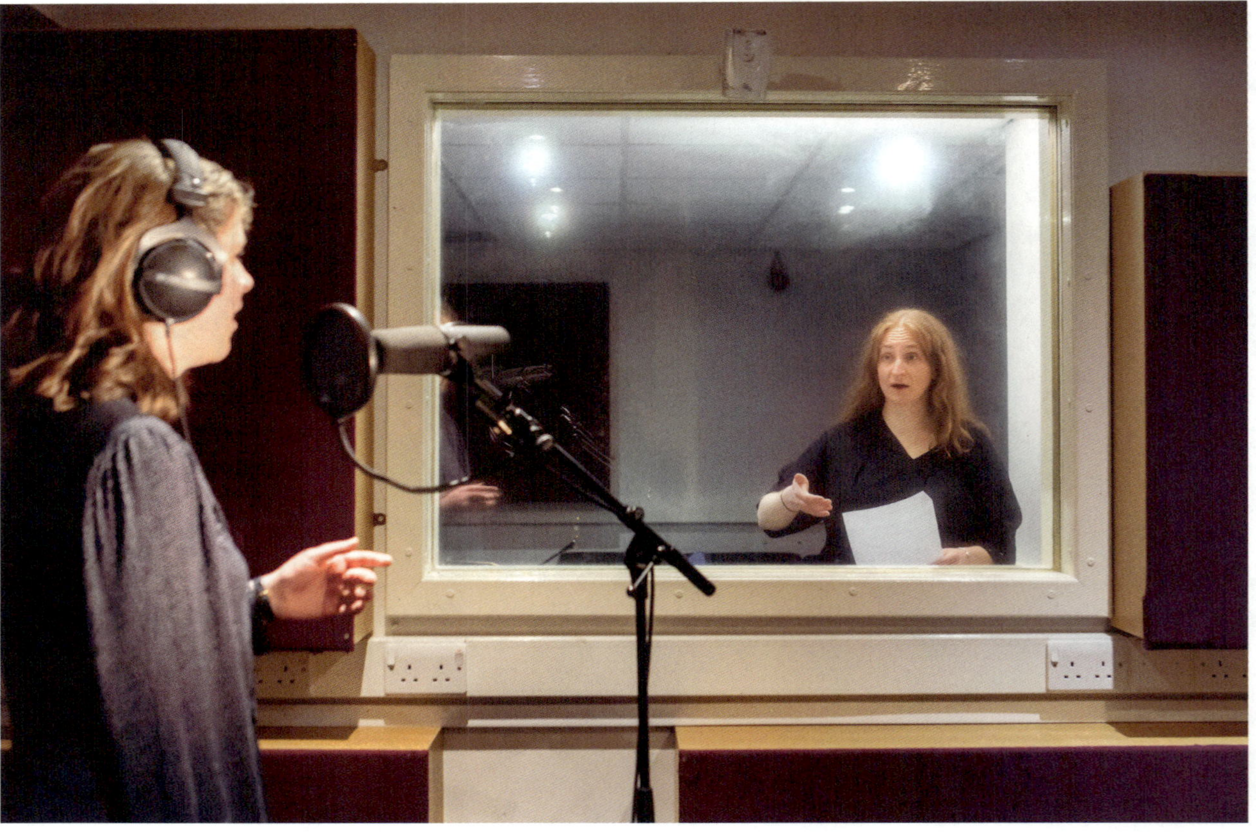

Recording session at Reid School of Music, Edinburgh College of Art
Top: Gavin McCabe
Bottom: Annemarie Klein and Katy Lavinia Cooper

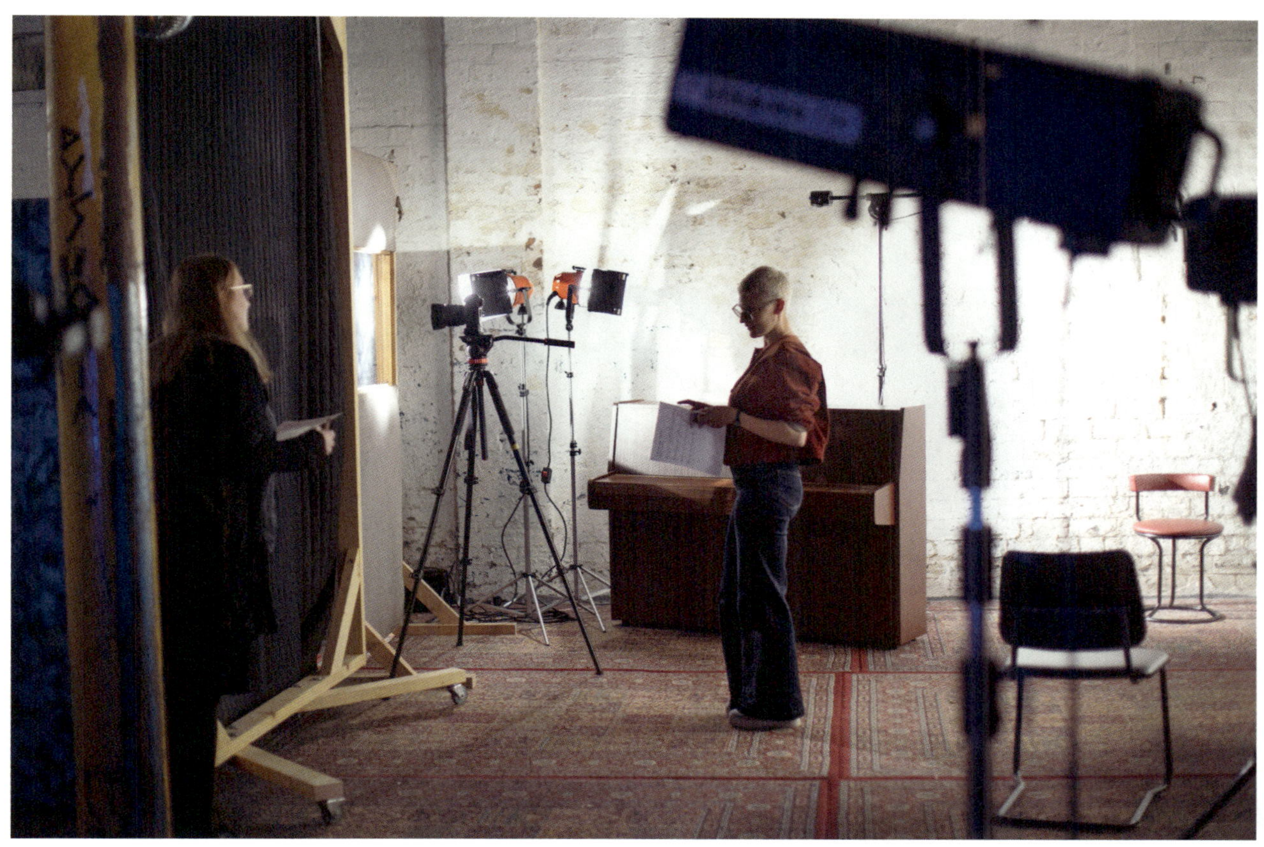

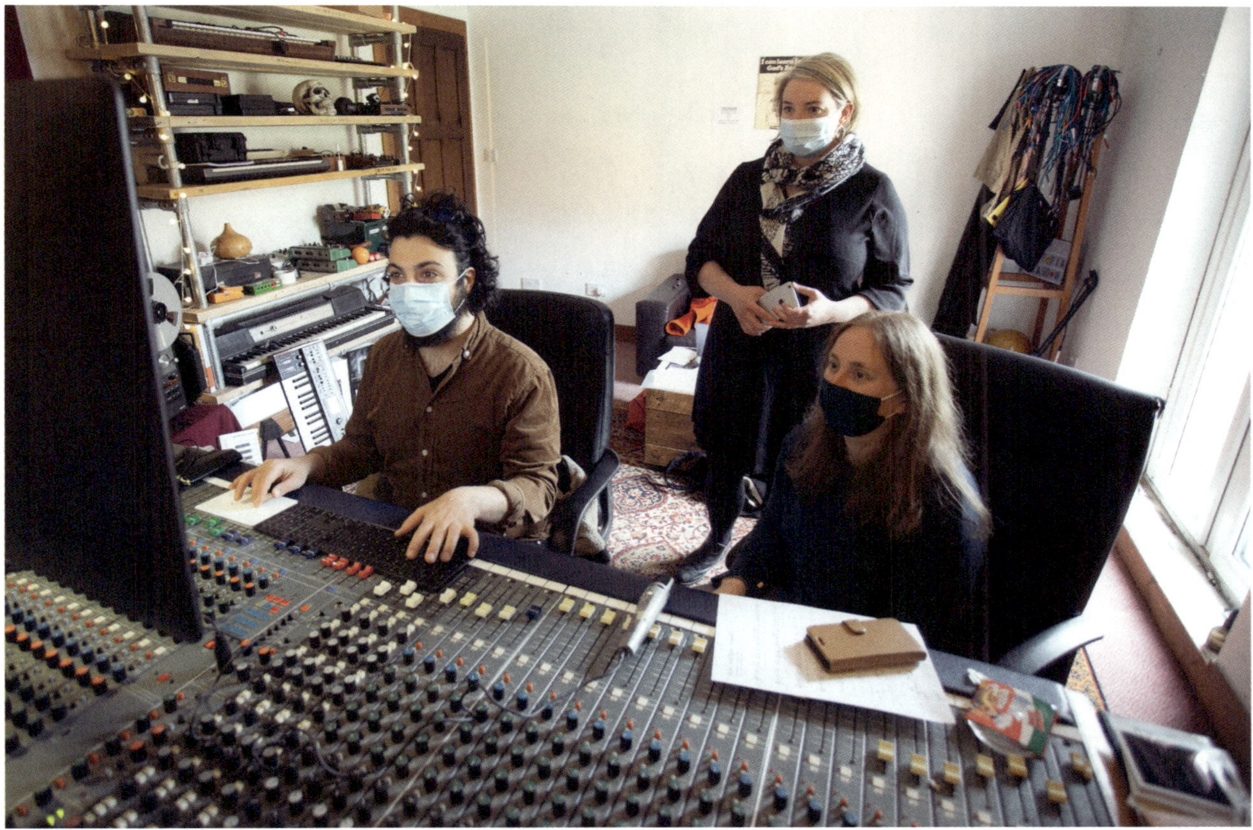

Recording session at Dystopia Studios, Glasgow
Top: Katy Lavinia Cooper, Tova Svanfeldt
Bottom: Luigi Pasquini, Melissa MacRobert, Katy Lavinia Cooper

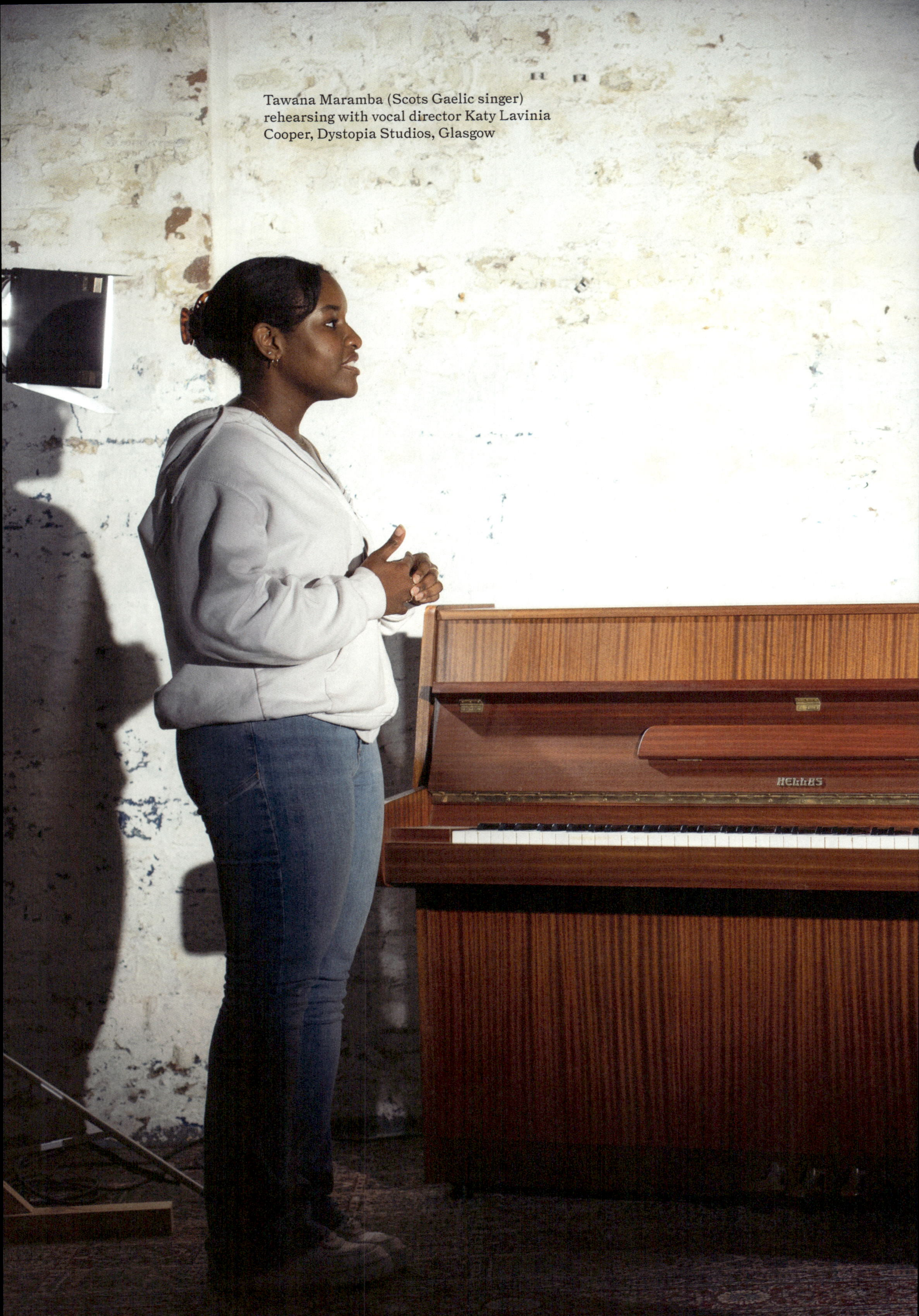

Tawana Maramba (Scots Gaelic singer)
rehearsing with vocal director Katy Lavinia
Cooper, Dystopia Studios, Glasgow

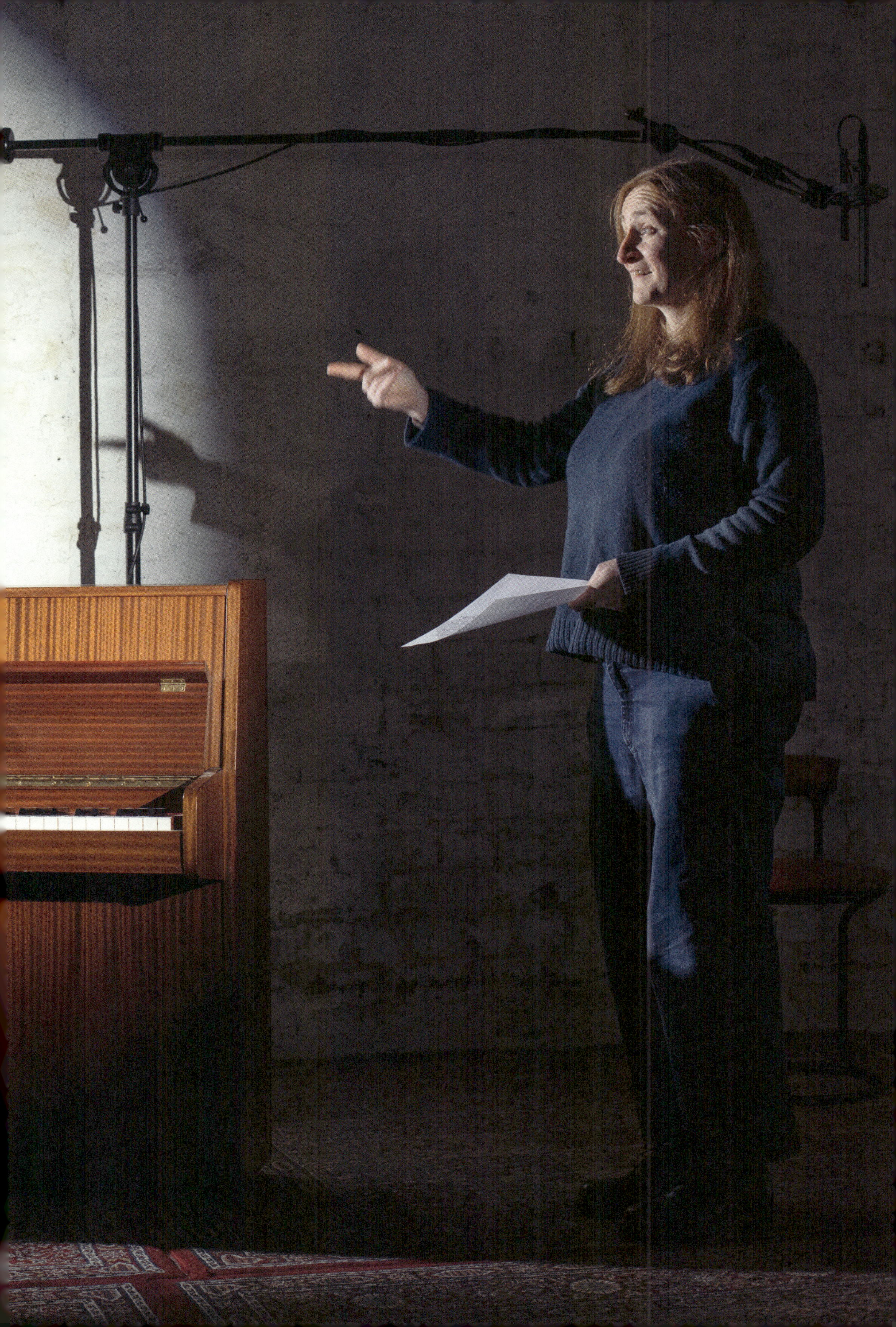

Scots Gaelic

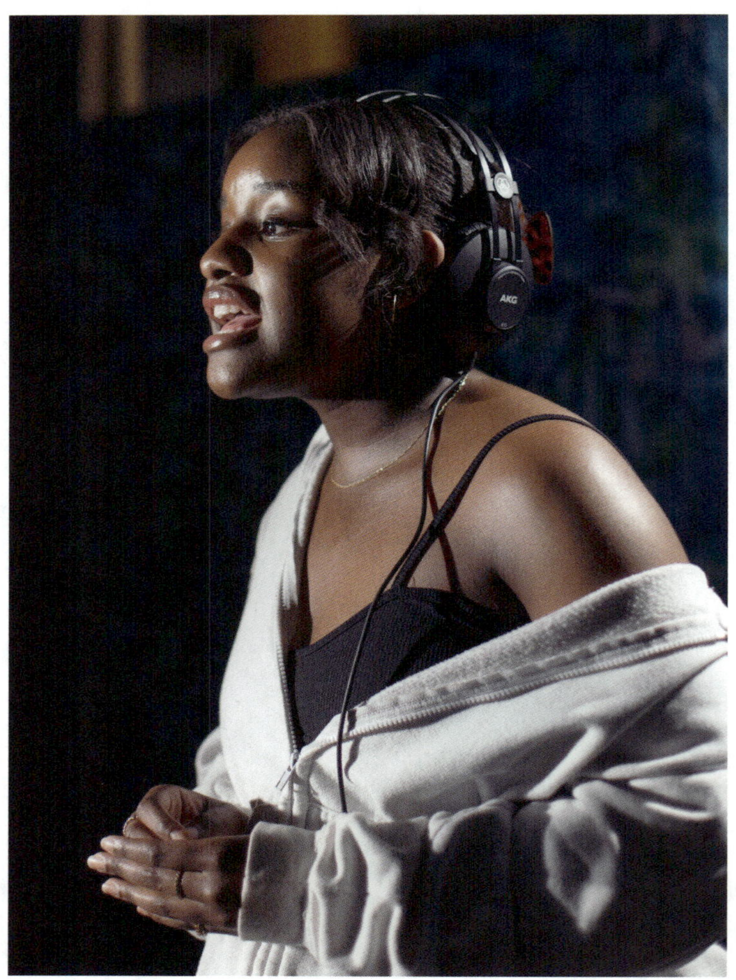

Tawana Maramba

Na Làithean a Thréig

Robert Burns (1759–1796)
Translated by Henry 'Fionn' Whyte, Eanraig MacGhille-bhàin (1852–1913)

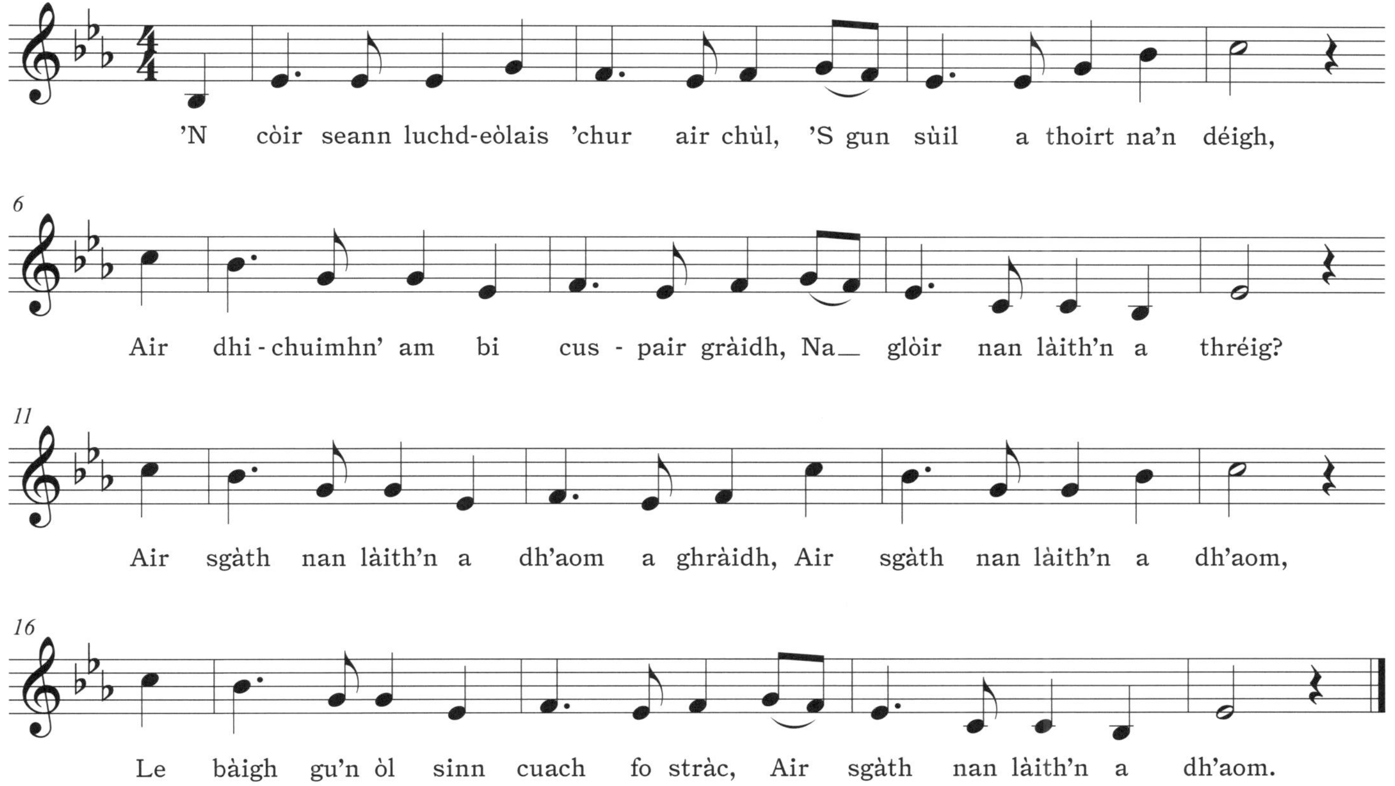

'N còir seann luchd-eòlais 'chur air chùl,
'S gun sùil a thoirt na'n déigh,
Air dhi-chuimhn' am bi cuspair gràidh,
Na glòir nan làith'n a thréig?

Air sgàth nan làith'n a dh'aom a ghràidh,
Air sgàth nan làith'n a dh'aom,
Le bàigh gu'n òl sinn cuach fo stràc,
Air sgàth nan làith'n a dh'aom.

Wales

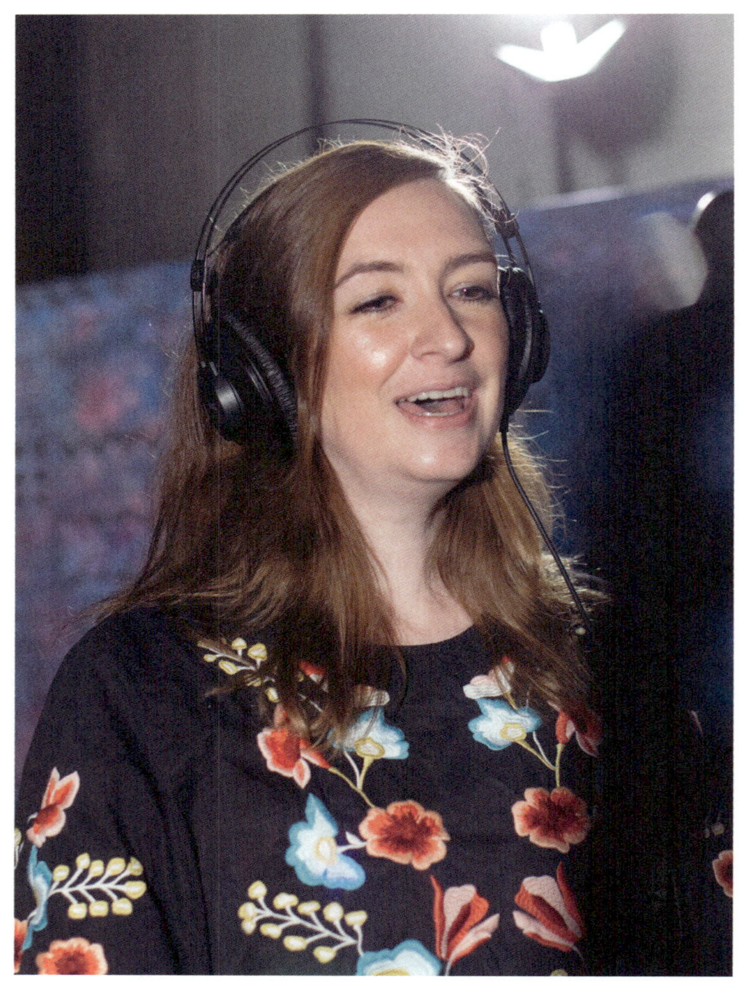

Gwen Màiri

Coffâd i'r Oesoedd Cynt

Robert Burns (1759–1796)
Translated by Arwel Roberts

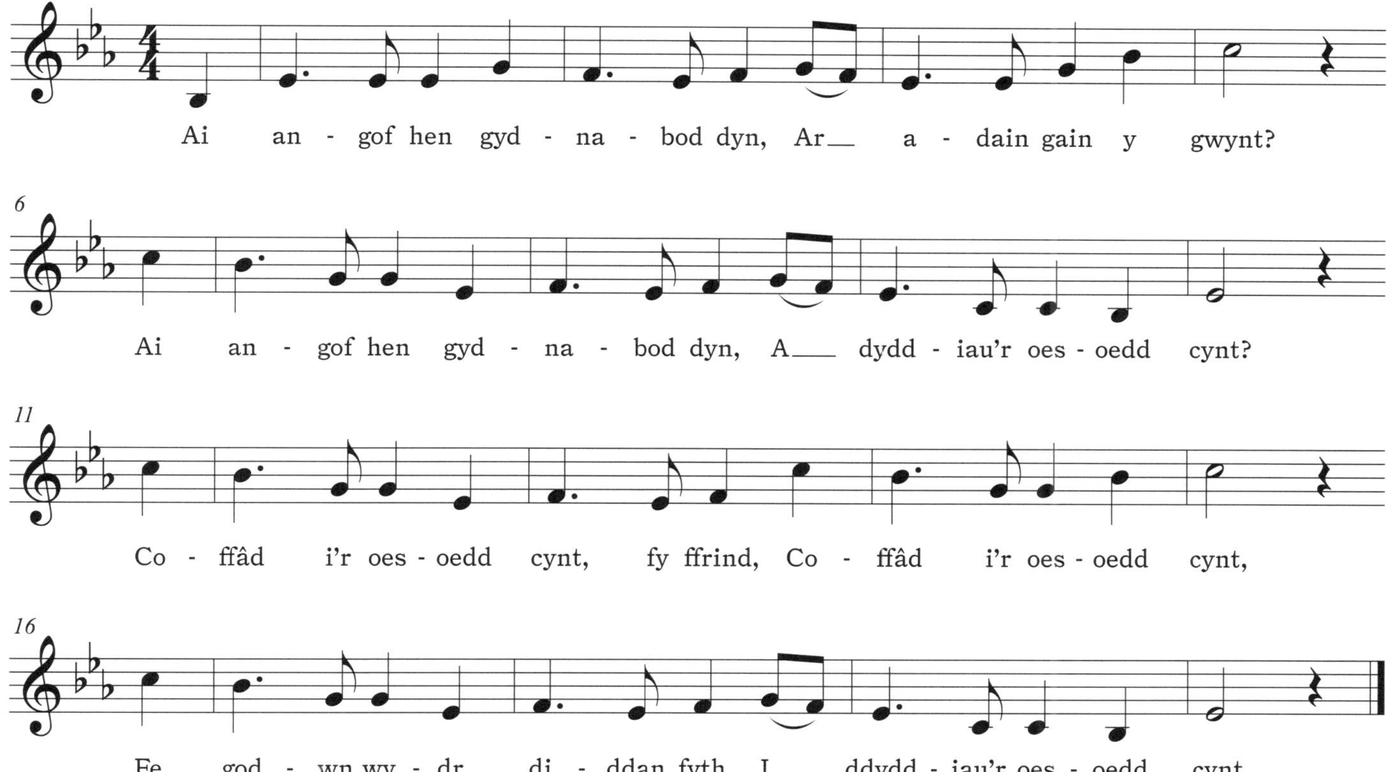

Ai angof hen gydnabod dyn,
Ar adain gain y gwynt?
Ai angof hen gydnabod dyn,
A dyddiau'r oesoedd cynt?

Coffâd i'r oesoedd cynt, fy ffrind,
Coffâd i'r oesoedd cynt,
Fe godwn wydr diddan fyth,
I ddyddiau'r oesoedd cynt.

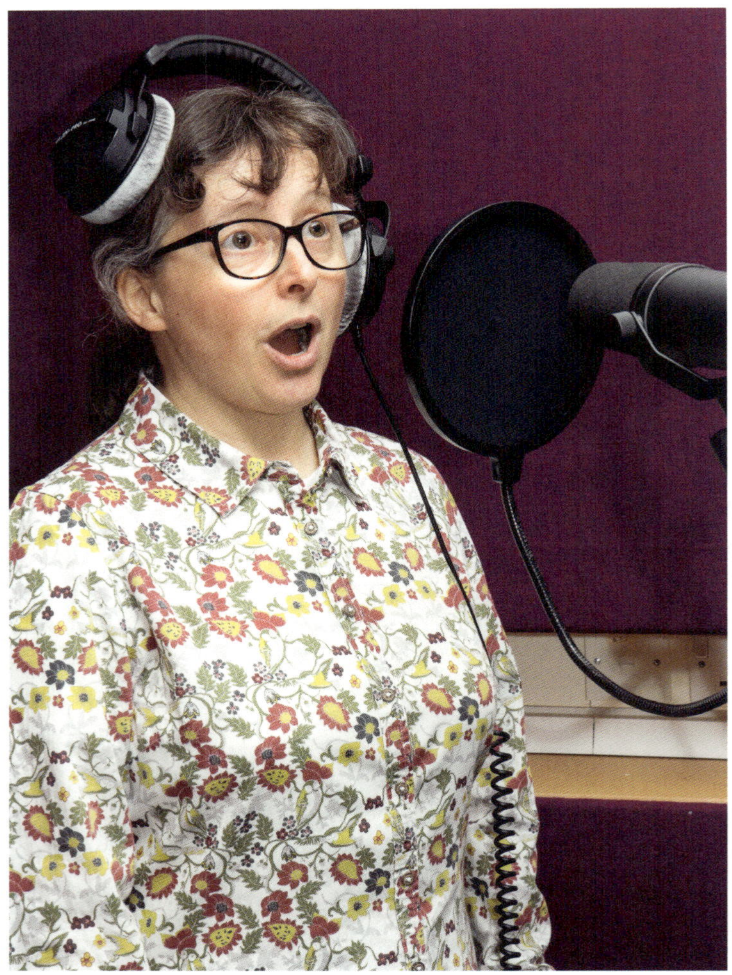

Jenny Nex

Auld Lang Syne

Robert Burns (1759–1796)
Published in vol. V of James Johnson's *Scots Musical Museum*, 1796

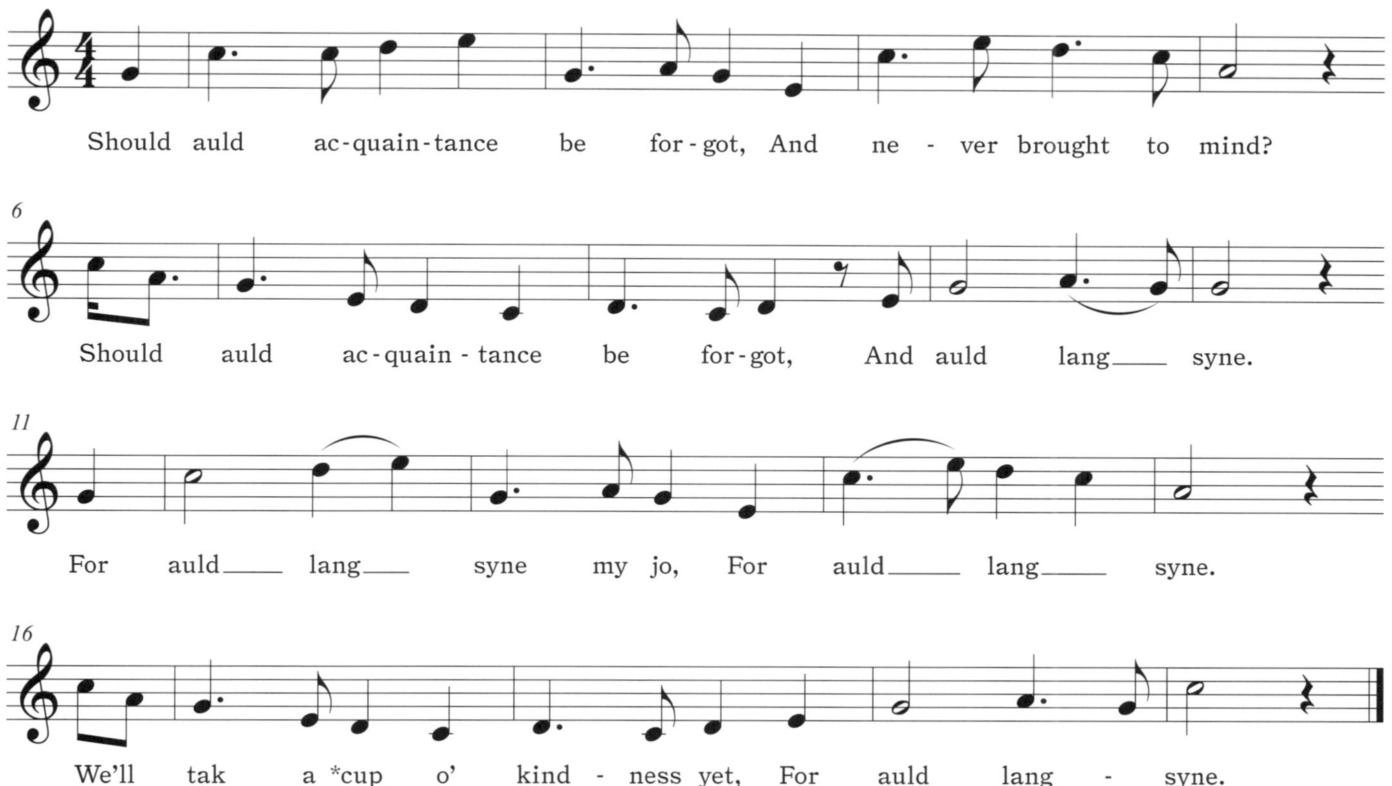

And surely ye'll be your pint-stowp!
    And surely I'll be mine!
And we'll tak a cup o' kindness yet,
    For auld lang syne.
      For auld, &c.

We twa hae run about the braes,
    And pou'd the gowans fine;
But we've wander'd mony a weary fit,
    Sin auld lang syne.
      For auld, &c.

We twa hae paidl'd i' the burn,
    Frae morning sun till dine;
But seas between us braid hae roar'd
    Sin auld lang syne.
      For auld, &c.

And there's a hand, my trusty fiere!
    And gie's a hand o' thine!
And we'll tak a right gude willie waught,
    For auld lang syne.
      For auld, &c.

*Some Sing, Kiſs, in place of Cup.

Of Possessing and Being Possessed

Negotiating Language and Translation with Emeka Ogboh

Bonaventure Soh Bejeng Ndikung

> English
> is my mother tongue.
> A mother tongue is not
> not a foreign lan lan lang
> language
> l/anguish
>   anguish
> —a foreign anguish.
>
> English is
> my father tongue.
> A father tongue is
> a foreign language,
> therefore English is
> a foreign language
> not a mother tongue.

M. NourbeSe Philip – excerpt from 'Discourse on the Logic of Language'

After about eight minutes of serious heavy-matter instrumental drives with drums, synths, keyboard and varying horn arrangements, Fela Kuti – who at some point dropped the middle name Ransome and replaced it with Anikulapo in what, these days, one might call a decolonial gesture – finally gets to the crux of his seminal piece 'Mr. Grammarticalogylisationalism is the Boss' from the 1976 album *Excuse O*. One could indeed argue that Fela's 'Mr. Grammarticalogylisationalism is the Boss' is one of the most, if not the most, astute critiques of language within the postcolonial condition: a condition that reveals the violence and wounds of our colonial legacy every time we open our mouths. Towards the middle of that piece, Fela Anikulapo Kuti calls on us, begs us, his brothers and sisters, to listen to him:

> Wey talk oyinbo well well to rule our land o (...)/ Him talk oyinbo pass English man!/ Him talk oyinbo pass America

man (him talk oyinbo pass English man)/ Him talk oyinbo
pass French man (him talk oyinbo pass English man)/
Me I say him talk oyinbo pass Germany man (him talk
oyinbo pass English man)/ The better oyinbo you talk/
The more bread you go get (...)

He goes on to sing of how the coloniser's language and the strive
to become even more colonial than the colonialist – which he
will call in another song 'colo-mentality' – has taken hold of us
and translates to economic value, the way the language affects
the people that rule us, our academic structures, our daily
news, our quotidian. He sings about the bogus languages that
have filled the pages of newspapers, that express things that
teachers, traders, labourers, people of all walks of life, will not
understand. There is something uncanny about the displacement
reaction that happens when a colonial language displaces the
mother tongue of the colonised, and the postcolonial being, in
that equation or reaction one might call communication. When
all books (especially the Bible), all signage, basically everything
written or spoken, are in a language that is not yours, and when
you are even banned from speaking your mother tongue in school,
then you realise that the notion of coloniality[1] is most effectively
planted and blossoms in and through language. What becomes
evident is that this imposition of language on others means that
their original language is no longer significant, and some other
person's language becomes most significant. But if language can
be an imperial force that disrupts, it can also be an anti-imperial
force that disrupts empire through resistance. It is this anti-
imperialising force of language that I have observed in Emeka
Ogboh's work over the past half decade.

In 2015, upon invitation by curator Okwui Enwezor to the 56th
Venice Biennale, titled *All the World's Futures*, Emeka Ogboh
presented the work 'The Song of the Germans' in an eighteenth
century tower situated at the far end of the Arsenale. This sound
installation comprised ten speakers from which emanated
ten voices singing the German national anthem in ten African
languages – Bamoun, Douala, Ewondo, Igbo, Kikongo, Lingala,
Moré, Sangho, Twi and Yoruba. A conceptually, vocally and
technically brilliant work of art, 'The Song of the Germans'

1. A term propagated by Latin American scholars like Anibal Quijano, Walter Mignolo
and others to describe the continuum of the colonial enterprise and the impacts it has
on our epistemic, social, cultural, political and economic bearings even post independence.
Coloniality gives us a term for the perpetuity and amoebic structure of colonial systems
of power.

played in a shifted loop, ie continuously but arranged differently
after every run, whereby one singer begins singing, followed
by others successively until all ten voices accumulate to form
a full choir. Each speaker was placed at the corresponding head
height of each singer, and the closer the listener went towards
the speaker, the more distinct the voice became – as if the
singer was giving them a private concert. In the centre of the
circular installation of speakers was a book containing images
of the singers in rehearsal and recording sessions, and also
translations of the German national anthem into each of
the languages. This piece has possessed my thoughts since
I first experienced it in 2015, and in my state of possession,
I have been thinking about language's capacity for possession;
to be possessed by language and to possess language. It is from
these two vantage points that I would like to consider Emeka
Ogboh's work.

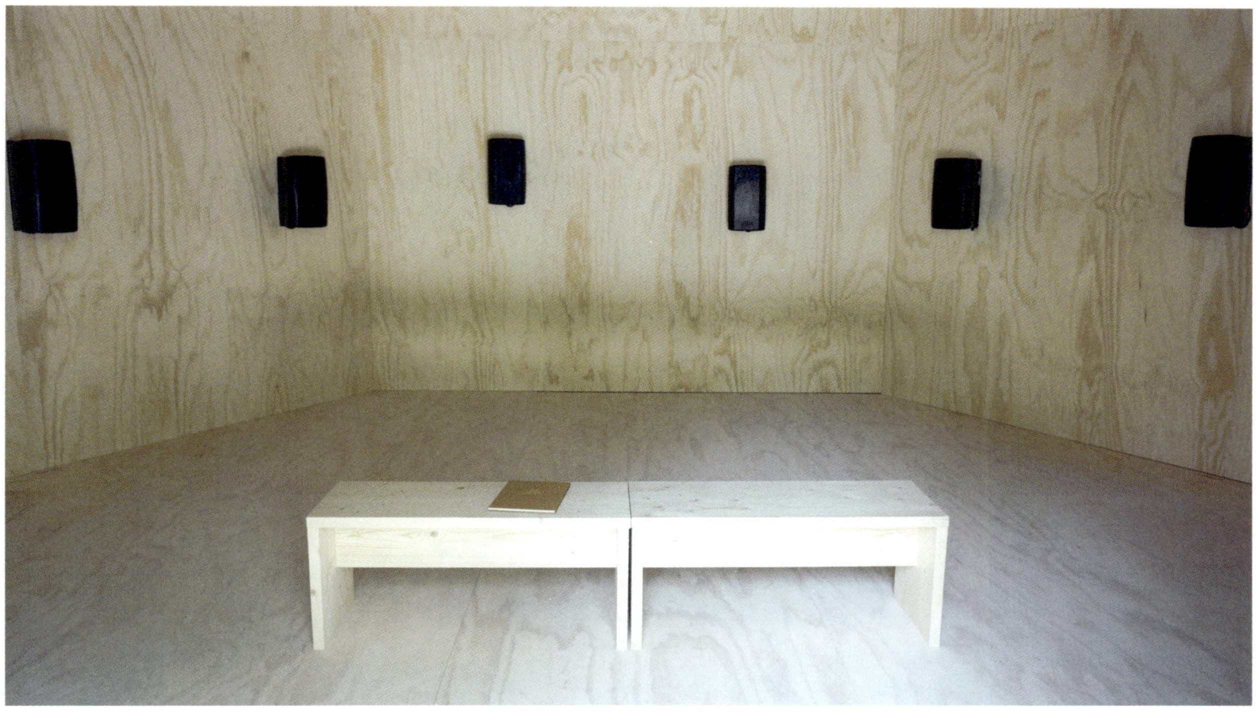

Emeka Ogboh, 'The Song of the Germans', 2015
10-channel sound installation
All The World's Futures, 56th Venice Biennale, 2015, curated by Okwui Enwezor

The first mode of possession is to take or seize something and
make it yours. This is the condition of the colonial enterprise,
whereby this mode of possession is always accompanied by
its mirror image: dispossession. The second mode of possession
is to be wholly gripped by something, akin to the religious
sense of being possessed by a spirit, which is to say one is

95

Douala

Jalatane, té me lá sim, wonja

Oñol' Ekombo a Jaman!

Ba be biso be se mpéte,

Boñango bo be bwasam!

Jalatane, té me lá sim, wonja

Bebókédi ba mutam!

Paña na mun mutam ó mwe ne n,

Paña Ekombo a Jaman!

Emeka Ogboh, 'The Song of the Germans (Deutschlandlied)', 2015
Publication containing German national anthem lyrics translated into ten African languages
Above: 'Deutschlandlied' translated into Douala, a Bantu language spoken in Cameroon

Do = F
transcribed in Tonic sol-fa
by Danny Wazolua L.K.
Unisson

Music:
Joseph Haydn
Lyrics:
Heinrich Hoffmann von Fallersleben

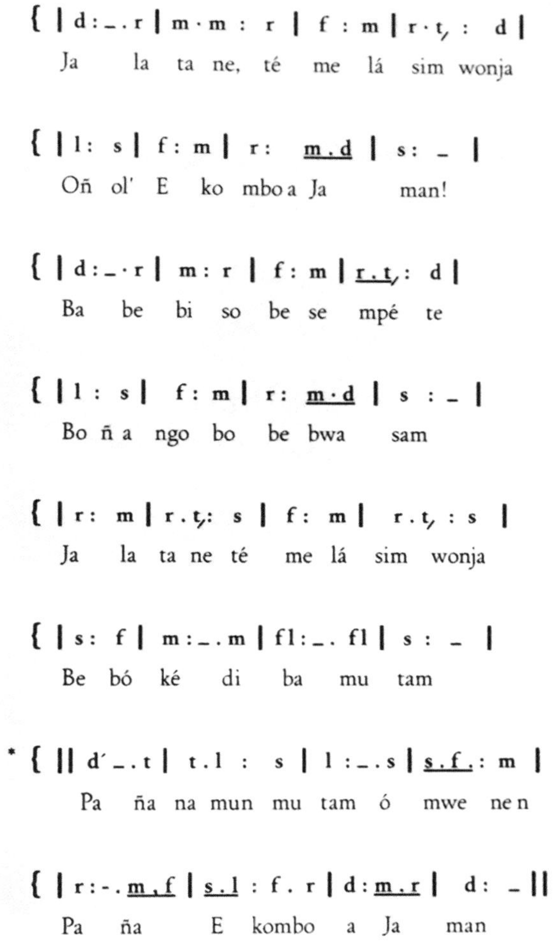

{ | d : _ . r | m · m : r | f : m | r · t₁ : d |
Ja   la ta ne, té me lá sim wonja

{ | l : s | f : m | r : m . d | s : _ |
Oñ ol' E ko mbo a Ja   man!

{ | d : _ · r | m : r | f : m | r . t₁ : d |
Ba   be   bi so be se mpé te

{ | l : s | f : m | r : m · d | s : _ |
Bo ñ a ngo bo be bwa   sam

{ | r : m | r . t₁ : s | f : m | r . t₁ : s |
Ja   la ta ne té   me lá sim wonja

{ | s : f | m : _ . m | f l : _ . f l | s : _ |
Be bó ké di ba mu tam

* { || d' _ . t | t . l : s | l : _ . s | s . f . : m |
Pa ña na mun mu tam ó mwe ne n

{ | r : - . m , f | s . l : f . r | d : m . r | d : _ ||
Pa ña   E kombo a Ja man

Transposition and reproduction:
Bona Deus Berlin, February 2015

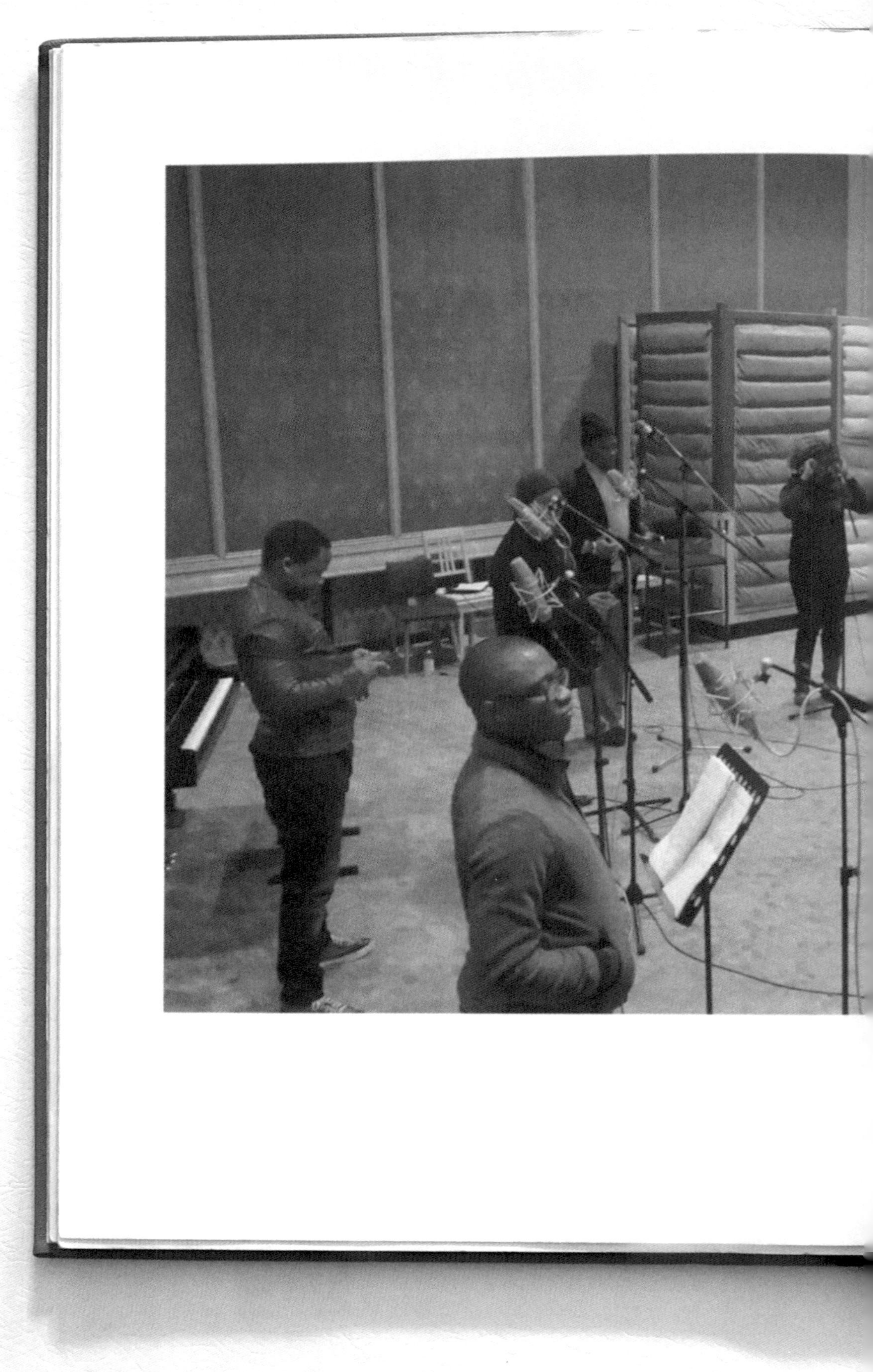

Emeka Ogboh, 'The Song of the Germans (Deutschlandlied)', 2015
Choir in Berlin singing German national anthem in ten African languages:
Bamoun, Douala, Ewondo, Igbo, Kikongo, Lingala, Moré, Sangho, Twi and Yoruba

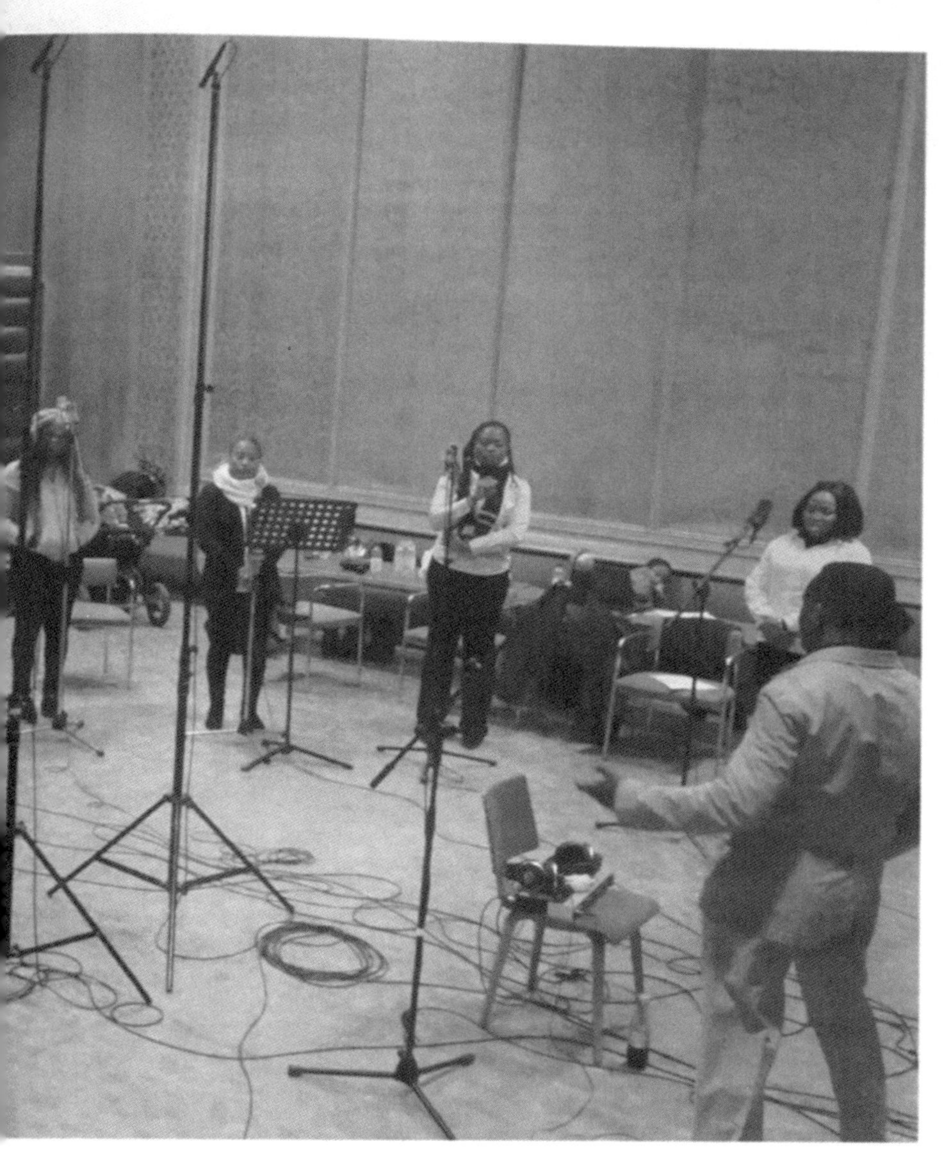

completely consumed. So, what does it mean to be consumed by a language? Fela's 'Mr. Grammarticalogylisationalism is the Boss' is a revelation, and critique of a society consumed by a language that is not theirs. Emeka Ogboh's 'The Song of the Germans', in my opinion, is a possibility of language's ability to disrupt through possession and repossession. The ten African singers not only take possession of the German national anthem by singing it, but in translating and singing it in their own languages, the anthem is possessed by the languages in which it is sung. As we know, anthems have become some of the most potent signifiers of nationhood. When the German anthem – or any other national anthem for that matter – is sung, there is a collective shiver that runs down the spines of the masses, and a collective pride for, honour of, and love for country that rises to the heads of the masses singing. People stand at attention, with their hands on their hearts as if sculpted for some kind of grand salutation, as the national hymn is chanted. Besides the content, it is the language that gives form to every national anthem. If the anthem is a liquid, then it is the national language that is the container, giving the liquid its form. So what Ogboh did was to pour that liquid into varying vessels, thereby destabilising and disrupting the content. What does the German anthem signify and what is its worth when sung in Bamoun, Douala, Ewondo, Igbo, Kikongo, Lingala, Moré, Sangho, Twi and Yoruba, the languages of people violently partitioned like a piece of cake on a table in Berlin in 1884–1885 when Otto von Bismarck summoned representatives of the 14 'great' nations to engage in a quest for their place in the sun?

Fast-forwarding six years, in 2021 Ogboh is invited to the Talbot Rice Gallery in Edinburgh to present a new sculptural and sonic installation. What Ogboh encounters in Scotland is a context, a history, a politics very different but also similar. A cocktail of imperial reverberations and calls, wishes and strives for independence, all spiced up, accelerated, catalysed and aggravated by the Brexit complex.

As I write, the results of the Scottish parliamentary elections are becoming clear, and though the pro-independence Scottish National Party did not gain the majority it needed to singlehandedly push for a new referendum to split from the United Kingdom, there is still hope that if they make a coalition with the Scottish Greens, the question of independence will still challenge Scottish politics over the coming years. As Stephen Castle wrote in a *New York Times* article of 8 May:

The millions of votes cast across Scotland Thursday could
be among the most consequential in recent times, and not
because of their impact on things like health, education and
fisheries. The greatest issue facing the country, and the one
that was really at stake, was nowhere to be found on the
ballot, and that is the future of its 314-year-old union with
England.[2]

Make no mistake … though in recent years many have compared
Scotland's relationship to England as akin to colonialism,
it cannot be compared to the relationships that England has
had with its colonies in Africa, Asia and America. Still, the
relationship between Scotland and England has not been
a kosher one from the outset. Having been an independent
kingdom and resisted assimilation by England for a large part of
the Middle Ages, it was only with the forging of the 1603 personal
union that the Scottish king, James VI, became England's king,
James I, with a political union following over a hundred years
later in 1707 uniting the two kingdoms. But since the 1800s
there have been recurring calls for independence: the devolution
referendums of 1979 and 1997, the establishment of the devolved
Scottish Parliament in 1999 and the 2014 Scottish independence
referendum being the most notable. With the UK choosing to
leave the EU following the June 2016 Brexit vote, calls for another
independence referendum have become louder.

This is the context in which Emeka Ogboh, like many of us,
found himself over the past five years, and this reality became
even more pressing and tangible upon his visit to Edinburgh,
in early 2020 for a site visit. During a visit to the monument
of the great Scottish poet Robert Burns, it was noted by gallery
director Tessa Giblin that 'Emeka has strong opinions about
Brexit, and as we were standing in the Burns Monument, we
started to riff off the memory that on the last day of the UK's
presence in the European Parliament, the day they voted
in the Withdrawal Agreement, while the Brexiteers waved
their Union Jacks and turned their backs, the rest of the MEPs
gathered rose to their feet, held hands, and sang "Auld Lang
Syne" – a song written by Robert Burns.'[3]

2. S. Castle, 'Of Brexit and Boris: What's Driving the Call for Scottish Independence',
The New York Times, May 2021, www.nytimes.com/2021/05/08/world/europe/brexit-
scotland-independence.html

3. Email to the author from Tessa Giblin, Director, Talbot Rice Gallery.

For this project, Ogboh implements the paradigms of possession
of language and possession by language which he implemented
for 'The Song of the Germans' in 2015.

Ogboh takes this iconic poem and song, 'Auld Lang Syne',[4]
which is often sung to bid farewells of all kinds – at funerals,
the end of the year, graduation, departures – and allows for
it to be possessed by the 27 languages of the 27 member states
of the EU, as well as for it to take possession of these languages.
With the recording installed at the Burns Monument and the
sound of the 27 languages emanating from the speakers on site,
the listeners cannot escape being possessed by the multiplicity
that makes up Europe.

With Brexit, England taps from its deepest crevices its instincts
and rationale of empire, because England has often thought that
by being part of the EU, they were being held down. The Great
British Empire felt it deserved more and if it couldn't get that
from the EU, it might get it from a so-called Commonwealth in
which the wealth is not, and never has been, common. We hereby
witness that instinct to forge new, old alliances with African
and Asian countries – relationships that have historically
been fashioned by asymmetry and exploitation. As we await
our corrupt politicians on the African continent falling prey to
another amoebic form of the colonial enterprise, Ogboh stages
a choir of 28 voices, including the 27 shunned nations, bidding
farewell to the British. But as 'Auld Lang Syne' is sung in the
28 languages, including the original Scots, the opening line of the
song, which is supposed to be the posing of a rhetorical question,
('Should auld acquaintance be forgot…' – is it right that old
friends be forgotten?) shifts from a question and becomes more
imperative. The conditionality of 'should', in the languages of
those shunned by the rest of the UK but loved by Scotland, seems
to become 'must'. But, most interestingly, since the expression
'auld lang syne' is also used as a narrative tool in storytelling
to mean 'long, long ago', it seems Ogboh is orchestrating a multi-
voiced and multilingual story that will be told for generations
to come, throughout the EU.

Besides the possessed-possession complex, Ogboh also employs
the device of translation as a core element of both 'The Song

4. 'Auld Lang Syne' exists in Scottish cultural memory long before Robert Burns
in the writings of Robert Ayton (1570–1638), Allan Ramsay (1686–1757),
and James Watson (c. 1664–1722).

of the Germans' and the current work 'Song of the Union'.
It would be a fallacy to think that what concerns Ogboh is
simply an effort to make something intelligible in another
language. Far from it. Translation in itself has long ceased
to be a mere transformation of words from one language to
the other, but must be understood as an alteration of states,
of substance, of figures and forms; translation as transmutation,
as translocation and transfiguration. When Ogboh instigates
the translation of the German national anthem into ten African
languages, or collects the translations of 'Auld Lang Syne'
from 27 European languages, there is an underlying political act
that cannot and should not be overlooked. In order to understand
these deeper ramifications of translation, it is worth calling
upon Naveen Kishore to share with us his thoughts on
translation:

> Translation as midwifery, then? Perhaps. Challenge
> the language you have so carefully cultivated. Revisit
> the meaning of words you have since childhood imbibed as
> universal truths. Consider the act of translation as impulse,
> as motivation, as a 'telling' of that which would otherwise
> remain 'untold'. So: speaking out and speaking about the
> forbidden? Maybe. Even perhaps. Do not the frames that
> rule the act of translating from one language into another
> blinker your vision into thinking the job is done? Translation
> as action. As activism. As a tool for translators who take
> up causes. *Body phele debo* as a translatable act of not
> just the *body* being thrown into the fray should the situation
> demand this of you – but the soul too. The soul translated
> as body made visible. Made passion. So: translate your
> passion. Singular. Plural. It doesn't matter. What matters
> is the subverting of the status quo. Translation therefore
> as subversion.[5]

There are four tenets in Naveen Kishore's statement that I would
like to relate to the context of Emeka Ogboh's practice, or better
said, four prisms through which Ogboh's recordings can be seen
and heard:

We must reckon that Ogboh's translation of the German national
anthem into ten African languages, and collecting 'Auld Lang

5. N. Kishore, 'Translation Rights that Which is Wrong. It Describes the Injustices Hidden
in the Dailyness', *Scroll*, January 2018, https://scroll.in/article/866975/translation-rights-
that-which-is-wrong-it-describes-the-injustices-hidden-in-the-dailyness

Syne' in 27 European languages, offers the possibility to 'tell' that which would otherwise remain 'untold' in those languages.

We must reckon that Ogboh's translation of the German national anthem into ten African languages, and collecting 'Auld Lang Syne' in 27 European languages, provides the possibility for speaking out and speaking about that which is forbidden.

We must reckon that Ogboh's translation of the German national anthem into ten African languages, and collecting 'Auld Lang Syne' in 27 European languages, makes 'enacting' possible; making an action come to life. This is a form of activism. The mere act of bringing bodies, voices, people together, as a loose or tied choir, to sing together is an action, a collective action. It is enacting performativity. And it provides the possibility of calling upon the voice to act.

We must reckon that Ogboh's translation of the German national anthem into ten African languages, and collecting 'Auld Lang Syne' in 27 European languages, is a subversion. In the case of 'The Song of the Germans' one imagines migrants of African origin, who might not even be German passport holders, singing the German national anthem in their own language at one of the most prestigious art events in the world, and subsequently as part of several museum collections. That is subversion of the notion of German-ness and what it stands for, *par excellence*. And consider the United Kingdom – deciding to turn its back on Europe, only to find out that it is not that united; Scotland is possibly on the verge of disuniting the union, and as if that was not enough, the farewell song of the Scots is placed into the mouths and languages of your former EU partners, to bid you farewell in their 27 languages. That too is subversion *par excellence*.

The two strands of translation and possession in the work of Ogboh can be tied together through the writing of Ilya Kaminsky when he discusses the translation of work by Russian poet Marina Tsvetaeva: 'If translation – as most translators are eager to claim, is "a closest possible reading," then it is not translation, it is notation, a midrash. To translate is to inhabit.'

To translate is to inhabit. To be inhabited is to be possessed. Translation becomes a phenomenological practice. That which is translated in Ogboh's work is not just read by the audience but listened to and felt by the audience, as the sound waves from the speakers break through air and not only head towards the ears of the beholder but also hit them physically to take possession.

It would be short-sighted to see the bidding of farewell in those 28 languages as just a celebration of the UK's departure. It is about language and song as/in memory. For if 'Auld Lang Syne' is about transition, saying goodbye, etc, it is most effectively about memory. After all, language is NOT apolitical. Bidding farewell in those 28 languages must be understood, too, as an expression of anguish – a deep anguish, which we as survivors of the British Empire know all too well. This deep anguish is expressed by Fela Kuti in 'Mr. Grammarticalogylisationalism is the Boss', and ultimately, it is this emotion that NourbeSe Philip talks about in 'Discourse on the Logic of Language' when she writes of English as a foreign anguish.

Robert Burns
and the Song of Union

M. J. Grant

When the referendum on leaving the EU took place in June 2016,
I was ineligible to vote. By that point, I had been living in Germany
as an EU migrant from the UK for over 15 years and had therefore
lost my right to vote in UK elections. In fact, I had never used
that right during my years in Germany; it didn't seem appropriate
since I did not live in the UK and initially had no plans to return.
But the EU referendum was different: a vote to leave had the
potential to strip me of many of the basic rights I enjoyed in my
country of residence. And yet, like the other EU migrants whose
renditions of 'Auld Lang Syne' form the basis of Emeka Ogboh's
sound installation, I had no voice – at least, not officially.

As it happened, I returned to Scotland the following year to take
up a post at the University of Edinburgh. Among the boxes and
bags and laptop bags I carried with me were the notes from my
research into the cultural history of 'Auld Lang Syne' – research
supported by the German funding authorities. The resultant
book is about to be published.[1]

*

As is commonly known, the song that we now recognise as
'Auld Lang Syne' is indebted to the songwriter and poet Robert
Burns. However, Burns never claimed authorship: introducing
it to correspondents, he would often refer to it as an 'old song',
adding, to the publisher George Thomson, that he had '[taken]
it down from an old man's singing'.[2] The earliest extant version
of the song in his hand came in a letter to his friend and corres-
pondent Frances Dunlop in December 1788.[3] At that time,
Burns and his young family were living at Ellisland Farm
near Dumfries. Burns sent this version of the song – text only –

---

1. M. J. Grant, *Auld Lang Syne: A Song and Its Culture*, Cambridge,
Open Book Publishers, 2021.

2. Robert Burns, letter to George Thomson, September 1793; J. De Lancey Ferguson
and G. Ross Roy (eds.), *The Letters of Robert Burns*, 2nd edn, vol. II, no. 586,
Oxford, Clarendon Press, 1985, p. 246. Burns also referred to it as an 'old song'
in the letter to Frances Dunlop referenced below.

3. Robert Burns, letter to Frances Dunlop, December 1788, in *Letters*, vol. I, no. 290.

in response to a letter in which Dunlop recounts an unexpected meeting with an old childhood friend. This version of the lyrics differs in small though significant ways from the version Burns would eventually submit for publication: for instance, it includes an exhortation to 'hae a waught o' Malaga' (a sweet wine) at the end of the first verse.

First page of earliest extant version of 'Auld Lang Syne' written by Burns and sent to Frances Dunlop in December 1788

Burns revised this version of the song for publication (and we
do not know how many revisions, or additions, he had introduced
even before the version he sent to Dunlop). It appeared not long
after his death in 1796, in the fifth volume of James Johnson's
The Scots Musical Museum, with the tune to which Burns
originally wrote the song. The tune most people know, however
– and which forms the basis of the versions recorded for Ogboh's
installation – first appeared with Burns' text in 1799, in the
collections of another of his collaborators, the publisher George
Thomson. Quite why Thomson changed the tune is unclear; the
tune he picked can be found, with some slight differences, in a
number of late-eighteenth-century publications, often but not
exclusively bearing the title 'Sir Alexander Don's Strathspey'.

George Thomson was an avowed connoisseur of the latest
European art music, and his volumes of Scottish song
featured arrangements from some of the leading continental
composers of the day. In the case of Burns' 'Auld Lang Syne',
this included a setting by Leopold Koželuch, and, in a much
later volume, Ludwig van Beethoven. A setting by Joseph Haydn
also appeared in 1806, in a collection published by Thomson's
competitor William Whyte. Haydn's arrangement, like other
early nineteenth-century arrangements of the Burns song,
are interesting not least because they demonstrate how quickly
the tune Thomson had picked was becoming established.

*

These, then, are the origins of the song as we now know it;
but where, in turn, did that song come from?

Although Burns claimed to George Thomson that the song had
never been in print, he must have recognised its relationship to
other songs in circulation in the eighteenth century. For the two
most significant elements of the lyrics in the song as it is sung
to this day – the phrase 'auld lang syne' itself, and the opening
line, 'Should auld acquaintance be forgot' – are shared with a
number of earlier songs. The earliest direct connections that
we can still evidence are to two songs published at the opening
of the eighteenth century, but with roots in the seventeenth.
One is printed on a broadside now held in the National Library
of Scotland, published c. 1701;[4] the other appears in the third

4. NLS shelfmark Ry.III.a.10(070). It can be viewed online at 'Broadside Ballad Entitled "Old
Long Syne"', *National Library of Scotland*, https://digital.nls.uk/broadsides/view/?id=14548

Auld lang syne.

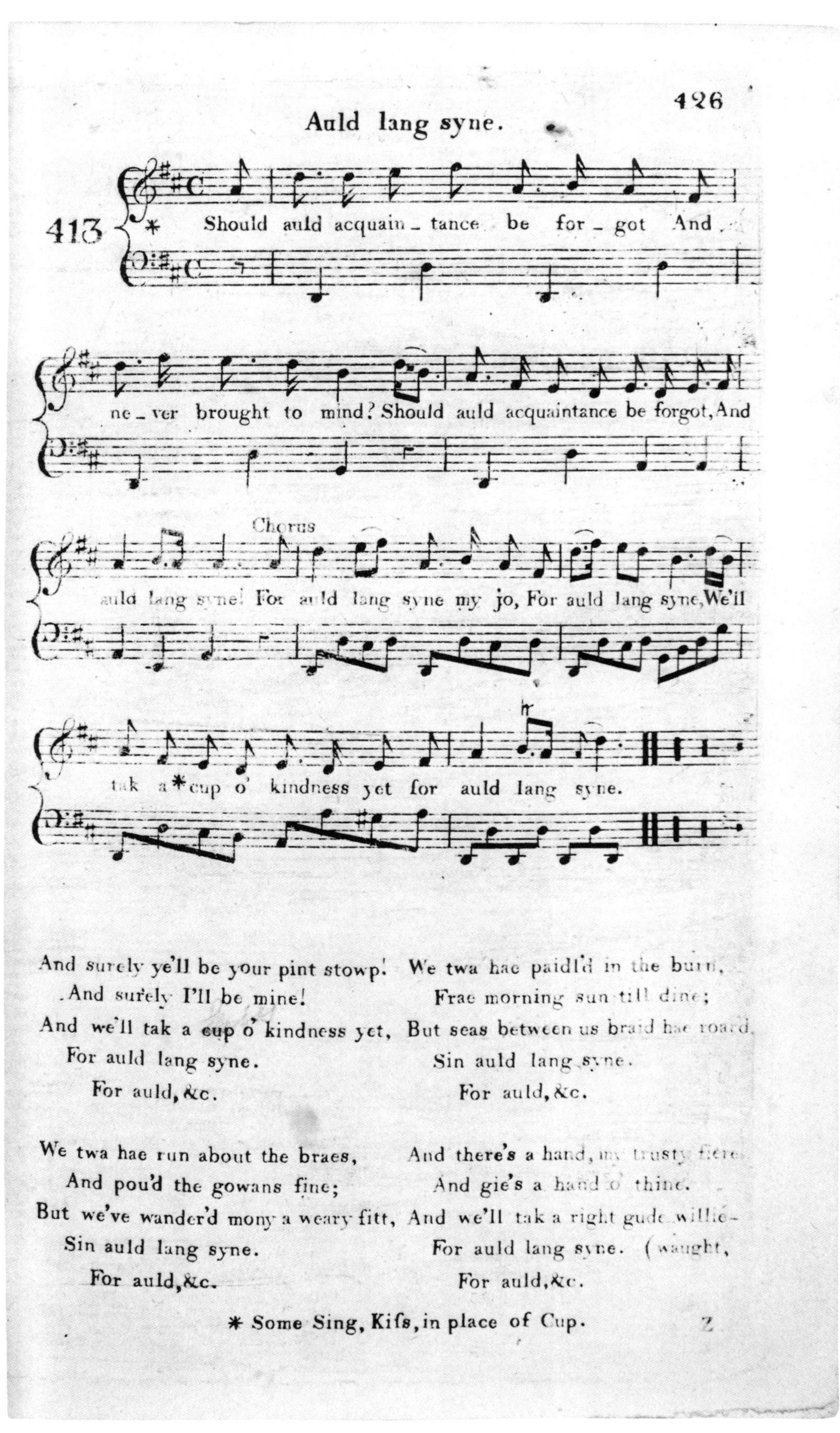

And surely ye'll be your pint stowp!
  And surely I'll be mine!
And we'll tak a cup o' kindness yet,
  For auld lang syne.
    For auld, &c.

We twa hae run about the braes,
  And pou'd the gowans fine;
But we've wander'd mony a weary fitt,
  Sin auld lang syne.
    For auld, &c.

We twa hae paidl'd in the burn,
  Frae morning sun till dine;
But seas between us braid hae roar'd,
  Sin auld lang syne.
    For auld, &c.

And there's a hand, my trusty fiere,
  And gie's a hand o' thine.
And we'll tak a right gude willie-
  For auld lang syne. (waught,
    For auld, &c.

    * Some Sing, Kifs, in place of Cup.

z

'Auld Lang Syne' as first published in *The Scots Musical Museum in Six Volumes: Consisting of Six Hundred Scots Songs with Proper Basses for the Piano Forte &c. / Humbly Dedicated to the Society of Antiquaries of Scotland by James Johnson*, vol. V, 1796, p. 426.

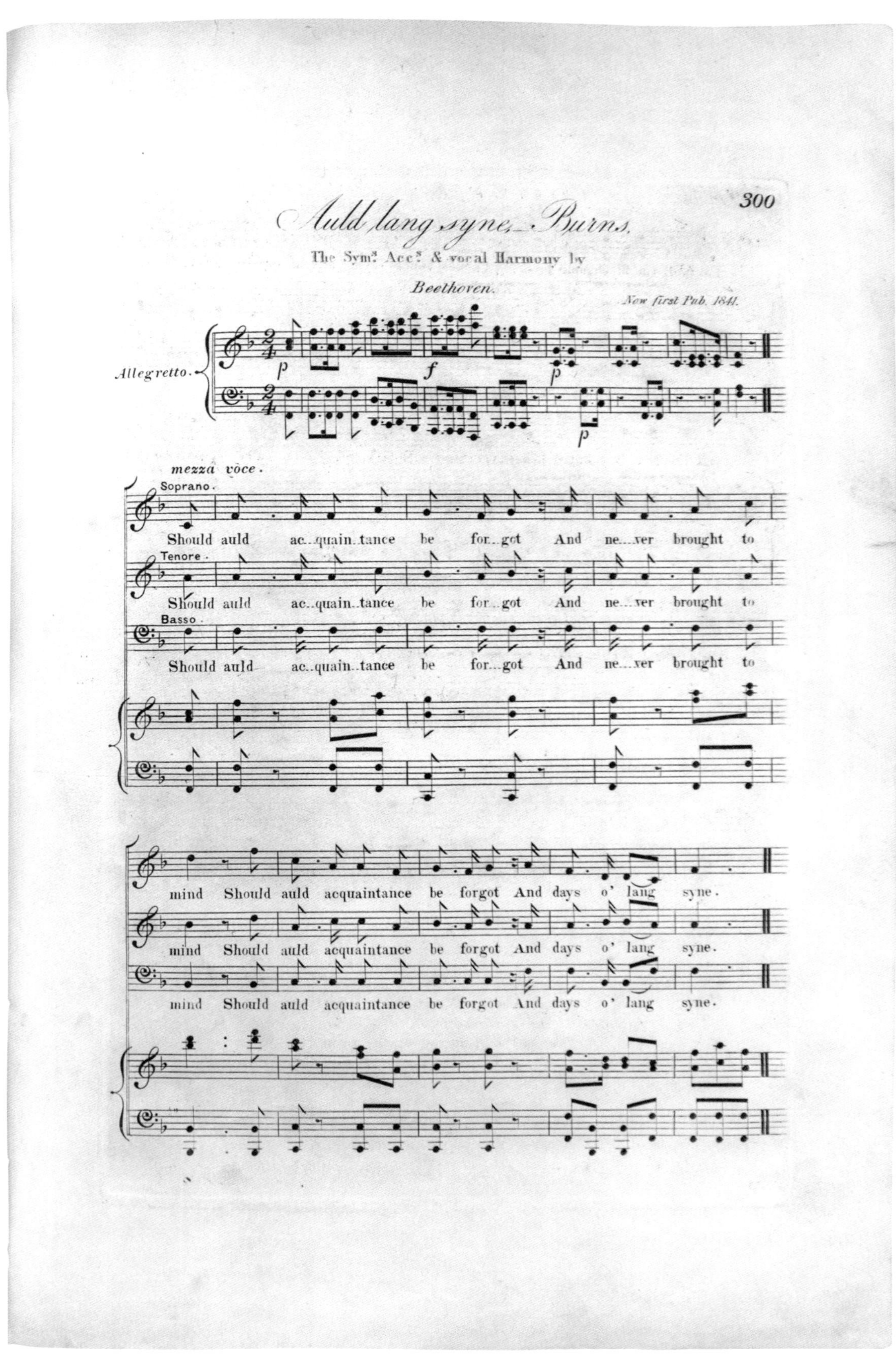

'Auld Lang Syne' arrangement by Ludwig van Beethoven. Thomson ed. *Volume Sixth of The Melodies of Scotland: with Symphonies and Accompaniments for the Piano Forte, Violin, &c / by Pleyel, Haydn, Beethoven, Weber, Hummel, &c. The Poetry Chiefly by Burns. The Whole Collected by G. Thomson, ... in Six Volumes*, 1841.

CHORUS.

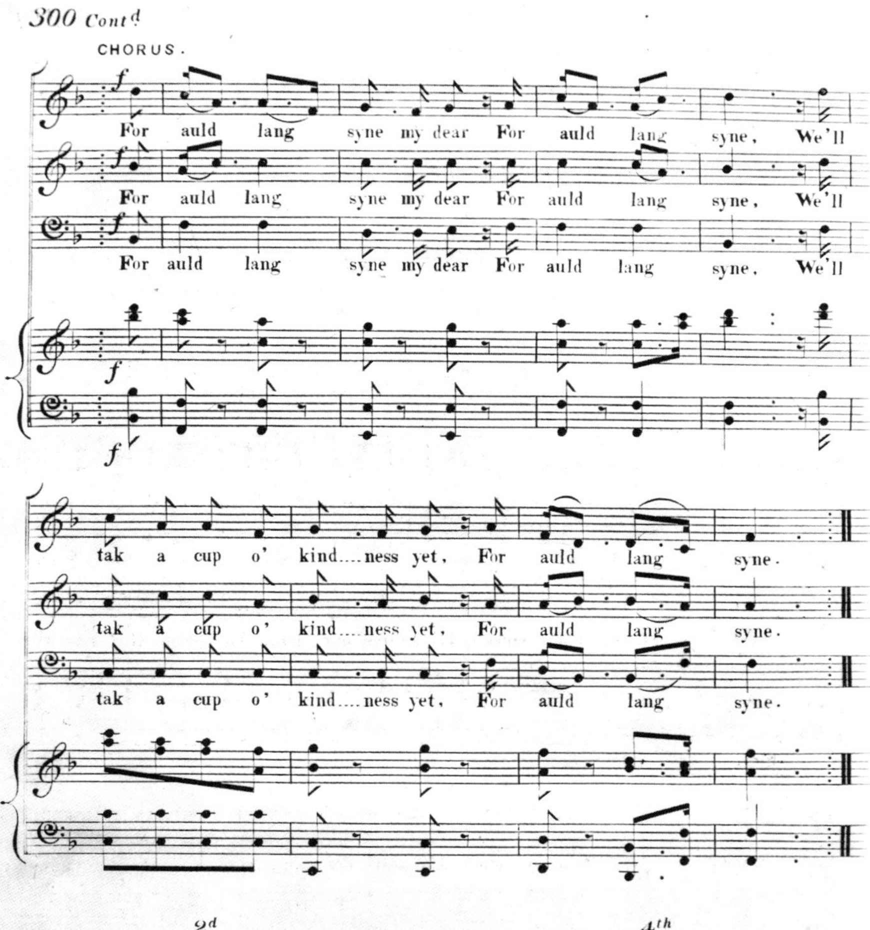

2^d

We twa hae run about the braes,
And pu'd the gowans fine,
But we've wander'd mony a weary foot
Sin' auld lang syne.
    CHO.^s For auld lang syne, &c:

3^d

We twa hae paidl'd in the burn
Frae morning sun 'till dine;
But seas between us braid hae roar'd
Sin' auld lang syne.
    CHO.^s For auld lang syne, &c:

4th

And there's a hand my trusty fiere,
And gie's a hand o' thine;
And we'll take a right good-willie waught
For auld lang syne.
    CHO.^s For auld lang syne. &c:

5th

And surely you'll be your pint stoup,
And surely I'll be mine;
And we'll take a cup o' kindness yet
For auld lang syne.
    CHO.^s For auld lang syne. &c:

* This admirable song is differently accompanied in a preceding volume.

volume of James Watson's *A Choice Collection of Comic and Serious Scots Poems Both Ancient and Modern*, published in Edinburgh c. 1711. In both cases, the song is entitled 'Old Long Syne'. Some elements of the song have, however, been traced back as far as a sixteenth-century poem with verses that each end with the statement that 'auld kyndnes is quyt foryet' (old kindness, or possibly kinship, has been quite forgotten). Versions of this poem appeared in several eighteenth-century publications as well. Burns would certainly have known a further eighteenth-century version, written by Allan Ramsay and first published in his song collection *The Tea-table Miscellany* in 1723.

There are many differences between these earlier songs and the one we know today in terms of structure and lyrics; another significant difference is the tune. As mentioned previously, the tune to which Burns' version of the lyrics was originally published was different to the one that became standard in the nineteenth century. The first tune – the one published by Johnson – is a simplified version of a tune known in the eighteenth century (and before) as 'Auld Lang Syne'. It is to some version of that older tune that these earlier songs are likely to have been sung. We know this quite definitively in the case of Ramsay's song, as he published the music to his *Tea-table Miscellany* in a separate volume.

Ramsay's is probably the most famous of these earlier songs. It is a love song, which Burns' is not, but both share a positive and uplifting take on reunion. The same cannot be said of many of the other early versions: many are complaints about an apparently inviolable social contract that has, in fact, been broken. In these cases, auld acquaintance has indeed been forgot. Some of these songs have been linked to Jacobitism; others (including Burns') tell of a return from an extended period overseas (which could also function as a Jacobite metaphor, given that the Stuart dynasty was exiled in continental Europe). Sometimes, the returning complainant is in straitened circumstances: hence the need to reactivate old ties and old support networks; hence the anger at discovering old acquaintances to be, in fact, mere fair-weather friends. But occasionally, as in Burns' song, the reunion is a happier one.

Like many of its predecessors, Burns' song is implicitly a song not just about friendship and reunion, but about migration, as one of the middle verses – rarely sung these days in communal contexts – indicates:

> We twa hae paidl'd in the burn,
> Frae morning sun till dine;
> But seas between us braid hae roar'd,
> Sin auld lang syne.
>
> (We two have paddled in the stream
> From morning sun until dinnertime
> But the broad seas between us have roared
> Since 'auld lang syne'/the time long ago).

This was a century of colonial expansion, including military campaigns and postings aimed at gaining and maintaining colonial territories. It was also the period of the British slave trade. Prior to the successful publication of his first book of poems in 1785, Burns himself had signed up to a position on a Jamaican plantation that would have placed him in direct authority over enslaved people.[5] The monied classes of Edinburgh and elsewhere who subscribed to the elaborate volumes of music and song discussed here would often have made their fortunes directly from stolen lands, and from slavery; others would have profited more indirectly. We are all implicated in this story in some way. The British nation is oddly protective of its own borders and boundaries considering how brazenly we have, in the past, disregarded those of others.

*

Perhaps the most fascinating aspect of the story of 'Auld Lang Syne' is how and why it spread around the world, and was adopted and adapted in the different places it landed. There is nothing particularly unusual about this process; song researchers have long noted the propensity of songs and their constituent elements – especially their tunes – to cross national, social and functional borders as people use and reuse them. Relatively rarely, however, does a song have quite the reach, and quite the level of use, that 'Auld Lang Syne' has achieved.

In part, but only in part, this is due to the legacy of Burns. His reputation as the 'ploughman poet' encapsulated many of the ideals not only of Romanticism, but also, as the nineteenth century progressed into the twentieth, other social and political

5. For more on this, and the broader context, see eg. M. Morris, 'Robert Burns: Slavery, Freedom and Abolition, 1786–1800', *Scotland and the Caribbean, c.1740–1833*, New York, Routledge, 2015, pp.98–140.

ideals as well. For example, an interest in national and regional cultures: the popular Danish version of 'Auld Lang Syne' was written by Jeppe Aakjær – closely following Burns' original – in the dialect Jutlandish; it was written in 1922 and first published in a 'workers' songbook'.[6] Europe's minority languages are further represented by several translations of the song into Jèrriais, a relative of the original Norman language which is spoken on the island of Jersey. Early translations of Burns' work into German, including 'Auld Lang Syne', were the basis of a choral work by Robert Schumann which does not reference either of the tunes to which the song was published back in Britain. It was only in the later twentieth century that German versions of the song became well established – with the common tune this time – and how and why this happened reveals much about the kinds of social processes responsible for the journey that 'Auld Lang Syne' has taken round the globe.

*

The tradition of using 'Auld Lang Syne' – originally a song of reunion – as a song of parting was not well established before the mid-nineteenth century. Without a doubt, this practice has been one of the main factors in 'Auld Lang Syne's' continuing fame and use in so many places around the world including in Japan, where the tune is often played to signal the close of business in shops, clubs and other commercial spaces. A further tradition, linking the song to the celebration of new year, emerged in the late nineteenth and early twentieth centuries, and has provided yet more impetus to the song.

But back to its use at occasions of parting. It was this tradition which led to it being sung as UK MEPs took their leave of the European Parliament. 'Auld Lang Syne' is also traditionally sung at the end of the annual meeting of the British Trade Unions Congress, and, unofficially, to close the Last Night of the Proms. In the early twentieth century, it was also sung at the first ever World Jamboree of the Boy Scouts, held in 1920. This Scouting connection lies behind the most popular French version of 'Auld Lang Syne', written by Jacques Sevin, one of the early promoters of Scouting in France. Polish Scouts also sing a version that contains a specific reference to the campfire,

---

6. Specifically, in a volume called *Arbejder Sangbogen* published in various editions by the Workers' Educational Association in Denmark. For more information on this and the other versions discussed in this section, see Grant, *Auld Lang Syne*, chap. 9, chap. 10.

and the two most common German-language versions also
emerged in connection with Scouting: one in Germany and
the other in Austria. Some of these localised versions have been
absorbed into the wider cultural repertoire of songs from their
origins in Scouting.

Like many organisations with a comparable structure (including
Freemasonry, which played a significant role in Burns' career
and legacy), Scouting combines membership of a local group
with ties to a national and international movement. These
ties are often not merely invoked, but enacted, through singing
a common repertoire of songs. What better choice, here, than
a song which in its very bones is about the ties that bind us
to others, and the strength that comes with those ties?

*

Sound installations are often about place as much as they
are about sound. They may, in fact, be created specifically for
a particular setting, drawing inspiration from its history or
physical characteristics while subtly changing the place they
inhabit, through their interpretation of it, and their presence
within it. But even beyond such site-specific manifestations,
sound installations are necessarily about being in a specific
place at a more or less specific time – the place and time of
the installation itself.

Music, on the other hand, is often discussed and approached as
something disembodied, not tied to place. (Music can, of course,
evoke place – very strongly in fact – but the music does not have
to be *in* this place to create this connection.) There are several
reasons for this notion of music as something disembodied.
One is the enormous influence of a strand of music aesthetics
that emerged primarily among German-speaking critics in
the nineteenth century, which viewed music as the ultimate
transcendent art. These critics regarded instrumental music in
the European classical tradition as the unsullied pinnacle of the
art form: music for the mind, not the body. Another contributing
factor, which emerged only slightly later, is sound recording.
Sound recording effectively severs the link between sound and
the bodies that originally produced it, thus furthering the idea
of musical communication as somehow disembodied.

Sound recording and broadcasting are also generally regarded
as the prime movers and shakers in processes of musical

globalisation. What drew me to researching the history of 'Auld Lang Syne', however, was the fact that the globalisation of this song could not be explained by recording and broadcasting alone. Its spread began much earlier; and even in the twentieth century, as the discussion of Scouting's role has shown, it is clear that the secret to the success of 'Auld Lang Syne' lies in singing, not just listening. The active, embodied practice of the song is what led to its spread through Scouting, and this is just one example of many. These are not just imagined communities, but sung communities.[7]

From its roots in songs about the persistent ties of friendship and kinship, Burns' version of 'Auld Lang Syne' has become associated with larger communities built around the same principles of mutual assistance, and the promise of maintaining these. This, ultimately, is why a song of reunion could end up as a song of parting – because implicit in that newer tradition is the idea that the company soon to be parted will remain connected and will reunite again. I wonder how many of those who joined hands to sing 'Auld Lang Syne' in Brussels on 29 January 2020 were aware of that.

7. M. J. Grant, 'Sung Communities', in K. Bicher, J-A. Kim and J. Toelle (eds.), *Musiken: Festschrift für Christian Kaden*, Berlin, Ries & Erler, 2011, pp. 81–93. 'Imagined communities' refers, of course, to Benedict Anderson's classic text on nationalism; Anderson actually mentions the singing of national anthems as an aspect of that imagining, but does not consider the physical enactment of community that singing together entails.

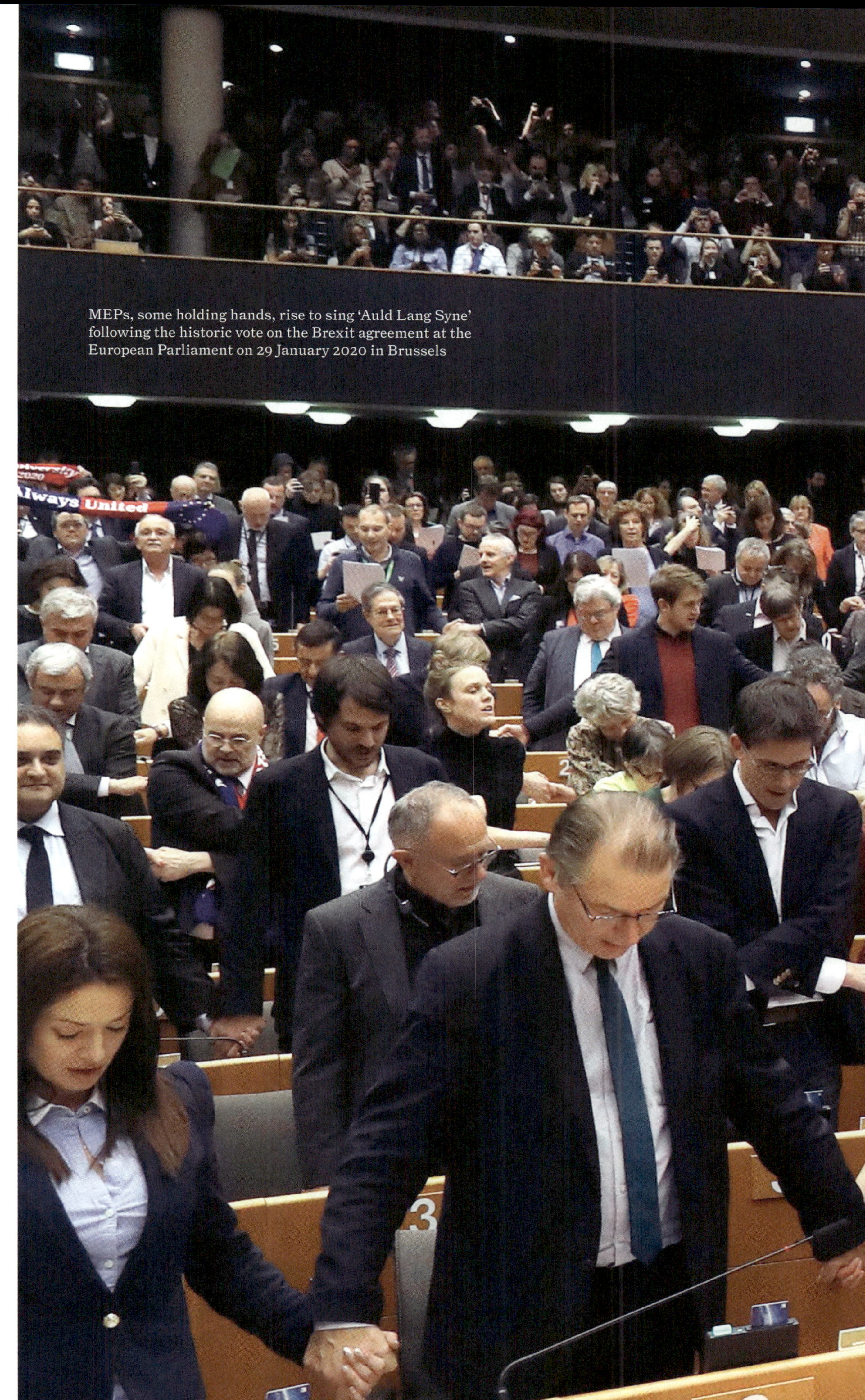

MEPs, some holding hands, rise to sing 'Auld Lang Syne'
following the historic vote on the Brexit agreement at the
European Parliament on 29 January 2020 in Brussels

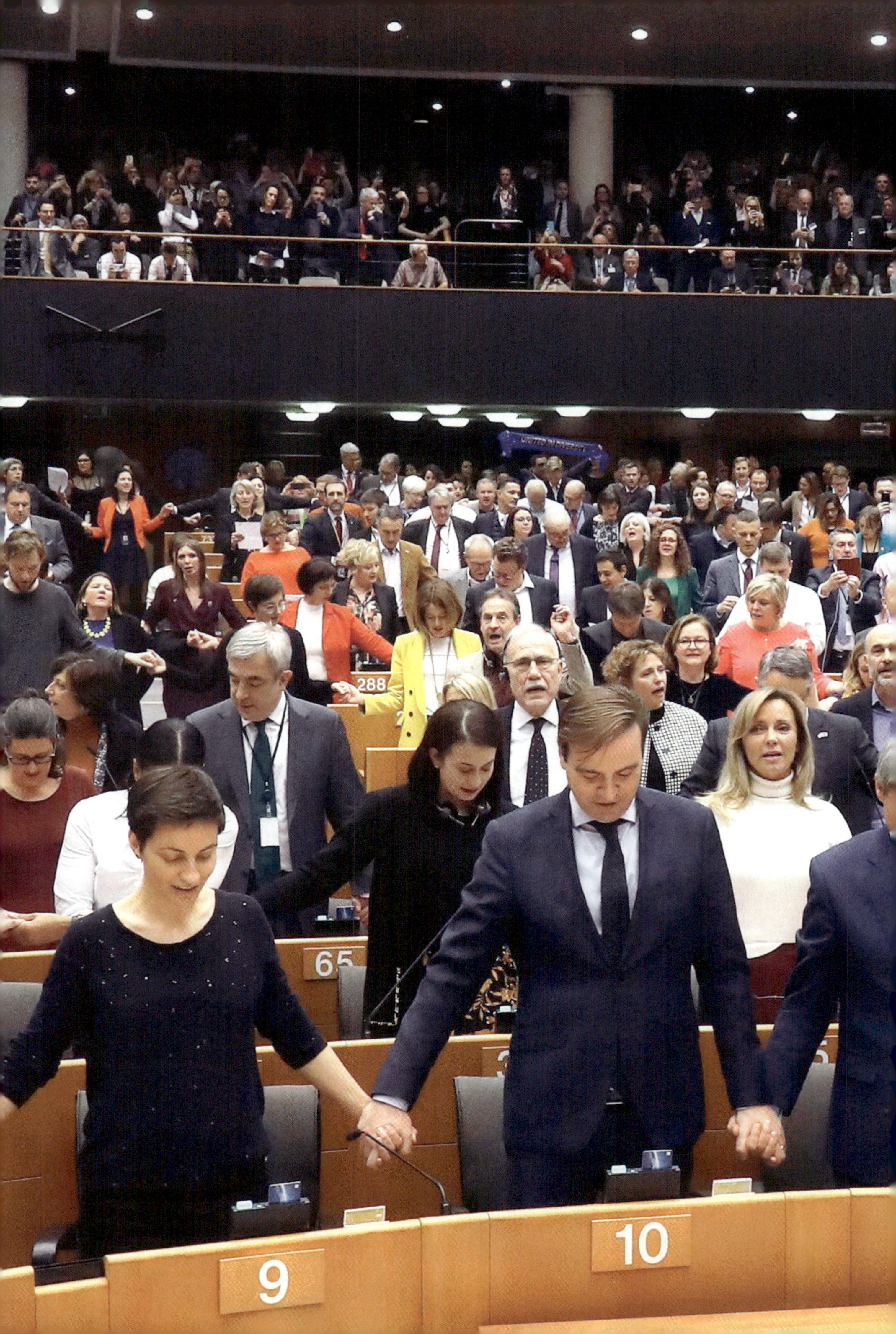

UNITED IN DIVERSITY
288
65
9
10

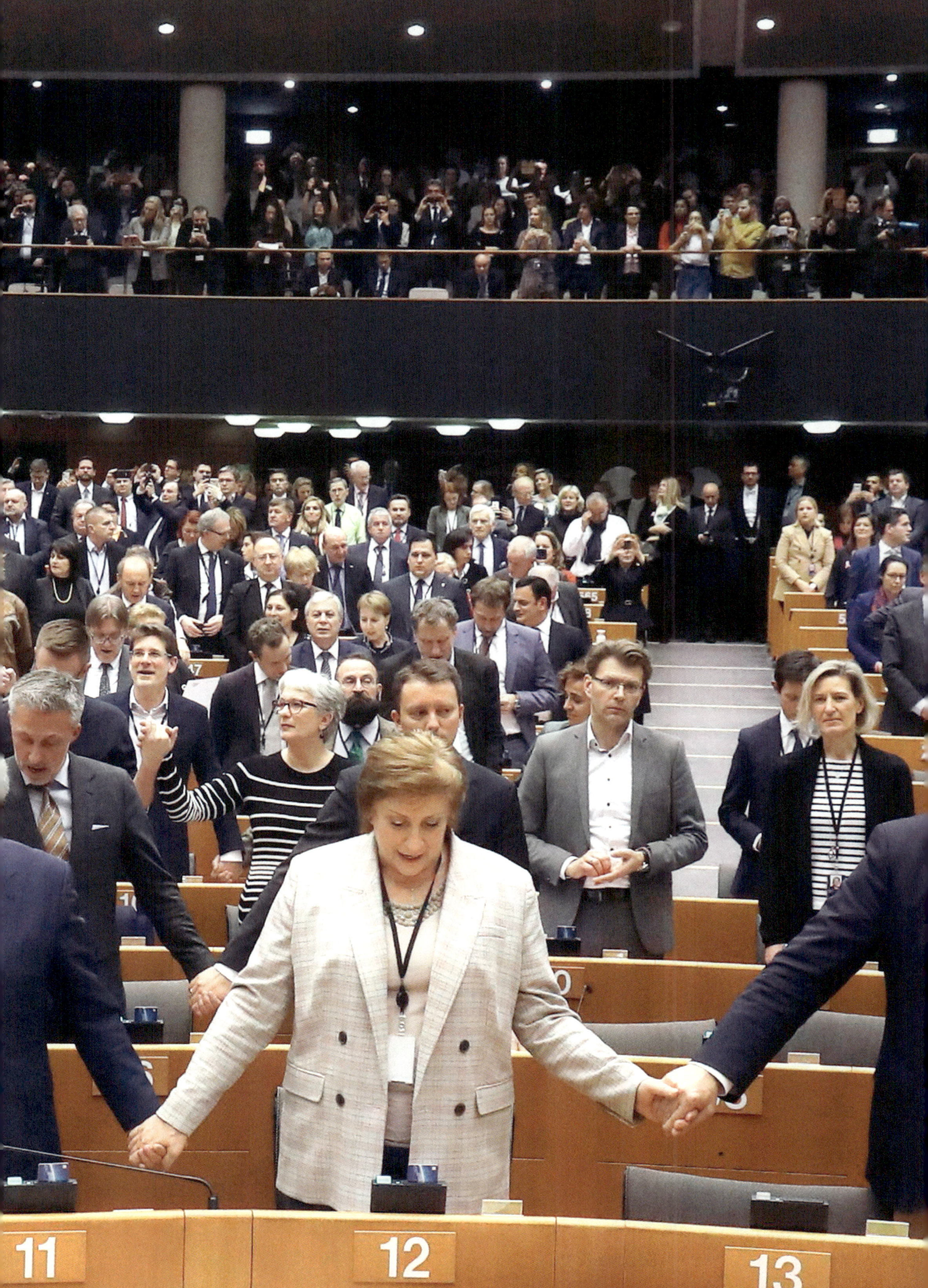

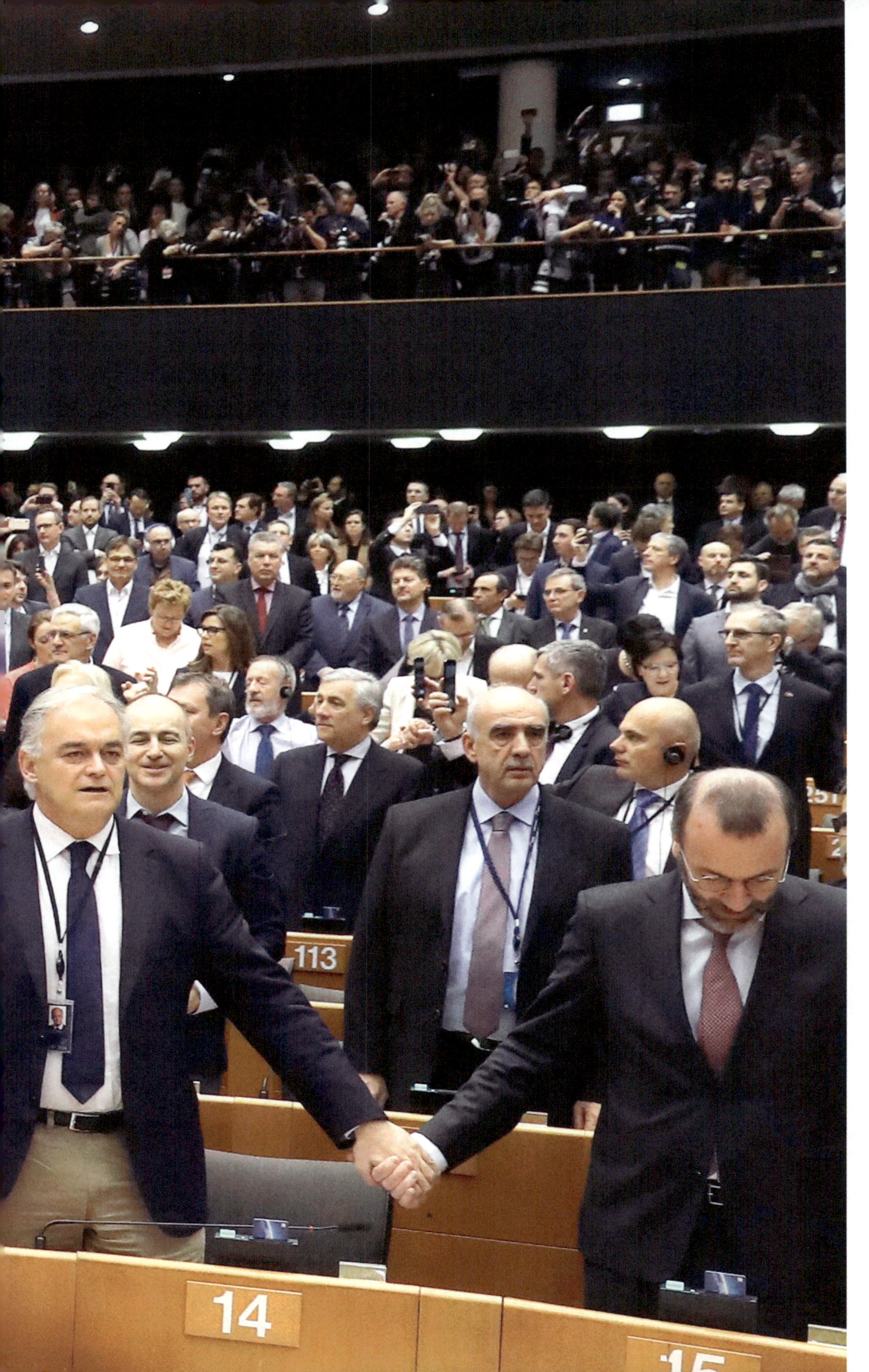

Scotland, the UK and Brexit: What Happened and Where Next?

Kirsty Hughes

The UK left the EU after 47 years on 31 January 2020. It was an extraordinary act, and has resulted in major and continuing damage to the UK's economy, international reputation and relationships with its former European partners. It has also led to deep divisions within society and in British politics throughout the last five years, as well as strongly exacerbating existing constitutional tensions across the four nations of the UK.

It was a decision taken in the 2016 Brexit referendum by a small majority across the UK: 52% voted to leave the EU while 48% voted to remain. Turnout was high – at 72% (although the 'leave' vote represented just 37% of the whole electorate eligible to vote). It was a decision that Scotland did not support, voting by an almost two-thirds majority to stay in the EU. Yet, despite the narrow majority for 'leave', only three of the UK's 12 regions and nations had a majority voting to remain in the EU – Northern Ireland, Scotland and London. The UK looked, and was, seriously fractured.

The vote for the UK to leave the EU has reverberated and impacted on British politics – and that of the European Union too – since 2016. David Cameron, who as Prime Minister had chosen to call the referendum, resigned immediately. His successor, Theresa May, presided over a chaotic, unstable and damaging three years of British politics before she too stepped down and Boris Johnson took over; the subsequent two years bringing UK–EU relations to an unprecedented low point.

The Brexit referendum led to deep divisions across the UK. Not only had voters in England and Wales voted to 'leave' while Scotland and Northern Ireland's voters wanted to 'remain', but the public were deeply divided in multiple ways: twice as many younger people supported staying in the EU than older people; large cities wanted to remain; smaller towns and rural areas mostly voted leave. To some extent, those on lower incomes, and those with fewer educational qualifications voted to leave too but there were also a significant number of wealthy older voters who bought into the 'Brexiter' ideology that UK sovereignty would be reclaimed by leaving the EU.[1]

In Brussels, and across the EU's 27 member states, the UK decision to leave a union in which it had played a major and influential role, was seen as baffling.[2] It was not only damaging to the UK's economy but also, albeit to a lesser extent, to the economies of many of its EU partners – not least those with whom it traded significantly, such as Germany, France, the Netherlands and Ireland. The peculiarity of what the UK had done and the damage to its reputation was visible internationally.[3]

There were fears, initially, that Brexit would also be damaging to the EU's structures and political unity. Might other states follow where the UK had led? In the event, and on the contrary, Brexit if anything led to a substantial and sustained display of unity across the EU27 as they negotiated with an unstable and unpredictable UK government on how and when the UK would leave the EU. In addition, the chaotic impact the Brexit decision had on UK politics meant that, fairly rapidly, those far right and populist groupings in other EU member states, including in France and Germany, that had toyed with leaving the EU soon dropped or denied they ever had that policy.[4]

Where Did Brexit Come From?

The European Economic Community (later known as the EU) was founded by six countries in 1957. At the time the UK chose not to join but – after an initial attempt to do so in the 1960s was vetoed by France – joined in 1973 alongside Ireland and Denmark. The UK rapidly became an influential member state. Alongside France and Germany, it was one of the 'big three' in the European Union – a respected and strategic, if periodically difficult, player.

1. P. Moore, 'How Britain Voted at the EU Referendum', *YouGov*, June 2016, https://yougov.co.uk/topics/politics/articles-reports/2016/06/27/how-britain-voted

2. K. Hughes, 'European Union Views of the UK Post-Brexit and of the Future EU–UK Relationship', *Scottish Centre on European Relations*, November 2020, www.scer.scot/database/ident-12883

3. N. Westcott, 'Britain Needs African Partners after Brexit – it Must Not Neglect the Continent Now', *The Conversation*, May 2020, https://theconversation.com/britain-needs-african-partners-after-brexit-it-must-not-neglect-the-continent-now-137568

4. R. Mac Cormaic, 'How the UK Killed Euroscepticism Across Europe', *Irish Times*, June 2019, www.irishtimes.com/opinion/how-the-uk-killed-euroscepticism-across-europe-1.3910882

Yet there had long been a wing of the Conservative party, strongly encouraged by a substantial part of the UK's media, that was Eurosceptic and had railed against what they saw as the overweening power of Brussels (a power that was held, ultimately, by the EU's member states including the UK).

There are long historical roots to this band of Eurosceptics who in 2016, now labelled 'Brexiters', finally achieved their ideological aim. Back in 1962, the then US Secretary of State Dean Acheson said that, since the Second World War, the UK 'had lost an empire and failed to find a role.' His message was clear – that the UK needed to work with its European allies. Yet the Eurosceptic Brexiters hark back to some nostalgic, fantasy vision of a 'global Britain' untrammelled by EU cooperation and common rules which they see as an affront to UK sovereignty.

These Eurosceptic views had been a minority part of the UK Conservative party but over time the influence of this grouping grew. Demands started to be heard for a referendum on EU membership, despite the fact that the UK had negotiated a series of opt-outs for steps, such as the introduction of the euro, with which it was uncomfortable. There was, however, no significant public demand for such a vote in the years before the referendum. While Conservative voters were much more Eurosceptic than the rather pro-EU Labour and LibDem voters, the EU was not of high salience according to polls – ranking low in issues of importance to voters.[5]

Even so Nigel Farage, the populist anti-EU campaigner, succeeded in tapping into considerable discontent especially amongst Tory voters, giving a much higher profile to the idea of Brexit. This led to concern in the Conservative Party as to how to stop their voters defecting to Farage's party. In the 2015, general election, Farage's UK Independence Party (UKIP) came a surprise third with 12.6% of the vote, ahead of the LibDems.[6] Infighting after the 2016 vote then led to the establishment of the Brexit Party in 2018, which came top in the European Parliament elections in the UK in May 2019, giving the Brexit Party 29 MEPs – a rowdy presence during the UK's last months in the EU.[7]

5. B. Clements, P. Lynch and R. Whitaker, 'The Low Salience of European Integration for British Voters Means that UKIP Will Have to Expand Their Platform to Gain More Support', *London School of Economics*, March 2013, https://blogs.lse.ac.uk/europpblog/2013/03/08/low-salience-european-integration-british-voters-ukip-expand-platform-support/

6. 'Election Results 2015', *BBC*, www.bbc.co.uk/news/election/2015/results

7. 'European Election 2019', *BBC*, May 2019, www.bbc.co.uk/news/uk-politics-48403131

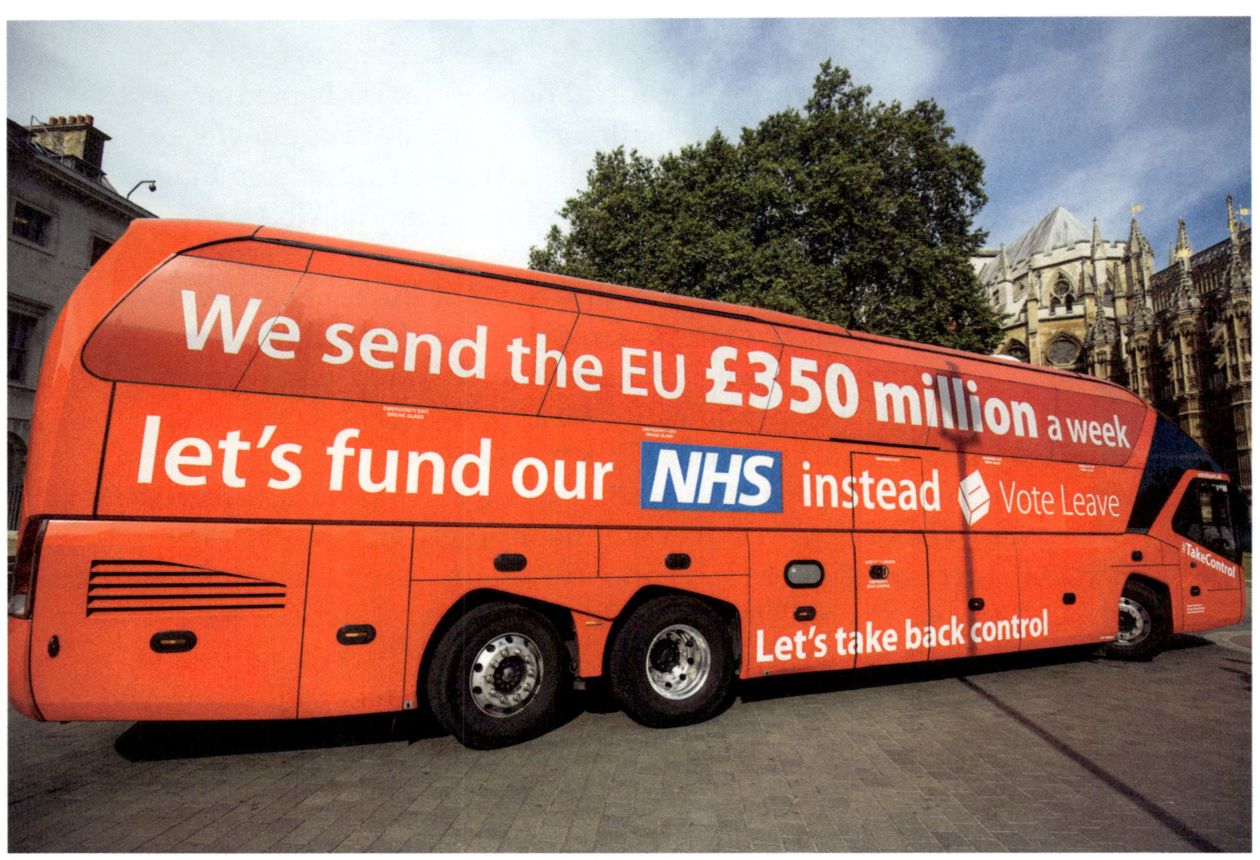

A Vote Leave bus parked outside the Houses of Parliament in Westminster, 2016

The 2016 EU Referendum Campaign

David Cameron, having won a majority in the general election
of 2015, chose to go ahead with his manifesto commitment
to hold such a referendum. It was a move that was designed
to resolve the divisions over the EU within the Tory party.
Or, as Dutch MEP Guy Verhofstadt colourfully labelled it
'a catfight in the Conservative party that got out of hand,
a loss of time, a waste of energy, stupidity.'

In the 2016 referendum campaign, the Conservatives dealt with
their splits on whether to stay or leave by allowing ministers
to campaign for leaving the EU, even though the Cameron
government was formally in favour of remaining within the union.
Boris Johnson notoriously wrote two draft versions of a newspaper
column – one backing leave and one remain – before he made his
career-defining move to lead the leave campaign. Even so, with
the opposition Labour party also supporting remaining in the EU,
albeit under its then rather Eurosceptic, left-wing leader Jeremy
Corbyn, it should have been a relatively easy vote to win.

But, in the event, the crucial vote was lost. The 'remain' side had the best economic arguments – indeed the 'leave' side never even spelled out what the future UK–EU relationship would look like. But the public mood was sour after several years of cuts in public spending and austerity after the 2008 international financial crisis, and with the EU struggling through the subsequent euro crisis. And the 'leave' campaign made several dishonest and misleading claims, such as, that the UK's annual contribution to the EU budget would be spent, post-Brexit, on the National Health Service.

Migration also became a key issue. The EU had faced a so-called migration crisis in 2015, when over a million refugees, many of them escaping the civil war in Syria, came to the EU (though mostly not to the UK). The vote 'leave' side rather deliberately, and with a xenophobic tone, linked this crisis with Turkey's faltering bid to join the EU, and with the fact that over three million EU citizens had made the UK their home since the enlargement of the EU to central and eastern Europe in 2004. The reality that these EU citizens had made a significant contribution to the UK, both economically and socially, filling a range of jobs, was presented negatively by the Brexiters and their media backers.

In Scotland, the presence of EU citizens was seen more positively. EU citizens in Scotland had halted demographic decline and had contributed to a wide range of sectors, from universities to tourism to agriculture. Scotland's First Minister Nicola Sturgeon underlined that EU citizens were welcome in Scotland both before and after the Brexit vote. But this was not the message they received in England. Nor could EU citizens in the UK (except those from Ireland, Cyprus and Malta) vote in the referendum – they only had the right to vote in local and European elections. Given the closeness of the referendum result, if they had been included it might well have resulted in the UK voting to stay in the EU.[8]

In the end, an ideological and populist campaign, rooted in sound bites, exaggeration, dishonesty and lack of detail or realistic plans for the future succeeded in the face of a solid but lacklustre campaign to stay in the EU. It set the scene for UK political instability, fragmentation and decline in the five years since then.

8. A. Low, 'In Some Respects the Brexit Referendum Was a Violation of Human Rights', *London School of Economics*, February 2017, https://blogs.lse.ac.uk/europpblog/2017/02/09/brexit-referendum-human-rights/

The initial response to the Brexit vote was one of deep shock both in the UK and in the EU. Theresa May took up the reins as Prime Minister and rapidly uttered one of her more notorious phrases: 'Brexit means Brexit'. The emptiness of this sound bite spoke both to her wish to reassure Brexit voters that their vote would be respected, but also showed the lack of preparation or ideas on what Brexit would and should look like.

Despite having backed the 'remain' campaign, Theresa May rapidly moved to set out 'red lines' that meant a very hard-line Brexit; the UK, she said, would not stay in the EU's single market or its customs union, it would chart its own course. This version of Brexit was one that would do substantial damage to EU–UK trade and to businesses and other organisations across the UK compared, for instance, to the option of staying in the EU's single market as Norway does.

But it was also a Brexit vision that ignored the political reality of Northern Ireland. The Good Friday Agreement in 1998 had brought relative peace to Northern Ireland – and though it was an agreement between the UK and the Republic of Ireland, it was one that was also strongly underpinned by the fact that both countries were in the EU. Theresa May's version of Brexit threatened to put a hard border where there was no visible border at all on the island of Ireland. This, it was clear, would undermine or fully collapse the Good Friday Agreement and risk the hard-won peace process.

May and her government struggled with the challenge they had set themselves: to keep the Irish border open, to leave the EU's single market and customs union, and not to have a border between Britain and Northern Ireland. May also made the fatal mistake of holding an early general election in June 2017. She lost her majority and not only became dependent upon the votes of the rather hard-line, pro-Brexit Northern Ireland Democratic Unionist Party (DUP) but was also at the mercy of her divided Conservative backbenchers – both the extreme Brexiter wing and the smaller more moderate 'remain' wing.

Finally, by the end of 2018, May negotiated a Withdrawal Agreement with the EU that covered three main issues: money (what the UK owed the EU as it left); the rights of EU citizens living in the UK and UK citizens living in the EU; and Northern

Ireland. Contrary to her initial aims, the agreement set out
that the UK would stay indefinitely in a customs union with
the EU. This solved the Irish border problem but it outraged
the Brexiters – it was not 'proper' Brexit.

A year of political chaos ensued. Theresa May could not get the
Withdrawal Agreement through the House of Commons – it was
voted down three times due to a group of hard-line Brexiter Tory
MPs siding with the opposition. Adding to the pressure, the UK
was due to leave the EU at the end of March 2019; the government
had triggered the EU's treaty clause for leaving in March 2017
and the time limit was two years. Fears were spreading of a
chaotic 'no deal' Brexit. In the end, the UK agreed a transition
period with the EU until the start of 2020.

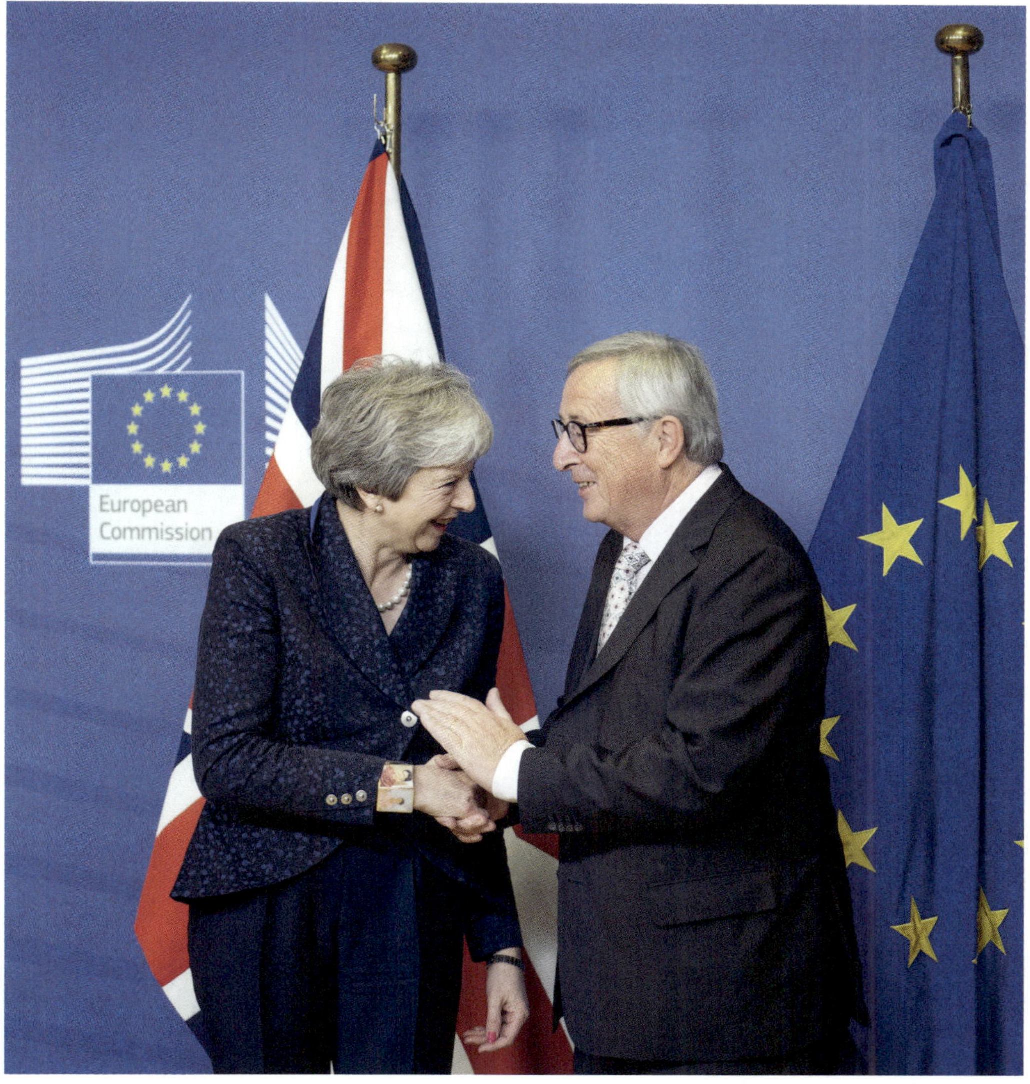

Theresa May, UK Prime Minister, left, shakes hands with Jean-Claude Juncker,
President of the European Commission, during a meeting ahead of Brexit negotiations
in Brussels, Belgium, 24 November 2018

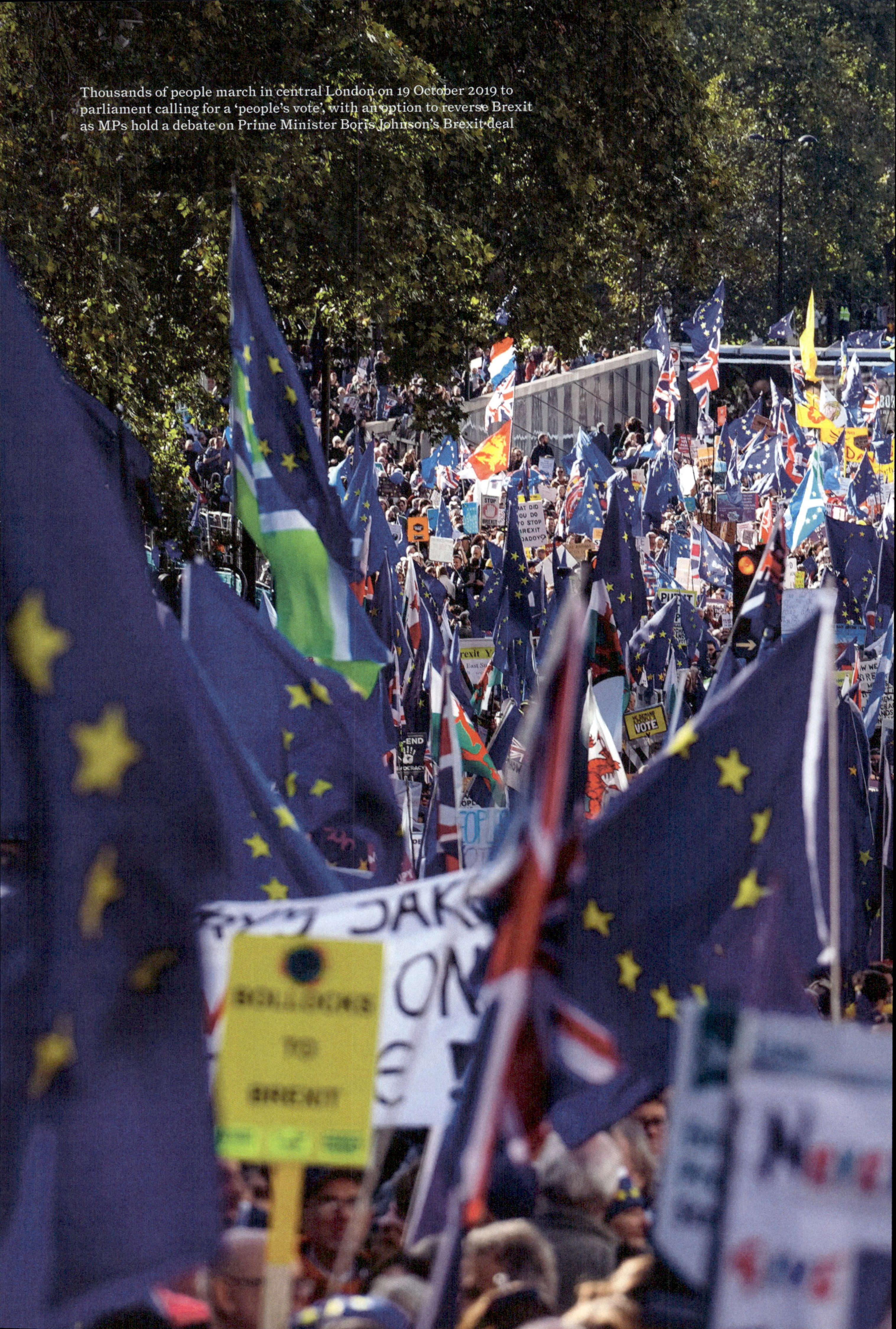

Thousands of people march in central London on 19 October 2019 to parliament calling for a 'people's vote', with an option to reverse Brexit as MPs hold a debate on Prime Minister Boris Johnson's Brexit deal

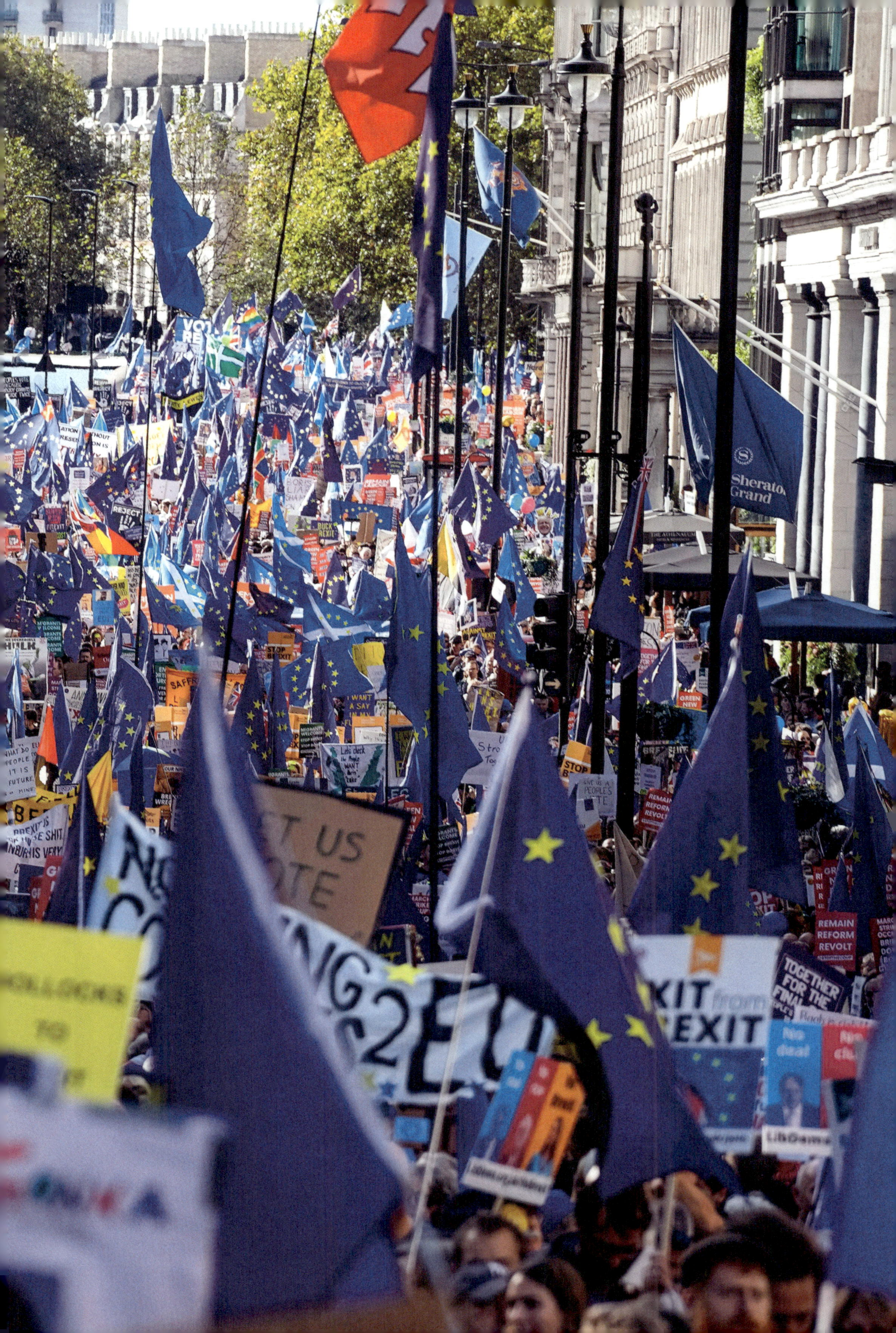

Sheraton
Grand
THE ATHENAEUM
LET US
VOTE
NO
2EU
XIT from
REXIT
REMAIN
REFORM
REVOLT
TOGETHER FOR THE FINAL
No
deal
STOP
BREXIT

The public were deeply divided as opinion polls showed – though from the start of 2018 there was mostly a small majority in favour of staying in the EU. Public and political demands started to be made to hold another referendum – a 'people's vote' as it came to be called. Large demonstrations were held in London, in favour of 'remain' and a people's vote, with one in October 2019 said to have attracted one million people. The pro-EU demonstrators were peaceful, good humoured, often bringing their families, including young children, their dogs and their home-made signs. Ironically, the UK now had one of the largest most active pro-European movements in Europe.

But it was not to be. The opposition parties at Westminster were deeply fractured and Labour itself was divided, with its leader Corbyn resistant to a change of tack that would support remaining in the EU. May's inability to command the support of her cabinet ministers and her backbenchers, or to get her agreed deal with the EU through Westminster, finally led to her resignation in May 2019. Two months later Boris Johnson became the UK's rather unlikely new Prime Minister.

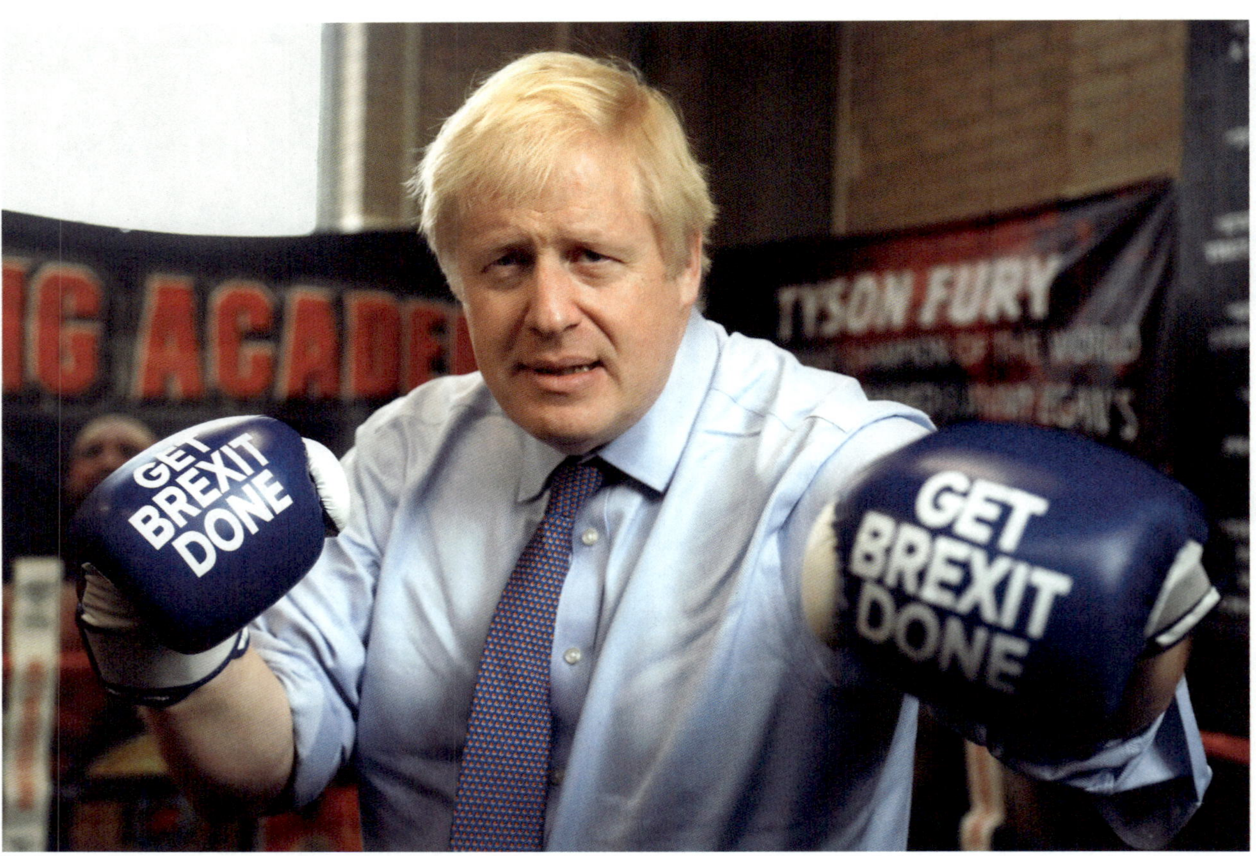

British Prime Minister Boris Johnson wears boxing gloves emblazoned with 'Get Brexit Done' as he poses for a photograph at Jimmy Egan's Boxing Academy in Manchester, England on 19 November 2019

Johnson, though, faced the same challenge as May: how to get a deal through an unstable, fissured Westminster without a reliable majority. In a move with deepening ramifications today, he agreed a Withdrawal Agreement[9] with the EU that would effectively keep Northern Ireland in the EU's single market for goods and its customs union even though Britain (England, Wales and Scotland) would leave both the single market and the customs union. This meant a trade border would be erected between Britain and Northern Ireland ie fragmenting the UK's own internal market. So, a Conservative Prime Minister had agreed to put a border between Britain and Northern Ireland, ie within the UK. At the same time, as an indication of the type of leader Johnson was going to be, he denied that there would be a border of any kind.

In the face of continuing political instability, Johnson managed to get agreement at Westminster to hold another general election in December 2019 and won a substantial majority with his slogan of 'Get Brexit Done.' His deal went through and the UK left the EU on 31 January 2020. Still, the economic impact was not yet fully felt as the UK stayed in the EU's single market and customs union for a transition year until 1 January 2021. It was a transition that, on ideological grounds, Boris Johnson chose not to extend in 2020 despite, by then, the COVID-19 pandemic being centre stage.

The Withdrawal Agreement was effectively the divorce deal. Next the UK and EU had to agree a new trade agreement. Negotiations proved difficult. Brexit had happened but the UK government still adopted trenchant, even aggressive Brexiter rhetoric in its dealings with the EU – and its negotiating goals were not always clear. The soft deadline of October 2020 for a deal was missed and fears of another 'no deal' Brexit rocked politics and the economy as Johnson threatened to renege on some parts of the Northern Ireland deal in the Withdrawal Agreement. The EU was appalled – the Withdrawal Agreement was an international legal treaty and a UK Prime Minister was threatening to break it. In the end, Johnson backed off from this but the reputational damage to the UK was done.

9. 'Agreement on the Withdrawal of the United Kingdom of Great Britain and Northern Ireland from the European Union and the European Atomic Energy Community', November 2019.

Finally, in late December, a trade deal was struck – the Trade and Cooperation Agreement – which rapidly came into effect on 1 January 2021.[10] A hard Brexit had finally happened. Trade had already been badly impacted by the pandemic and now, in the first few months of the year, major regulatory and customs barriers were now in place, impeding trade and reducing exports and imports between the UK and EU (even though there were, in principle, no tariffs).

The internal border from Britain to Northern Ireland also caused substantial technical as well as political troubles as goods, including for supermarkets, could no longer flow freely between the two. In April 2021 there were several days of street riots in Northern Ireland as a range of discontents bubbled over and focused on the new internal border as a target of their anger.[11] The UK and EU continued to be locked in fractious talks over how to make the Northern Ireland protocol operate more fluidly.

Meanwhile, total UK trade in goods with the EU started to look badly affected by the new trade deal (as many had predicted). In the first three months of 2021, compared to 2018, trade with the EU was down 23% – while with non-EU countries it was only down 0.8%, suggesting Brexit, not the pandemic, was already having a dramatic, negative impact on trade.[12]

In May 2021, there were local elections in England, Scotland and Wales: the Conservatives did well in England, Labour won in Wales and the Scottish National Party (SNP) won in Scotland. Together with the pro-independence Scottish Green party, the SNP now has a clear majority in the Scottish Parliament and a mandate from voters to hold another independence referendum. But, for now, Boris Johnson is refusing to agree to another vote. Yet pressures are likely to build in the coming years, leading to growing constitutional and political divisions across a still deeply divided UK.

10. 'Trade and Cooperation Agreement Between the European Union and the European Atomic Energy Community, of the One Part, and the United Kingdom of Great Britain and Northern Ireland, of the Other Part', December 2020.

11. P. Foster and J. Brunsden, 'London and Dublin Call for Calm after Fresh Riots in Northern Ireland', *Financial Times*, April 2021, www.ft.com/content/001ab788-15ba-4059-88c0-80995a4dbb9b

12. 'The Impacts of EU Exit and the Coronavirus on UK Trade in Goods', *Office for National Statistics*, May 2021, www.ons.gov.uk/businessindustryandtrade/internationaltrade/articles/theimpactsofeuexitandthecoronavirusonuktradeingoods/2021-05-25

Where Next?

Brexit was and is an ideological project, one that projects the
UK as an influential global player rather than a cooperative
European one, pooling sovereignty to common ends within
the EU. Alongside the economic damage, and the damage
to its international reputation and ties to its European
neighbours, Brexit has fractured the UK. There is more
discussion of the possibility of Irish reunification, and in
Scotland the independence movement has grown stronger
as some voters, who would previously have voted to stay
part of the UK, now prefer the choice of an independent
Scotland in the EU.

For now, the UK government has chosen a path of substantial
economic damage and major frictions with its former European
partners. But the UK is an island off the European continent.
The EU is its major trading partner. The EU and UK will have
to continue to cooperate.

And it is possible a future UK government will aim to negotiate
much closer cooperation with the EU compared to the approach
Johnson has chosen. Perhaps in a generation the option of
rejoining the EU may be discussed again. But whether in
20 years the UK will still exist – or whether an independent
Scotland may have left the UK and re-joined the EU, and
Northern Ireland may also be in the EU as part of a reunified
Ireland – is one more debate and consequence of Brexit that
will reverberate through the coming years.

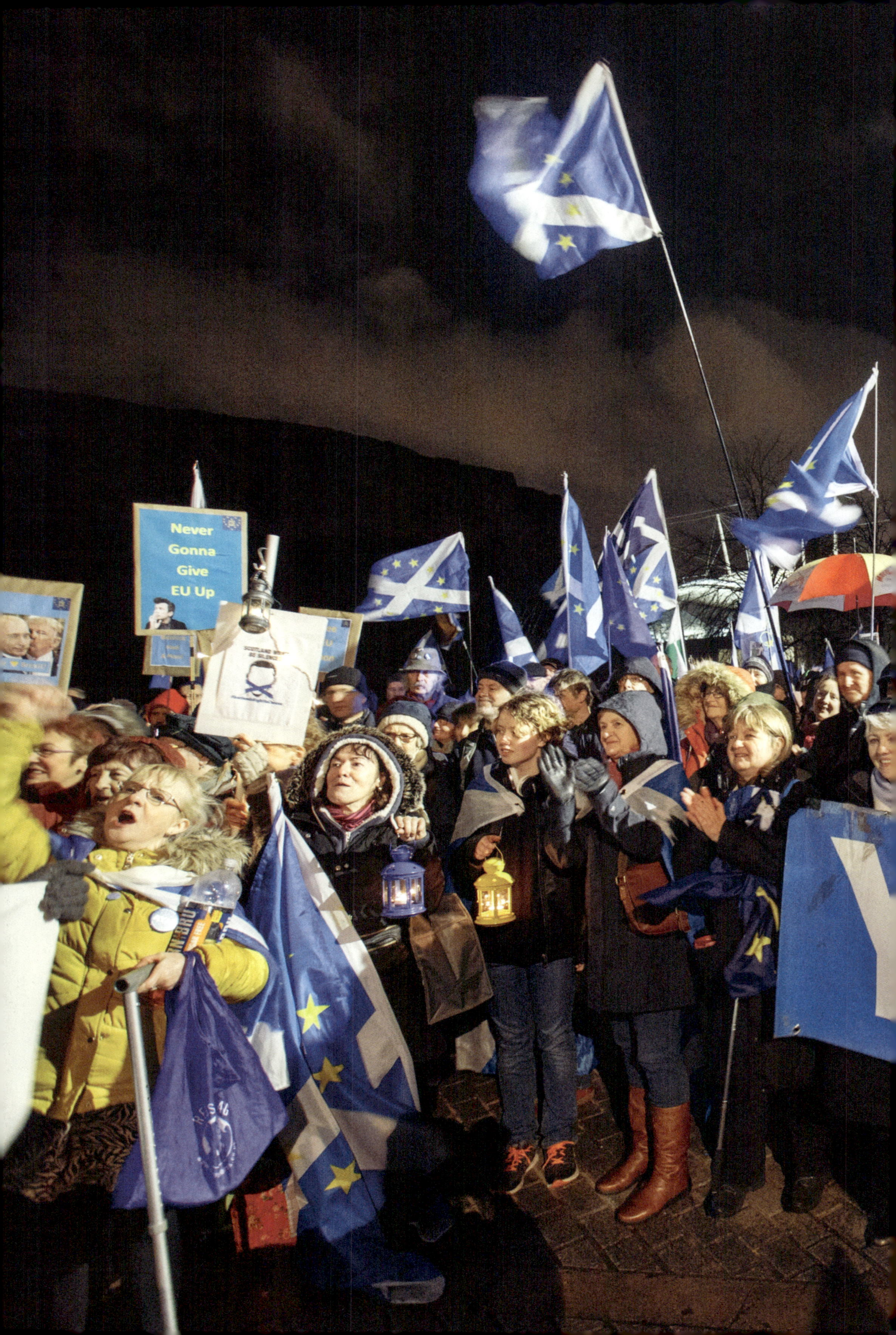

Never
Gonna
Give
EU Up
SCOTLAND

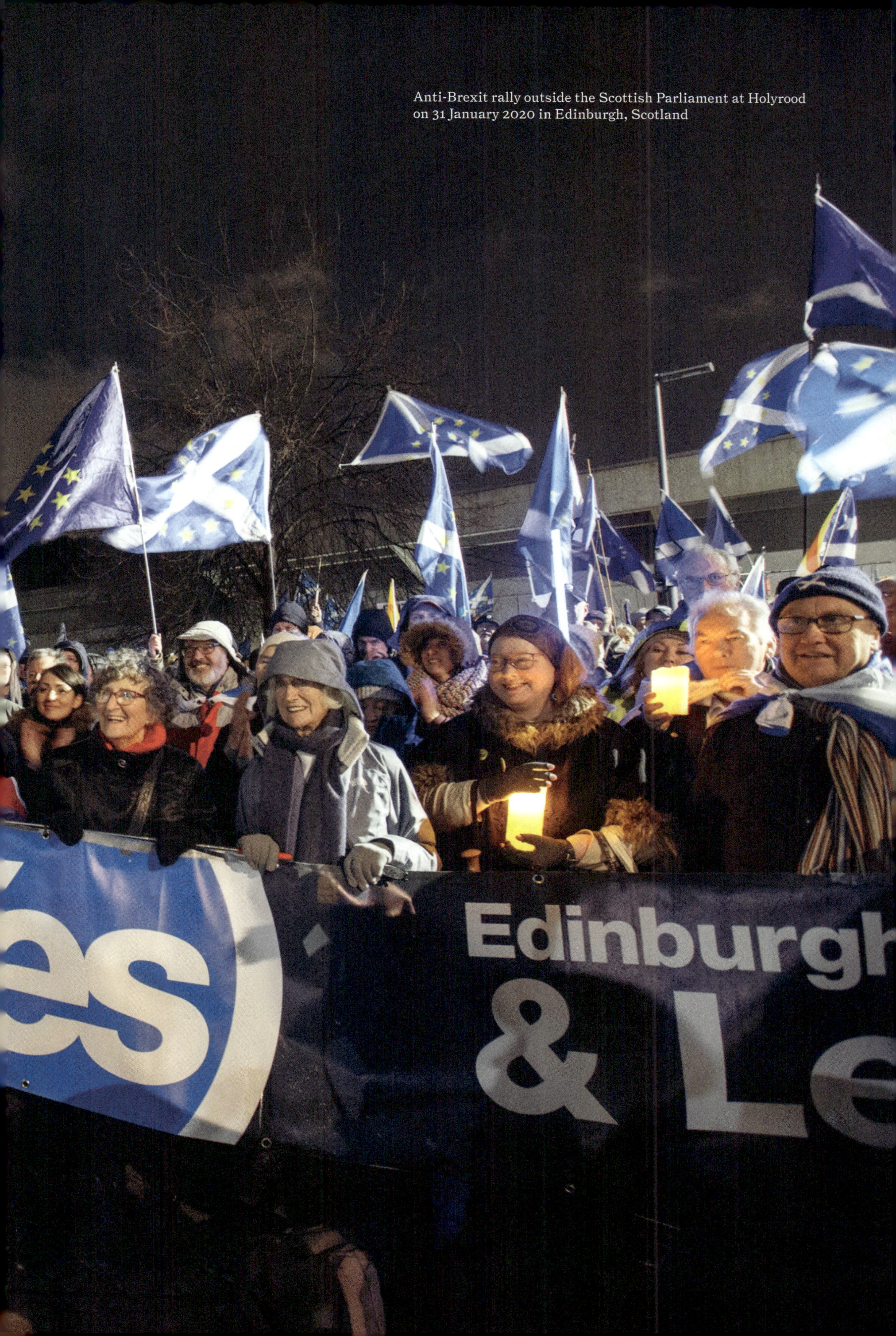

Anti-Brexit rally outside the Scottish Parliament at Holyrood on 31 January 2020 in Edinburgh, Scotland

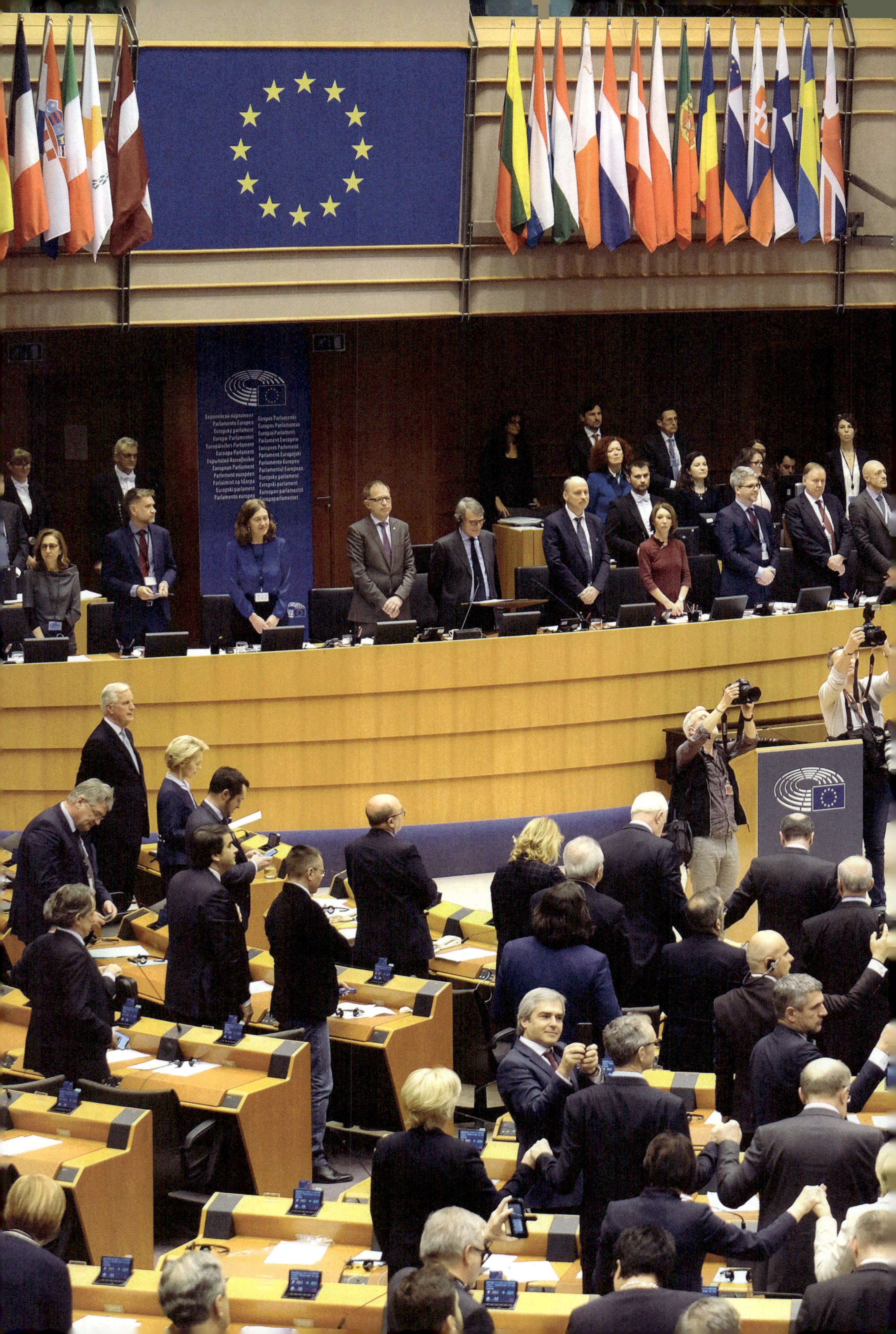

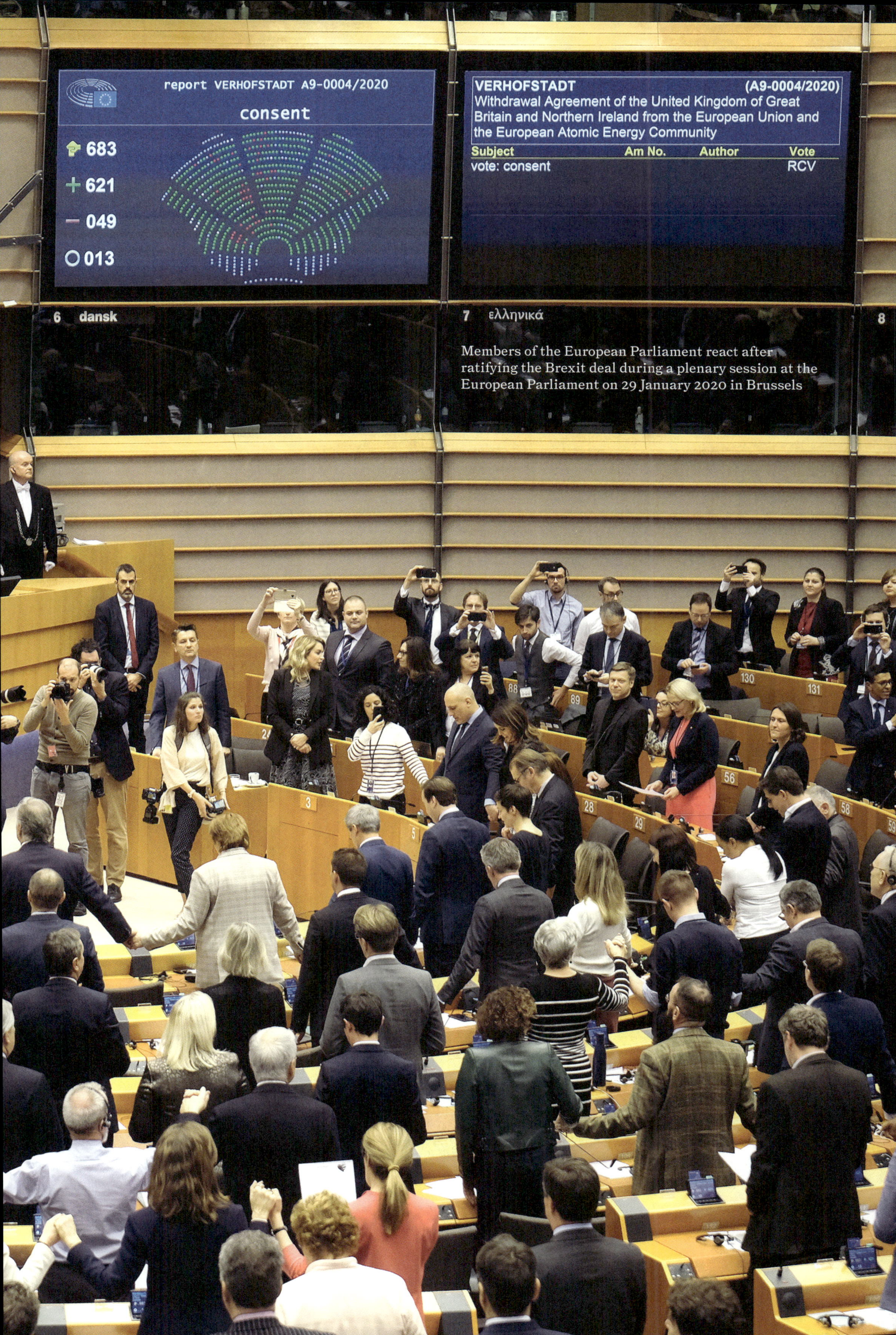

Members of the European Parliament react after ratifying the Brexit deal during a plenary session at the European Parliament on 29 January 2020 in Brussels

Formation of the European Union

1957 EU Founding Members

In the aftermath of the Second World War there was a strong urge to ensure peace in Europe for the future. This led to the creation of the Council of Europe in 1949, focused on upholding human rights and democracy, and to some initial economic cooperation via the European Coal and Steel Community in 1951.

The European Economic Community (EEC), which later was called the European Union (EU), was established in 1957, through the Treaty of Rome, by Belgium, France, Germany, Italy, Luxembourg and the Netherlands. It aimed to establish a Common Market between its members.

Belgium, France, Germany, Italy, Luxembourg, Netherlands

First EU Enlargement

In 1973, the EEC enlarged for the first time to include three new member states. The UK, having chosen not to join the EEC in 1957, had applied in the 1960s but faced a veto (twice) from France's President de Gaulle. All three countries – Denmark, Ireland and the UK – had been in the European Free Trade Association (EFTA) but over time saw the benefits of being part of the EEC both economically and in having a political say in the future development of the Common Market.

1973
Denmark, Ireland, United Kingdom (UK departed January 2020)

1980s Enlargement Waves

The 1980s saw the next two waves of enlargement. The three countries who joined had all returned to democracy after years of authoritarian and fascist rule. Joining the EEC was seen not only as an economic benefit but as becoming part of the club of European democracies and underpinning the renewed democracy in these countries.

1981
Greece

1986
Portugal, Spain

The EFTA Enlargement

In 1995, three countries that had been part of the European
Free Trade Association – Austria, Finland and Sweden – decided
to join the European Union. The EU had created a deeper, more
integrated single market in 1992 and these countries saw the
benefits of having a political say in how that market developed
in the future. At the same time, the European Economic
Area (EEA) was established – and Iceland, Liechtenstein and
Norway decided to be EEA members and not to join the EU.

1995
Austria, Finland, Sweden

The Fall of the Berlin Wall
and Enlargement in the 2000s

After the Berlin Wall fell in 1989 and the Soviet Union collapsed
in 1991, the decades-long division of Europe was finally over.
Many of the new democracies in central and eastern Europe
wanted to join the EU to underpin their transition to becoming
democracies and social market economies. It took time. But
in 2004 and 2007, ten central and eastern European countries
joined the EU in its largest ever enlargement. Two other small
states – Cyprus and Malta – joined at the same time in 2004.
And in 2013, Croatia joined the EU, its most recent accession.

2004
Cyprus, Czech Republic, Estonia, Hungary, Latvia, Lithuania,
Malta, Poland, Slovakia, Slovenia

2007
Bulgaria, Romania

2013
Croatia

Biographies

Emeka Ogboh (b. 1977, Enugu, Nigeria) currently lives and works between Lagos and Berlin. His work has been shown in solo exhibitions at Fraeme, Marseille (2021); Cleveland Museum of Art, Cleveland (2019); The Power Plant Contemporary Art Gallery, Toronto (2018); Imane Fares Gallery, Paris (2018); Tate Modern, London (2017); Staatliche Kunsthalle Baden-Baden, Germany (2017); Ludlow 38, New York (2016); Smithsonian National Museum of African Art, Washington, DC (2016); Modern Art Museum, Gebre Kristos Desta Center, Addis Ababa (2016) and ifa-Galerie Berlin (2015), among others. His work has also been featured in recent group exhibitions at the Busan Biennale (2020); Sharjah Biennial 14 (2019); Palais de Tokyo, Paris (2019); Museum für Moderne Kunst, Frankfurt (2018); Dakar Biennial (2018); Monument Lab, Philadelphia (2017); documenta 14, Athens and Kassel (2017); Skulptur Projekte 2017, Münster (2017); Galerie des Galeries, Paris (2017); Oslo Architecture Triennale (2016); SAVVY Contemporary, Berlin (2016) and Le FRAC Centre-Val de Loire, France (2016). Ogboh's work is part of the permanent collections of the Centre Pompidou, France; Sharjah Biennale; MMK Frankfurt; Museum Ludwig, Cologne; Tate Modern, London; Smithsonian National Museum of African Art, Washington, DC; Federal Republic of Germany and Le FRAC Centre-Val de Loire, France. Ogboh is a founding member and director of Video Art Network Lagos. He holds a BA in Fine and Applied Arts from the University of Nigeria, Nsukka (2001).

Tessa Giblin is the Director of Talbot Rice Gallery (TRG) at the University of Edinburgh, where she holds a Senior Lectureship with Edinburgh College of Art. At TRG she has recently curated solo exhibitions of Samson Young, Lucy Skaer, David Claerbout and Jesse Jones, and is working towards exhibitions of Emeka Ogboh, Angelica Mesiti and Céline Condorelli. Recent group shows have included *The Normal* (reflecting on the impact of the pandemic); *Borderlines* (art in the age of Brexit), *At the Gates* (on women and power), *Riddle of the Burial Grounds / Hall of Half-Life* (art in relation to the Anthropocene and nuclear waste burial). She was commissioner and curator of Jesse Jones' *Tremble Tremble* for Ireland at the Venice Biennale 2017, which has since continued to tour internationally. She is part of the acquisitions committee of the Frac Bretagne 2020–2022, and from 2006–2016 was Curator of Project Arts Centre in Ireland. She was raised in Christchurch, Aotearoa / New Zealand, where she graduated from Canterbury University School of Fine Arts and emerged as a curator through the national network of artist-run spaces.

Dr Bonaventure Soh Bejeng Ndikung is an independent curator, author and biotechnologist. He is founder and artistic director of SAVVY Contemporary in Berlin and the artistic director of sonsbeek20–24, a quadrennial contemporary art exhibition in Arnhem, the Netherlands. Ndikung was the curator-at-large for Adam Szymczyk's documenta 14 in Athens, Greece and Kassel, Germany in 2017; a guest curator of the Dak'Art biennale in Dakar, Senegal, in 2018; and the artistic director of the 12th Bamako Encounters photography biennial in Mali in 2019. Together with the Miracle Workers Collective, he curated the Finland Pavilion at the Venice Biennale in 2019. He is currently a professor in the Spatial Strategies MA programme at the Weissensee Academy of Art in Berlin and is also a recipient of the first OCAD University International Curators Residency fellowship in Toronto in 2020.

The musicologist M. J. Grant is a Chancellor's Fellow in Music at the University of Edinburgh. Her research in the sociology and historical anthropology of music includes work on the social functions of songs and singing, music in Scotland, and the musicology of war and violence. She has also published extensively on the theory and aesthetics of avant-garde and experimental music since 1950. She is a member of the Editorial and Advisory board of the Musica Scotica Trust. Her second monograph, *Auld Lang Syne: A Song and its Culture*, is forthcoming from Open Book Publishers.

Dr Kirsty Hughes is a researcher, writer and commentator on European politics and policy. She is Director and founder of the Scottish Centre on European Relations and has worked at a number of leading European think tanks, including as Senior Fellow at Friends of Europe, Brussels; Senior Fellow, Centre for European Policy Studies; and Director, European Programme, Chatham House. She is a fellow of the Royal Society of Edinburgh. She has published extensively, including books, reports and policy papers, as well as contributing to a wide range of national and international media outlets.

Song of the Union

Song of the Union, Emeka Ogboh, 2021
7-channel sound installation, duration infinite

Featuring the 28 voices of (in order of joining EU)
Dorothee Nys (Belgium), Bianca Morantin (France),
Ursula Böser (Germany), Alberto Sarti (Italy),
Annemarie Klein (Luxembourg), Kristine
Mackenzie-Janson (Netherlands), René Sommer
Lindsay (Denmark), Lori Sky (Ireland), Rory
Haye (United Kingdom), Isidora Bouziouri (Greece),
Carla Mendonça Ward (Portugal), Amaya López-
Carromero (Spain), Ulrike Wutscher (Austria),
Outi Smith (Finland), Tova Svanfeldt (Sweden),
Crystalla Lola Serghiou (Cyprus), Štěpán Janča
(Czech Republic), Greteliis Kattus (Estonia),
Bado Réti (Hungary), Anna Marta Šveisberga
(Latvia), Julija Straizyte (Lithuania), Laura
Cioffi (Malta), Monika Niemczynowicz (Poland),
Lucia Šmatláková (Slovakia), Rahela Horvat Toš
(Slovenia), Gergana Vasileva (Bulgaria), Alexandra
Dodu (Romania), Elizabeth Malnar (Croatia).
Sincere thanks also to Jenny Nex, Lois Barr,
Gwen Màiri and Tawana Maramba.

Concept: Emeka Ogboh
Curator: Tessa Giblin

TRG Exhibition Manager: Melissa MacRobert,
supported by acting Gallery Manager Corinne Orton
and Gallery Assistant Charis de Kock

TRG Gallery Technician: Colm Clarke,
supported by Catriona Gilbert

Vocal Director: Katy Lavinia Cooper

Recorded by Gavin McCabe, Louis McHugh,
Roderick Buchanan-Dunlop at Reid School of Music,
Edinburgh College of Art, and Luigi Pasquini at
Dystopia Studios, Glasgow

Software programmer: Dr Robin Price

Co-commissioned with Edinburgh Art Festival

Produced by Talbot Rice Gallery,
University of Edinburgh, 2021
www.trg.ed.ac.uk

Emeka Ogboh and Tessa Giblin would like to thank
all of the singers without whom this project could
not have happened. With warm thanks also to Katy
Lavinia Cooper for her invaluable input throughout,
directing all the vocalists and working with the
TRG team to prepare the 'Auld Lang Syne' scores
in so many languages. Thanks to Gavin McCabe
and Louis McHugh at Reid School of Music;
to Luigi Pasquini and his team at Dystopia Studios
in Glasgow. Thanks to all the Talbot Rice Gallery
team, especially Melissa MacRobert, Colm Clarke
and Corinne Orton, to Sorcha Carey and Jane Connarty
from Edinburgh Art Festival and to Fraser Muggeridge
and Michael Kelly. And thanks also to Annie-Claire
Geisinger, Bonaventure Ndikung, and Ugochukwu-
Smooth Nzewi for the discussions, as well
as Morag Grant, Kirsty Hughes, Jenny Nex,
Martin Parker, Juan Cruz and Kirsteen McCue
and Moira Hansen from Centre for Robert Burns
Studies, University of Glasgow. Further sincere
thanks to former and current MEPs Terry Reintke,
Molly Scott Cato, Alyn Smith and Scott Ainslie
for their insight and reflections.

Translations

Flemish: Published in L. van Dessel (Ed.),
Groot Vlaams Liedboek, Tielt, Lannoo, 1986
(translator unknown)

French: Jacques Sevin, 1920

German: *Lieder und Balladen von Robert Burns
aus dem Englischen von K. Bartsch*, Karl Bartsch,
Leipzig und Wein, Bibliographisches Institut, 1865

Italian: Alberto Sarti

Luxembourgish: Veruschka Uliczay in association
with First Edition Translations Ltd, Cambridge, UK

Dutch: Juliette Van Gurp in association with
First Edition Translations Ltd, Cambridge, UK

Danish: Jeppe Aakjær. *Under Aftenstjernen:
Digte [Under the Evening Star: Poems]*,
Copenhagen, Gyldendal, 1927

Irish: The Translation Room Ltd

Scots: *Select Collection of Original Scottish Airs*,
published by George Thomson, 1799

Greek: Boy Scouts Repertoire (translator unknown)

Portuguese: Ana Vozone in association with
First Edition Translations Ltd, Cambridge, UK

Spanish: Courtesy of Centre for Robert Burns
Studies, University of Glasgow

Austrian German: Ulrike Wutscher

Finnish: Translator unknown

Swedish: *Några dikter af Robert Burns,
traducido del inglés*, Magnus Gustaf Retzius,
Estocolmo, Klemming anticuario, 1872

Cypriot Greek: Greek Boy Scouts Repertoire
(translator unknown)

Czech: Josef Václav Sládek, 1892

Estonian: Ivi Leiar / Diskusija in association with
First Edition Translations Ltd, Cambridge, UK

Hungarian: Bado Réti

Latvian: Translation Empire. Edited by Kitty Brige
in association with First Edition Translations Ltd,
Cambridge, UK

Lithuanian: Courtesy of Centre for Robert Burns
Studies, University of Glasgow

Maltese: Christopher Bezzina / Transcripta in
association with First Edition Translations Ltd,
Cambridge, UK

Polish: Translation Empire. Edited by Jadwiga
Ruchlewska in association with First Edition
Translations Ltd, Cambridge, UK

Slovak: Lucia Šmatláková

Slovenian: Tomi Dobaj in association with
First Edition Translations Ltd, Cambridge, UK

Bulgarian: Translation Empire. Edited by
Nataliya Nedkova in association with First
Edition Translations Ltd, Cambridge, UK

Romanian: Alexandra Dodu

Croatian: Fedja Imamovic in association with
First Edition Translations Ltd, Cambridge, UK

Scots Gaelic: Henry 'Fionn' Whyte, Eanraig
MacGhille-bhàin from *The Celtic Garland*,
published by Archibald Sinclair, Glasgow, 1881

Welsh: Arwel Roberts, Testun Cyf in association
with First Edition Translations Ltd, Cambridge, UK

For assistance with sourcing translations:

Moira Hansen, Kirsteen McCue, Françoise Molitor,
Doris Federanko, Monika Zimmerl, Johan Eeckeloo,
Olivia Wahnon de Oliveira, Dr Yordanka Velkova,
Dessi Stefanova, Maria Brankova, Jelena Sancic,
Inka Myyry, Stathis Makris, Sára Lengyel,
Kovácsné Sorossy Csilla, Virginia Blankenhorn,
Ieva Nagle, Saiva Cakure, Daiva Vyčinienė,
Dr Anna Borg Cardona, Andrew Pace, Martine
de Bruin, Ihor Loza, Ewa Lachiewicz-Walińska,
Dr Raquel Ribeiro, Cristine Morrison, Cathlin
Macaulay, Anja Gunderloch, Elizabeth Lawrence,
Jenny Nex, Maja Rančigaj Beneš, Anja Slapničar

Image Credits

This catalogue is published by Talbot Rice Gallery, University of Edinburgh on the occasion of the exhibition Emeka Ogboh 'Song of the Union' as part of Edinburgh Art Festival 2021 Commissions Programme.

29 July – 29 August 2021
Burns Monument, Edinburgh

Curated by Tessa Giblin,
Director of Talbot Rice Gallery

Talbot Rice Gallery
The University of Edinburgh
Old College
South Bridge
Edinburgh
EH8 9YL
United Kingdom

Editors: Tessa Giblin and Melissa MacRobert

Design: Fraser Muggeridge studio
Print production: Graphius
Copyediting: Miranda Blennerhassett

Published by Talbot Rice Gallery,
University of Edinburgh, 2021
Printed in Belgium
Edition of 1000
ISBN 978-1-8381232-3-9

This book is set in Triptych Roman and Triptych Italick designed by Ellmer Stefan in 2019, a revival and interpretation of *O.S. (Old Style) Antique No.7* by Miller & Richard of Edinburgh from 1858.

Vinyl record produced in conjunction with this catalogue:

Song of the Union
Limited edition of 500
Mastered by Marco Pellegrino,
Analogcut Mastering (Berlin)
Manufacture: Mother Tongue, Verona, Italy

Co-commissioned by Edinburgh Art Festival and Talbot Rice Gallery, as part of Edinburgh College of Art. Supported by the PLACE Programme, a partnership between Edinburgh Festivals, Scottish Government, City of Edinburgh Council and Creative Scotland. With additional support from Goethe-Institut Glasgow, ifa (Institut für Auslandsbeziehungen), Edinburgh College of Art and Museums and Galleries Edinburgh

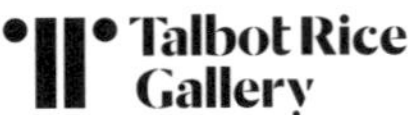
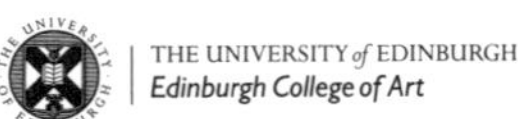
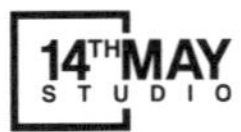
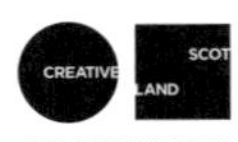
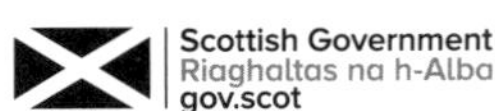
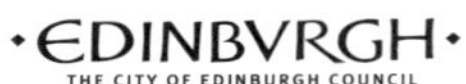
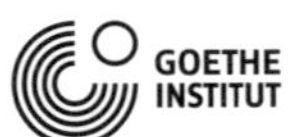
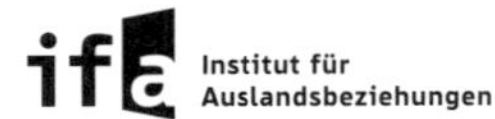